YES WE (STILL) CAN

YES WE (STILL) CAN

POLITICS IN THE AGE OF OBAMA, TWITTER, AND TRUMP

DAN PFEIFFER

TWELVE

New York Boston

Copyright © 2019 by Daniel Pfeiffer

Cover design by Jarrod Taylor
Cover images: Obama, Trump, basketball hoop © Getty Images; floor © Alamy
Cover copyright © 2019 by Hachette Book Group, Inc.

Hachette Book Group supports the right to free expression and the value of copyright. The purpose of copyright is to encourage writers and artists to produce the creative works that enrich our culture.

The scanning, uploading, and distribution of this book without permission is a theft of the author's intellectual property. If you would like permission to use material from the book (other than for review purposes), please contact permissions@hbgusa.com. Thank you for your support of the author's rights.

Twelve
Hachette Book Group
1290 Avenue of the Americas, New York, NY 10104
twelvebooks.com
twitter.com/twelvebooks

Originally published in hardcover and ebook by Twelve in June 2018
First trade paperback edition: June 2019

Twelve is an imprint of Grand Central Publishing. The Twelve name and logo are trademarks of Hachette Book Group, Inc.

The publisher is not responsible for websites (or their content) that are not owned by the publisher.

The Hachette Speakers Bureau provides a wide range of authors for speaking events. To find out more, go to www.hachettespeakersbureau.com or call (866) 376-6591.

Library of Congress Control Number: 2018932320

ISBNs: 978-1-5387-1170-5 (trade paperback), 978-1-5387-1172-9 (ebook)

Printed in the United States of America

LSC-C

10 9 8 7 6 5 4 3 2 1

To Howli and Kyla. I love our family so much.

We know the battle ahead will be long. But always remember that no matter what obstacles stand in our way, nothing can stand in the way of the power of millions of voices calling for change.

—*Barack Obama, "Yes We Can"*
speech, January 8, 2008

CONTENTS

INTRODUCTION

IF YOU'RE READING THIS, IT'S TOO LATE

My final visit to the White House during the Obama era was not at all what I'd imagined it would be.

Over the years, I had often thought about the moment when this chapter in my life and the country's history would come to a close. I imagined it to be bittersweet, but more sweet than bitter. I imagined it to be the triumphant end to a great era in American history—one that would be talked about with the reverence reserved for the great presidents.

This was the last day of the Obama presidency. But I wasn't headed back for a raucous good-bye party or even a sheet cake in the Roosevelt Room to pat ourselves on the back for years of good work.

We weren't celebrating at all. We were about thirty-six hours from Barack Obama, our first African American president, leaving and Donald J. Trump, racist reality TV star, assuming the presidency. Sure, I had thought about the possibility that Obama would be replaced by a Republican. It wasn't just possible, but historically probable. But I had never imagined something like this.

Donald Trump in the White House was worse than my worst nightmare.

And to make this visit even more surreal, I was back at the White

House to interview President Obama. For a podcast. A medium I barely knew existed when I first met him back in 2007.

I walked into the West Wing this one last time with my *Pod Save America* cohosts, Jon Favreau, Tommy Vietor, and Jon Lovett, all of whom had been with me on Day 1 of the Obama presidency.[1]

There is something powerful about walking through the doors of the White House—even if you do it every day for six years—but this time felt even more consequential. This was the last time I would walk into a White House staffed by friends and colleagues—people with whom I had shed blood, sweat, and tears in the service of making Hope and Change a reality. This was the last time I would walk into a White House where Barack Obama was president.

This might be the last time I ever walked into the White House period—the place that had been my home for almost my entire thirties; the place where I had experienced tremendous triumph and tragedy; the place where I had met and fallen in love with my wife.[2]

I am proud to say I never took working in the White House for granted. But up until this moment, it had never occurred to me that I might never again walk through those doors.

We arrived just in time for Obama's final press conference as president. This felt fitting. I hate press conferences. Sure, presidents taking questions from reporters is an important part of the democratic process. But I hate everything about them. I hate the process of preparing for them. I hate the questions that are asked. And I hate watching them. When I worked in the White House, I couldn't bear to be in the room when they happened. They made me too anxious, and I would watch in my office. I told people I did that so I could consume the press conference like the public—see how it played on TV. That was bullshit. I just wanted the

---

1   As is well known by all Friends of the Pod, Tommy and Favreau were original Obama campaign staffers while Lovett worked for Hillary in '08. We forgave him, but never stopped making fun of him.

2   You will meet her later—she's awesome.

ability to yell at the TV like a crazy, basement-dwelling C-SPAN viewer.[3]

On this day, I ostensibly had to watch in preparation for our pod interview, which would immediately follow the press conference. Even though I had no skin in this game, I was freaked out for the whole press conference, unable to sit still, and yelling at the TV when I thought the questions were inane or the answers too long. A fitting end to my role in Barack Obama's dance with the White House Press Corps.

I was mostly anxious about the interview. It was going to be his final interview as president of the United States, and this was a big deal for *Pod Save America*, which had just launched less than two weeks earlier.

Interviewing a president is hard. I have seen experienced, world-famous journalists melt the moment they walk into the Oval Office. We weren't experienced and we certainly weren't journalists. Our familiarity with the subject added to my anxiety. I know all too well how busy a president is—even on his or her last day in office. During my years working with Obama, one of the things I brought to the table was a finely honed sense of the exact moment when Barack Obama was tired of doing the thing he was doing. In staff meetings and prep sessions, I could always tell when Obama's brain had started to move on to the next item of his never-ending to-do list. It was often my role to bring the meeting or interview to an end before the length of the meeting exceeded Obama's patience.

I dreaded the idea of seeing that switch flipped before we were done. The last thing I wanted to do was be yet another annoying thing on his schedule. I had been the one to ask the president if he would do the interview, so I felt particularly tied to its success.

Or failure.

We had been working on questions for weeks. Obama is by his

---

3 Or the forty-fifth president of the United States.

very nature a storyteller, so I went looking for the perfect anecdote to set him up to put the Obama era in perspective and explain how and why we ended up with someone like Donald Trump as president.

When I left the White House in 2015, President Obama gave me a collection of photos from our time together, dating back to the early days of the campaign,[4] as a farewell gift.

One of the first photos in the book is from an early 2007 campaign trip to New Hampshire. Neither Obama nor I have any gray hair, and we both look so young. We are smiling and laughing—blissfully unaware of all that is to come—as we head into one of the endless series of meet and greets with voters that define the early days of presidential campaigns.

Each photo in the album is attached to a different moment in the Obama era—the good times and the bad; the funny and the sad; our successes and our failures.

I never found the magic question for the interview, but I did find the seeds of this book.

READER BEWARE

First, let's talk about what this book isn't.

It's not a history of the Obama years, because I'm not a historian.

It's not the inside account of the moments that will fill the history books, because that's Barack Obama's story to tell (and he will tell it much better).

And finally, it's not a "tell all" filled with gossipy scoops about the Obama White House, because I'm not an asshole.

Instead, *Yes We (Still) Can*[5] is a look back at my experiences on

---

4   Obama also gave me—a rabid Georgetown University basketball fan—a basketball autographed by Georgetown legends Patrick Ewing, Alonzo Mourning, and Dikembe Mutombo.

5   I am going to make the parentheses thing a thing. Just watch.

the Obama campaigns and in the White House to try to better understand the current state of politics and look at where we go from here. Much like *Pod Save America*, it's a no-bullshit conversation about politics in the era of Obama, Trump, and Twitter.

As I was doing my deep dive through the Obama years, I kept finding examples of Barack Obama trying to navigate the very forces that created an environment where someone like Donald Trump could be elected.

For eight years, Barack Obama dealt with:

- A dystopic, anything-goes media environment upended by the emergence of the Internet
- An intellectually bankrupt and increasingly rabid Republican Party
- A right-wing propaganda machine embodied by Fox News
- The rising tide of fake news and conspiracy theories
- The emergence of social media platforms such as Twitter that reward the loudest voices and penalize thoughtfulness and analysis

It became clear to me in those dark days after the election that embedded in the successes (and failures)[6] of our battles against these forces were lessons about how Democrats can ultimately defeat Trumpism.

This account is my best recollection of what happened and what people said. I didn't take notes or keep a diary, because at the time I had no intention of writing a book, but I like to think I have a good memory. I threw in some of my favorite fun stories, just cuz.

Finally, this book is also an argument to young people that politics is something very much worth engaging in. It's fun, fulfilling, and really damn important. We need another generation of young people to get in the game. Barack Obama inspired millions of young people to believe in the value of being part of something larger than

---

6   See footnote 5.

themselves. As the rapidly emerging gray hairs of myself and my former 2008 colleagues show, that generation is now older. It's time for a new generation to step up and take charge of our future.

I started writing this book in the days after that final presidential encounter with Obama. I didn't know what I was writing when I started; I just knew I wanted to say something about how we got to this moment in politics and how we could get past it. I was worried that it would be a depressing exercise, the equivalent of wallowing at home looking at photos of an ex after a bad breakup.

But it wasn't.

Not at all. Quite the opposite actually. I was inspired by something Obama said in the *Pod Save America* interview.

Toward the end of the interview, Jon Favreau asked Obama,

"Mr. President...you've talked a lot about how we're all trying to get our paragraph right in history. What do you hope that paragraph says about you?"

The president replied, "When I think about what will most gratify me, it will be if, twenty years from now, I can look back and I can say, wow, look at all these people who first got involved—maybe even when they were too young to vote—in government, politics, issues, nonprofits, public service, and that wave just kind of—a cleansing wave washes over the country. And if that happens, then the details of how we dealt with climate change, or whether the individual responsibility mandate on the Affordable Care Act was the right approach or not—that becomes less important. Because if we're getting the broad direction right, this is a pretty ingenious country, full of ingenious people, and we'll figure it out. And that's what I want—is I want everybody to feel like we can figure this out if we just don't waste a lot of time doing dumb stuff."

The idea of Trump and his coterie of Internet trolls, self-dealing Wall Street tycoons, and unrepentant racists wandering the halls of the White House doing dumb, mean shit is hard to stomach. Not a day has gone by since the 2016 election when I haven't been angry about the result and sad for the country.

My hope in writing this book is to show that it doesn't have to be this way. That if we learn the right lessons and, most important, people—especially young people—get involved in politics, we can ensure that Donald Trump is an aberration. A speed bump on the path to the America we all hoped for in 2008.

But it's up to us.

Yes we (still) can.[7]

---

7   Not giving up the parentheses thing.

CHAPTER 1

STARTED FROM THE BOTTOM

I don't believe in fate. But if I did, I would say it was fate that I ended up meeting Barack Obama at the exact moment when I most needed to meet someone like Barack Obama.

Since I don't believe in fate, I will chalk it up to being one lucky SOB.

I walked into my first meeting with Barack Obama in early 2007 with a good deal of skepticism. Ostensibly, I was there for him to interview me for a potential presidential campaign, but I wanted to see if Barack Obama, the man, matched up to Barack Obama, the hype. I was pretty skeptical that a rookie politician espousing a gauzy but vague message of hope and change had what it took to survive the brutal freak show of presidential politics.

Frankly, on paper it was insane that he was considering running for president. But that's why I was there.

I went into that meeting with a hard-earned cynicism from a decade in Democratic politics filled with defeats, disappointments, and a growing disillusionment. I was on the verge of quitting politics and trying my hand at something new—I had even started studying for the GRE and was looking at applying to grad schools.

Instead, I walked out of that meeting with a new job and a new reason to hope.

The rest is history, but I almost missed it.

This is embarrassing to admit now, but when the rest of the world was falling in love with Barack Obama in 2004, I wasn't paying any attention to him.

In fact, I didn't even watch the famous 2004 convention speech that skyrocketed Barack Obama into national politics. I didn't watch it in the days after when it was the talk of everyone in politics. And I didn't watch it in the ensuing two years when I was working in the Senate and seeing Obama on the weird Senate Subway,[1] which takes senators and their aides from their office buildings to the Senate Chamber.

In 2004, I was working day and night on Senate Minority Leader Tom Daschle's reelection campaign in South Dakota, and due to the obsessive tunnel vision that campaigns give you, I was paying very little attention to anything that wasn't in the Sioux Falls *Argus Leader* newspaper.

When *Dreams of My Father*, Obama's memoir, was rereleased to rave reviews in 2004, I didn't read it.

When *The Audacity of Hope*, Obama's instant best-seller of a follow-up book, was published, I didn't read it.

The first time I heard the name Barack Obama, I was sitting in the backseat of an SUV driving around rural South Dakota with my boss, Senator Daschle. Senator Jon Corzine of New Jersey, who was heading up the Senate Democrats' campaign committee, called Daschle to check in. After the call, I asked Daschle what Corzine had wanted and he said, "Jon has just met the most impressive candidate who is running in the Illinois primary. His name is Barack Hussein Obama." Daschle went on to convey Corzine's assessment of Obama's immense charisma, smarts, and oratorical skills, as well as Obama's unique background.

"Sounds amazing. Too bad he has no shot," I responded.[2]

---

1   It's really a short walk, but senators apparently need public transportation to get to votes on time. Like the worst ride at Disneyland.
2   Perhaps political predictions have never been my thing.

WHO AM I? WHY AM I HERE?[3]

My first encounter in politics was one befitting a Democrat: I got my ass kicked.

It was 1988, I was in seventh grade, and it was in Tokyo.

My family was living in Japan because my dad worked for DuPont and had been assigned to a four-year stint in the Tokyo office. I was attending the appropriately named American School in Japan, being that it was an American school that was most certainly in Japan. My civics teacher opened up class one day with an announcement.

A Japanese television network was doing a special on the American election, and as part of their programming, they wanted to put on a mock presidential debate with two students playing the roles of then vice president George H. W. Bush and Massachusetts governor Michael Dukakis. The debate would be carried in part on local Japanese television.

The teacher asked for volunteers and said the class would vote to choose the debaters.

"Who wants to volunteer to be Vice President Bush?"

About ten hands went up.

"Who wants to be Michael Dukakis?"

One hand went up.

Mine.

I'm not exactly sure why I volunteered. Maybe I thought being on TV would be cool.[4] I did enjoy debating or, as my mom would call it, being a "smart aleck."[5] There is a famous story in my family about a seven-year-old me finding out that Santa wasn't real and turning it into a debate about the existence of God. I stand by my view then that if Santa, the Easter Bunny, and the Tooth Fairy—all

---

3   In other words, why the fuck should you care?
4   It's not.
5   She is too Southern and proper to say "ass."

magical entities, never seen by people—were fake, I was right to ask the question. My mom disagreed.

Either way, I definitely did not think it through before I raised my hand. But now I was Michael Dukakis for the whole world or at least the whole of Japan to see. My parents were lifelong Democrats whose views had been shaped growing up in the South during the heyday of the civil rights movement and going to college in 1968, when activism against the Vietnam War swept the nation. We talked about politics and world events at the dinner table in part because my dad's job allowed us to see a lot of the world outside the United States. Prior to living in Japan, we had also spent three years in São Paulo, Brazil. My parents had ingrained in my younger brother and me the idea that Democrats were right and Republicans were wrong.[6] At this point, I had a very simple understanding of our two-party system: Republicans liked war and hated poor people.[7] Democrats hated war and liked poor people. I also knew that Democrats did not win elections very often. As for Dukakis himself, he was a mystery other than the fact that he was a Democrat, was losing, and once looked ridiculous riding in a tank.

I leaped into preparation. I didn't know a lot about life, but I knew enough to be aware that embarrassing yourself on TV was something you don't quickly live down in the cutthroat world of middle school. And beyond my own social standing, I hated losing in anything and everything.

When I was about ten or eleven, my family got the board game Trivial Pursuit and we would all play it together. Other than being able to answer some of the sports questions and some of the easiest questions on subjects like history that I studied in school, I was completely flummoxed. The questions were about books, movies, television shows, and events that happened long before I was born. I was bad at the game and I hated constantly losing.

---

6   Still, and always, true.
7   Also, still, and mostly true.

I took matters into my own hands.

When my parents weren't looking, I would take the cards with the questions from the box and go into my room and memorize the answers. I would read each card several times, repeating the answers to myself before moving on to the next card. I did this almost every day for weeks until the next family game night, which went something like this:

"What Byzantine city was renamed Istanbul after being captured by the Ottoman Empire?"

"Constantinople!"

And so it went. I answered the next ten or so questions without getting one wrong—including one about what movie won the Best Picture Oscar in 1944[8]—and won the game in record time. My parents couldn't tell if I was a remarkable genius or an inveterate cheater. By the end of the game, they were either sending me to juvee or early enrolling me in Yale.

I stand by the idea that this was in no way cheating (my dad disagrees[9]), but it definitely revealed my combination of nerdiness, obsessive compulsion, and competitiveness, which would define much of my adult life and help push me toward a career in politics.

This was the level of preparation that I brought to the role of Michael Dukakis. Because I lived in Japan and the Internet wasn't yet invented, the only way to learn about Dukakis was to go to an actual library and look at old newspapers and magazines. I printed reams of articles and made flashcards of the candidate's positions. My dad would quiz me at the dinner table about the finer points of Dukakis's policy papers.

Heading into the debate, I was very confident. The role of Bush was being played by one of the smartest girls in our class, but I was

---

8   It's not that hard. The answer is *Casablanca*, the only movie that old that anyone has heard of.
9   He's wrong.

sure there was no way she knew more or was better prepared for the debate—I could memorize an entire set of Trivial Pursuit cards.

I was right. I knew more about the issues and positions of both candidates. And in what should be an object lesson for generations of Democrats, I still got killed.

While I was trying to explain how Dukakis's plans were better for the middle class, my opponent was hammering me over the head claiming Dukakis was soft on crime, soft on the Soviet Union, and wanted to raise people's taxes.

I pushed back on those accusations with facts about Dukakis's plans, but I was on the defensive for much of the debate. It didn't matter that I was right on the facts; her message was much more compelling than my policy details. This is a lesson that I would need to relearn many times in my career.

After we'd finished, our civics class held a mock election based on what they'd seen in the debate. I lost by a margin not dissimilar to the ass kicking that the real Dukakis received in the real election.

A couple of years after my less than stellar performance, my family moved back to Delaware so that I could go to high school in the United States. When it came time to think about college, I didn't really know where I wanted to go to school. All I knew was that I wanted to get out of Delaware. After living in Tokyo, life in the second-smallest state in the Union—one best known for being the home of tax-free shopping—had started to feel suffocating.

I ended up at Georgetown University in Washington, DC.

I was pleasantly surprised when I was accepted. I wasn't great about turning my homework in on time, so my high school GPA was a little below their standards. Before the beginning of my freshman year, I went to an event for incoming students hosted by a local alumnus to introduce us to our new classmates and learn more about the school. When I introduced myself to the host, he said, "Dan Pfeiffer? I remember your application."

"Oh?" I responded.

"I have been serving on the acceptance committee for many years and I have never seen a report on an alumni interview like yours. It's why you got in."

Part of the application process involved an in-person interview with a local alumnus. These are usually scheduled for forty-five minutes or so. Mine lasted almost two hours. My bullshit abilities were at peak performance this day. We talked about everything—politics, the Gulf War, civil disobedience, the novel *Catch-22*, and what I learned about the world from living abroad. Everything I had ever read, experienced, and memorized came in handy that day.

I didn't think much of it at the time, but it was now clear that I might have just conned my way into college. I was immediately scared shitless that people would figure out that I didn't belong as soon as I stepped on campus.

This was the kick in the ass I needed. After gliding through high school doing just enough to do fine, I arrived at college with a chip on my shoulder to prove that I belonged and a strong desire not to flunk out.

Don't get me wrong, I had a lot of fun in college, but I never skipped a single class in four years—no matter how tired, sick, or hungover I was, I dragged myself to class. I couldn't control how smart I was or how hard the classes were, but I could give myself the best chance to succeed by being the guy who went to class every day.[10]

This was the same approach I'd taken in my decidedly mediocre high school basketball career.

When I was growing up, all I wanted in life was to be a great basketball player. To star for my high school team, go on to play in college, followed by a career in the game coaching, scouting, or commenting. Even at a young age, I knew that was as far as it was going to go.

---

10   Don't sign me up for the Nobel Prize—after my freshman year I never again had a class before 11:00 a.m. or on a Friday.

There are a certain set of physical attributes that are necessary to be a good basketball player: quickness, leaping ability, long arms, quick reflexes, and of course, height.[11]

I had almost none of them. I was slow and couldn't jump particularly high. I tried everything I could to improve. I jumped rope for hours in the driveway and worked out wearing those platform shoes featured in the back of *Sports Illustrated* that promised to make you able to dunk.

None of it mattered.

I realized pretty quickly that the only way I was going to make my high school team, let alone have any success at any level, was to work harder and care more than everyone else.

I spent every waking moment either playing basketball, watching basketball, or reading about basketball. For a while I slept with a basketball in my bed in the hope that somehow that extra bonding time would make me shoot better. I would record college and NBA games so that I could watch them repeatedly and break down what the players and coaches were doing. I ran shooting drills in my driveway long after the sun went down with my poor younger brother being forced to rebound for me. I had an encyclopedic knowledge of which park, gym, or YMCA had pickup basketball games on which day. I was going to will myself into a basketball player if it was the last thing I did.

I did make my varsity team and eked out a decent few years of ball, which might have gone better if I hadn't busted up my knee in my sophomore year. I tore my ACL in a drill trying to take a charge and then refused to see the trainer and tried to finish practice on it until my coach sat me down because my knee was the size of a grapefruit. In typically obsessive fashion, I rushed my rehab and came back too soon, never regaining what (very) limited bounce I had in my legs.

---

11   I was six feet tall in seventh grade and thought I was on my way to being six five or so, but I never grew another inch.

After the last game of my senior year, my coach—with whom I had an up-and-down relationship—said some perfunctory words about the seniors who were graduating.

When it was my turn, the coach said:

"Dan: I have never known a player who has made more out of less."

Most of the team took—and perhaps my coach intended—this statement as a slight.

Not me. I took it as a compliment. I had earned whatever limited success I had achieved by working for it. And I was going to do the same thing at Georgetown.

Despite the inadvertent caution of that alumnus, I ended up graduating with honors. As it turns out, the ability to memorize an entire set of Trivial Pursuit cards and being pretty good at bullshit combined with perfect attendance is the exact combo of skills needed to succeed in a liberal arts college with more than a touch of grade inflation.

Being in the nation's capital and the alma mater of Bill Clinton, among many other political luminaries, Georgetown was a magnet for wannabe politicians. There were so many kids who were prepping 24/7 to one day walk the corridors of power. There was student government, College Democrats and Republicans, mock debate, model UN, and a thousand other students for or against this or that groups. I did none of those things. Instead I preferred hanging with my friends, getting drunk at Georgetown bars like the Tombs, and playing pickup basketball during every free moment.[12]

As the prospect of graduation and being forced into the real world loomed, I realized that it was time to start thinking about what came next. Throughout college, I had assumed I would eventually go to law school. I don't really know why I assumed that other than it seemed like what I was supposed to do.[13]

---

12   In 2010, the Georgetown College Democrats named me their alumnus of the year. I had to tell them that I had never been a member.

13   Since I hadn't taken a real science or math class since high school, medical and business school seemed to be a bridge too far.

But before I signed up for more school, I wanted to spend at least a couple of years out in the real world. Again, I don't really know why I wanted to do that other than it seemed like what I was supposed to do.

In my junior year at Georgetown University, I met a guy named Chad Griffin.[14] He was a year ahead of me in school, but a few years older. He was moving into the famously pink row house we rented on Prospect Street right off campus. We needed a seventh guy to move into our group house so we could afford the rent, and he needed a place to live. Chad was from rural Arkansas and had been a student at Ouachita Baptist University in Arkansas when Bill Clinton decided to run. Chad interned for Dee Dee Myers, who was press secretary on that campaign and eventually in the Clinton White House. Chad was good at his job and got offered a full-time position on the campaign. When Clinton won, he went to the White House as a staffer at age nineteen, and among other things, he got to see the world, helping shepherd the media around during Bill Clinton's travels.[15] After a couple of years in the White House, Chad came to Georgetown to finish his college degree.

Chad had great stories about working on the Clinton campaign and in the White House. And it occurred to me that maybe working on a presidential campaign and maybe in the White House could be a good way station on the path to law school. Certainly better than being a paralegal in some law firm while taking practice LSATs on my lunch break. Not to mention that since my Dukakis debate, politics had become one of the subjects I followed with Trivial Pursuit–like intensity.

Old plan: go to law school, become a lawyer, probably hate my life.

New Plan: go work on a presidential campaign, work in the White House, go to law school, become a lawyer, hate my life, but have done and seen some cool things first.

---

14   Chad would go on to be the president of the Human Rights Campaign and lead the fight for marriage equity.

15   Interesting historical footnote: Chad's desk in the White House was the one that my wife, Howli Pfeiffer, would sit at twenty years later.

I had enough credits to graduate a semester early. Instead of venturing out into the real world, I took the first semester of my senior year off and Chad helped me land an internship at the White House in Vice President Al Gore's office. This was fortuitous timing (aided by Chad pulling a few strings for me) since Gore was going to be running for president in a couple of years.

Any internship, even one in the White House, boils down to copying, filing, and getting coffee for the people who get coffee for other people. Mine was no different. None of it is rocket science, and there is no real way to distinguish yourself from other interns as long as you show up on time and don't still smell like the previous night's party. For the first couple of weeks, I was assigned to do the "clips," which in those days meant actually cutting articles out of the newspaper, gluing them to pieces of paper, and then copying them for the staff.

Then I caught a break.

At that time, the White House was being investigated by the Republicans in Congress for potential violations of campaign finance law during the 1996 campaign. Amazingly, they were accused of selling access to the Lincoln Bedroom and raising money from Buddhist monks.[16] Gore was specifically implicated, and, therefore, his office was forced to produce reams of documents to investigators—schedules, memos, phone messages, and so on. Basically, anything that had anything to do with fund-raising of any sort.

This was a massive undertaking, and I was sent to help the counsel's office with this task. I worked on the top floor of the Eisenhower Executive Office Building next to the White House, out of a windowless room that was stacked floor to ceiling with binders full of documents.[17]

Each page of documents was assigned a number—something like

---

16 These things were sort of true, but not illegal. We definitely need new laws.
17 "White House intern" is a very broad term.

B-865—so that they could be tracked and filed appropriately. I was constantly copying, filing, and refiling these documents and became very familiar with them.

Gore was being investigated by several congressional committees, the FBI, and every news outlet on the planet. Every reporter and Republican wanted to muddy up the likely Democratic nominee. Every day, the office would get a request for some set of documents. Even with the tracking numbers, finding the requested memo or e-mail was very time intensive.

Early in my tenure, one of the attorneys in the counsel's office came in and asked for a very specific memo about a very specific fund-raising event that was under scrutiny.

"I need this by the end of the day," he said and turned to go.

"Wait. This will just take a minute," I said and walked over to the shelf, grabbed a binder, and opened it to a certain page.

"Is this the one you are looking for?"

He looked at me like I had a third arm growing out of my head. "How did you know where that was?"

"I have copied and filed these things so many times that I remember the numbers."

Word got around to the lawyers, researchers, and communications staff who needed quick access to the documents that I was the intern to ask. In hindsight, I was treated a little like Rain Man for this parlor trick, but at the time I loved it.

The same weird ability to memorize Trivial Pursuit questions happened to be something in great demand at this exact moment in the White House. I was offered a job but demurred because I wanted to finish school. Instead, my internship was extended to a second semester. I was nothing more than a paper jockey, but I was a valued one.

After college, I got an offer to work in the press office of a division of the Department of Justice, biding my time for what I assumed was a guaranteed job on the Gore campaign.

LOSING SUCKS AND OTHER STORIES FROM
THE CAMPAIGN TRAIL

When Al Gore announced his candidacy for president, I didn't get a job. When he did his second wave of hiring, I didn't get a job. When he fired half his staff and hired new ones, I didn't get a job. I got so worried that I wasn't going to get hired that I started looking for other campaign jobs. I had my boss at the Justice Department, who had worked closely with Hillary Clinton in the White House, send my résumé to her Senate campaign. No response. In Gob Bluth fashion, I thought I had made a huge mistake.

After Gore won the primary, I finally got the call from Chris Lehane, who was Gore's campaign press secretary and my boss when I was an intern. Chris told me to move to Nashville, where Gore's campaign was headquartered, and he would get me a job in the press office.

I was ecstatic. I quickly signed a temporary lease on an apartment in Nashville, packed up my car, and prepared to make the trek. One problem: Chris went dark on me and wasn't returning my calls or e-mails. I assumed it was because he was busy trying to win an election.

The day I was supposed to get in the car and start driving, I woke up, finished packing, and logged on to the Internet to check the news before hitting the road.

After patiently waiting for the Internet to dial up (which was a thing that used to happen), I checked the NBA scores from the night before and then started skimming the major papers to see the latest campaign news when something caught my eye.

Crap.

Lehane had gotten into a dispute with Gore's campaign manager and taken a temporary leave from the campaign with speculation that he would never return. The person who'd promised me a job was on the outs.

I had a decision to make. Should I delay my trip and wait for things to shake out with Lehane?

I had paid a security deposit on an apartment and had no other options, so I said, "What the hell?" and drove to Nashville and hoped Lehane had told someone about me.

He hadn't.

On my first morning in Tennessee, I drove to the campaign headquarters. I sat in my car in the parking lot for a good twenty minutes trying to get up the courage to go inside. This had the potential to be quite embarrassing.

Finally, I walked in and approached the woman sitting at the reception desk.

"Hi, my name is Dan Pfeiffer. Chris Lehane told me to come here for a job."

She looked at me with a blank stare for a minute and then asked, "How do you spell 'Lehane'?" I got the sense that this woman spent much of her day dealing with crazy people who wandered into the offices of the potential next president. On this day, I was just another crazy person.

I knew I was in trouble. No one knew who I was, why I was there, or that I had been promised a job. I was eventually passed off to the volunteer coordinator, who gave me two choices: go back home, or suck up my pride and join the kids and retirees who were volunteering on the campaign.

I was assigned to answer the phones in the press office with a very uninterested teenager who was there as part of a high school civics project and a very nice man in his late seventies who had volunteered on every presidential campaign since Adlai Stevenson, but was in the wrong job since he was very hard of hearing and couldn't pronounce the names of the callers.

It was pure chaos in the tiny broom closet masquerading as an office where we worked. The phone was ringing off the hook, messages weren't getting to the right people, and calls weren't getting returned.

On my second day, I took matters into my own hands and implemented a system for answering the phone, distributing messages, and tracking who got called back when. This caught the attention of some of the campaign aides.

Within a few weeks, I was offered a job working with the regional media. One big caveat in the job offer—they couldn't afford to pay me for my work for another four months or so, until after the convention, when the campaign would get an infusion of federal campaign funding. Thus began a lifelong habit of making terrible financial decisions in the service of a career in politics.

Within days, I knew I had found my calling. The campaign headquarters buzzed with excitement at all hours of the day and night.

Every decision felt massively consequential. My fellow campaign staff were young, energetic, and very smart.

Campaigns are meritocracies of sorts. Sure, some people get their job based on how much money their parents gave to the party or because they went to school with the candidate's kids, but once you're in the door, no one gives a shit who you know, where you went to school, or even how old you are. Things are just moving so fast that no one has time to worry about those things; hard work and smarts get rewarded with opportunities to move up to a bigger, better job with more responsibilities.

All of my new colleagues had real experience working in the White House, on Capitol Hill, or on other political campaigns. Most were at least a few years older than I was. I had done none of the above. Despite my new duties and actual desk with an actual phone, I still felt like a glorified volunteer. But I knew the drill—I had to prove myself by working harder and hopefully smarter than those around me.

I tried to be one of the first in and one of the last out of the office every day. Over time, I proved that I belonged and was treated as a real member of the team despite being someone who had wandered in off the street and still was, at best, a glorified volunteer.

Now, of course, some shenanigans in Florida and some bad campaign strategy decisions meant my position on the Gore campaign didn't end in the White House job I had hoped for.

My first campaign came to an end in an airport bar as I watched Al Gore concede the election to Bush while some drunks booed Gore. I was on my way to move back into my parents' house. I was unemployed, broke, and had nowhere else to go.

I lasted less than a week at my parents' house before I headed back to DC to sleep on the couches of friends and look for a job. This was a tough time to be an unemployed Democrat—thousands of us had just lost our jobs and were about to compete over a minimal number of positions in Democratic politics.

After playing a very small role helping elect Democratic governors in New Jersey and Virginia while working at the Democratic Governors Association, I got a call from Steve Hildebrand, who had been a top aide to Al Gore, asking if I had any interest in coming to work for him. I didn't know Hilde, as he was called, but his reputation as one of the best political minds in the party preceded him, and working for him would be a great opportunity to learn and get a leg up on the next presidential election.

"I'm looking to hire a communications director for a Senate race that I am managing," Hilde told me.

"Interesting. Where's the race?" I asked.

"South Dakota. I'm managing Senator Tim Johnson's reelect."

I tried to suppress a groan. South Dakota might as well have been the North Pole as far as I was concerned. I mean, I had never even really been to the Midwest. All I knew was that it was cold. Really, really cold.[18]

Hildebrand made a very compelling case about the importance of the race and the quality of the team he was putting together. I assumed that he'd tried and failed to convince a long list of more prominent and experienced political operatives to move to South Dakota before he got to me.

My initial thought was to turn down the job. But I wanted to

---

18   I underestimated how cold it was.

run communications on a Senate race, and no one else was exactly beating down my door. Once again, I said to hell with it, put all my possessions in my car, and drove to South Dakota.[19]

I knew so little about South Dakota that I told people for weeks that I was moving to Sioux City, before I learned that Sioux City is in Iowa. Sioux Falls was where I was moving.

Despite the cold and the geographic confusion, moving to South Dakota put me on the path to Barack Obama. It was just a *very* windy path.

BEING LEFT AT THE ALTAR

My cell phone rang on the morning after that election. It was a Washington, DC, number. I figured it was some reporter doing a postmortem on Tim Johnson's victory by less than 1/10th of a percent of the vote. Our come-from-behind win shocked everyone and was the rare bright spot on a very dark night for Democrats. Within hours of the election being called, folks were saying we had run the best campaign in the country.

"Hi, Dan. It's Tom Daschle."

"Umm, hello, sir," I responded to the Senate majority leader and the most powerful Democrat in the country. And the other senator from South Dakota.

After congratulating me on the victory, Daschle cut to the chase:

"Dan, I am thinking seriously of running for the White House, and I know you are going to have some other opportunities, but I would appreciate it if you wait until I make a decision before taking another job. If I do this, I want you on my team."

I was blown away. This was the Senate majority leader calling *me* and asking *me* to join his team—how could I turn that down?

---

19   South Dakota is a beautiful state filled with great people, but it is so cold that if you leave your car parked outside for too long, the engine freezes.

"Absolutely, sir. I'm flattered that you would ask." I responded too quickly and eagerly to be seen as playing it cool.

The week before Thanksgiving, I was summoned to the Capitol by Pete Rouse, Tom Daschle's top aide and a man so powerful that he was referred to as the 101st senator. Pete was such a big deal that his staff had to build a secret back exit to his office in the Capitol so that he could come and go without being harassed by senators hanging around to bend his ear. Despite his powerful persona, Pete might be the nicest, most thoughtful person in politics.

The Capitol was a ghost town because the Senate was out of session for the holiday. I met Pete in a Capitol coffee shop that was so empty, I thought it was closed. I had worn a suit and tie for the meeting. Pete showed up in jeans and cowboy boots.

After gruffly heckling me for being dressed like a kid at his confirmation, Pete laid it out for me.

"Tom has basically decided to run. His wife is supportive. He wants to make a final decision over the holidays, but it's a done deal. Hildebrand is going to manage the campaign, and we want you to play a senior role on the communications team."[20]

Before Pete could finish offering me the job, I accepted. It wasn't till later that I realized I had just signed up to move back to South Dakota—less than three months after returning to DC.

I spent the next six weeks on conference calls planning out the launch of the campaign. In the first week of January, we were in the final preparations for the announcement of Daschle's campaign for president. We had gone so far as to have the Winter Dance at Daschle's alma mater in Aberdeen, South Dakota, moved out of the gym so we could hold the announcement event there.

On the morning that I was going to fly to South Dakota to prepare for the event, I got an e-mail from a well-connected reporter

---

20   There was no specific job, but "senior role" certainly sounded important.

asking me about a rumor that Daschle had changed his mind about running. I laughed.

"How could that be true?" I thought. "I would certainly know that if it was." I got in my car and started driving to the airport. My cell phone rang and it was Steve Hildebrand calling to sheepishly tell me that, yes, the rumor was true and that Tom had changed his mind at the last minute and was going to stay in the Senate.

Two years later, I was still working for Daschle and eventually helped run his reelection campaign. It was a brutal, exhausting affair that ended with me being part of the group that had to tell Tom and his family that we weren't going to pull it off. The memory of consoling his mother still haunts me.

I missed the 2004 presidential race and instead had worked on the most high profile losing campaign in recent memory. Couldn't have played my cards worse if I'd tried.

BAYH-BYE

I was dark, fed up with politics, and thinking seriously about going to law school yet again. And then I got a fortuitous phone call that kept me out of the legal profession. This time it was Anita Dunn, an advisor to Indiana senator Evan Bayh, whom I had worked with on the Daschle campaign. Evan was thinking of running for president in 2008 and was looking to hire a communications director to help him prepare for that potential campaign.

I wasn't immediately sold on the idea of Bayh as presidential material, but I had just helped lead the first losing campaign for a Senate leader in fifty years, so I was mostly just glad someone wanted to hire me again. Bayh was a genuinely nice guy and I needed to pay my rent, which made it easier to swallow some of my concerns about his political centrism.

Learning from Losing

I had entered politics as a bleeding-heart liberal. In my high school, one of the requirements for graduation was undertaking a monthlong senior project. Some students wrote plays; others painted murals and conducted sophisticated science projects; I wrote and defended a thesis that argued for socialism as a better governmental system than capitalism.[21] My liberal idealism had been dulled by the presiding political strategy of the Democratic Party of the late 1990s and early 2000s— that the best way to win was to dull the edges of our liberalism and co-opt Republican issues to win over swing voters. It wasn't inspiring, and after defeats in the 2000, 2002, and 2004 elections, it was clear it wasn't effective either.

I also felt like I had something more to prove in politics. I had just gotten my ass kicked; Daschle had run a great race, but his opponent had bested us when it counted. I had learned some lessons from the defeat and was eager to test them out in a new arena.

After two years of plotting, planning, and many, many trips to small towns in Iowa and New Hampshire to build a network for those two states that play such a critical role in the nominating process, the Bayh for President train was about to leave the station.

Right about this time, Barack Obama popped up on my radar.

Obama had been out campaigning for Democrats in the 2006 election and drawing huge crowds everywhere he went. There was a budding grassroots Draft Obama movement on this new site called Facebook. From my perch, it all seemed ridiculous: what freshman senator would run for president?

Obama agreed to speak at Iowa senator Tom Harkin's annual Steak Fry. This event was a traditional proving ground for

---

21   I was young, dumb, and wrong.

presidential candidates looking to make a name for themselves. My old boss Steve Hildebrand, who had a lot of experience in Iowa, was staffing Obama on this trip. For all the people who make their living talking and writing about politics, this was a sure sign that Obama was going to run.

I was still a skeptic. Obama had a book coming out, and floating a presidential campaign is a *great* way to sell a book.[22]

On his way home from the Steak Fry, Hildebrand called me on my cell phone. I quickly answered because I was desperate to hear his scouting report on Obama.

"Hilde. How was it?"

Hildebrand is a stoic of Norwegian descent. It takes a lot to get him excited, but he was talking a mile a minute.

"Obama is the real deal. The greatest, most inspiring politician of my lifetime. Pfeiffer, you have to come do this."

"Do what?" I asked.

"Get Obama to the White House."

"Is he running?"

"He better. We need him."

It wasn't clear to me if "we" meant America or Hilde and me, since we were both still suffering from the emotional trauma of losing Daschle's race.

After getting left at the campaign altar by Daschle, I was pretty skeptical about joining a campaign that did not yet exist. Fool me once, and so on. Plus, after two years of working for him, I was loyal to Evan Bayh.

As the weeks went on, the momentum for an Obama run gained steam and Hildebrand's entreaties to me grew more frequent and impassioned. Pete Rouse was now Obama's chief of staff and was making a similar case. I was starting to develop serious FOMO. I didn't know Obama, but he was impressive and there was a

---

22 Ignore this admission if, by the time you read this book, I have floated myself as a potential candidate to juice up lagging sales.

palpable excitement around him beyond anything I had ever seen in politics. Plus, Obama was surrounding himself with some of my favorite people in politics.

A week after Bayh announced his presidential exploratory committee, we were scheduled to visit New Hampshire as part of our announcement tour. Then we got some bad news: Obama had just agreed to speak at a New Hampshire Democratic Party dinner and hold a book signing during our visit. This would, of course, lead to unpleasant comparisons about the size of our crowds and the enthusiasm for our candidacies. The press (and the public) was in a feeding frenzy of excitement over a potential Obama candidacy. We had already announced our trip, so canceling it was not an option. A story about Obama scaring us away was worse than one about his bigger crowds. I still doubted Obama would run, and the odds would be long, especially against the two front-runners—Hillary Clinton and former vice presidential nominee John Edwards. So off we went to take our lumps.

Turns out when you make chicken salad out of chicken shit, it still tastes like shit.

When I got to the gate at BWI Airport for the one nonstop flight to Manchester, New Hampshire, I saw more big-name reporters than one finds in the White House briefing room on a normal day.

I noticed there was a crowd of reporters standing around someone or something. When I got closer, I saw that it was Robert Gibbs, Obama's communications director, who was holding an impromptu press conference of sorts, while Alyssa Mastromonaco, Obama's scheduler at the time, stood by, watching with some amusement.[23] I had never met Alyssa before, but Rouse had been raving about her to me.

I stood off to the side, trying not to be noticed, when a reporter from USA Today came up to me.

---

23   I didn't know it at the time, but Alyssa would become one of the most powerful people in Obama's White House and one of my best friends.

"Dan. What are you doing here?"

"I'm headed up to New Hampshire to staff my boss on his first official swing through the state."

"I thought you worked for Bayh."

"I do. He's campaigning in New Hampshire this weekend."

"Hmmm, I had no idea," the reporter replied before going back to talk to Gibbs.

It went downhill from there.

On the final event of our trip, Bayh was participating in a meet and greet at the home of a state legislator. Bayh was on his game and impressed the crowd with his record of winning and governing in a red state. Maybe, I thought, there was an opportunity here to be the "electable" alternative to Clinton and Obama. As we were leaving, we asked one of the hosts of our event for directions back to the airport. He responded: "Normally, I would tell you to hop on the highway, but given the traffic for the Obama event downtown, I would suggest taking back roads."

Two weeks later, I was on a conference call with Bayh and his top advisors debating whether he should drop out of the race and stay in the Senate. It was clear he had already decided to leave the campaign. At one point, Bayh had to take another call and I used that break to walk out in the hall and leave an urgent message for Pete Rouse. "Pete, it's Pfeiffer. I don't know whether Senator Obama is going to run, but I would love to have a serious conversation with you as soon as possible."

Pete returned my call later that night after Bayh dropped out. We scheduled a coffee for the next week. And in what I felt was a real warning sign, the meeting was going to be in the exact same coffee shop where I had accepted the position on the never-to-be Daschle presidential campaign.

Pete and I sat down, and in one of the more surreal experiences of my life, he gave me the exact same pitch from four years prior.

"Obama is almost certainly going to run, his wife is onboard, he is going to make a final decision over the holidays, but it's a done deal." The thought bubble over my head said, "Are you fucking kidding me?" I was excited about the opportunity, but based on my recent disappointments, I was trying to keep my expectations in check. I just knew deep down that Obama wasn't going to run.

Around that same time, I got a call from John Edwards, the incredibly ambitious former senator who had been John Kerry's choice to be VP in 2004. Even if Obama ran, most political prognosticators thought that Edwards had the best chance to beat Hillary Clinton, who had been planning for this race for a decade and was certain to run. After a quick perfunctory interview with Edwards, he offered me the position of communications director.

I spent the holidays catching up on the Obama thing—reading Obama's two books, watching some of his speeches (including the 2004 convention speech, which I still hadn't seen) and interviews, and starting to fall into platonic, political love.

I was still torn between my head and my heart. I had been beaten down in recent years by some really painful campaign losses; the Democratic Party felt stale and uninspiring; and being out of power in Washington during the Bush years made everything I did feel futile. Even the campaigns I had won had felt like moving the pieces around the board without winning the game instead of being part of something bigger.

I had almost quit politics twice in the last two years, seriously explored a job at a nonprofit, and studied for the LSAT and the GRE. I had experienced professional success in the sense that I had gotten some "good" jobs and had built what I believed was a decent reputation among my colleagues. When "good" jobs came open, I often got a call. But if I was honest with myself, I had been in politics for a decade and what had I accomplished?

What difference had I made?

Whether it was from watching *The West Wing* on a loop or reading every book ever written about Robert Kennedy's 1968 campaign, I had an unrequited relationship with politics. I desperately wanted to experience a politics that felt more like a cause than a campaign. I had never felt anything resembling what I imagined that historic Kennedy campaign felt like. And I was dying to know what that was like.

I could point to playing a role in this fight or that fight that had helped prevent some harm being done to people by the Bush administration, but that's sort of like feeling good about a couple of defensive plays in a game you lost by three touchdowns. I wanted to be part of something that mattered to the world; something that actually helped people.

There is a quote from the HBO show *The Sopranos* that I kept coming back to in this period. Discussing his discontent with the state of his career as a mob boss, Tony Soprano says:

"It's good to be in something from the ground floor. I came too late for that and I know. But lately, I'm getting the feeling that I came in at the end. The best is over."

I was sick and tired of playing not to lose and losing anyway. There had to be something more.

GAME ON

Right after New Year's, I got a call from Obama's office asking to schedule a meeting with the senator. This could mean only one thing: he was in the race.

On the morning of the interview, I woke up feeling a little nauseous. At first, I thought I had a touch of the flu coming on, but it was just nerves. This was a big deal for me. This might be my last chance to be part of something special. Something different from everything I'd done before.

My first clue that Obama was cut from a different cloth was that he didn't send some eager beaver aide to fetch me for our meeting. At 11:00 a.m. on the dot, Obama himself walked out into the lobby with no jacket and his sleeves rolled up, introduced himself as Barack (which is pretty funny in hindsight), and shook my hand. I'd had hundreds of meetings with politicians and never before had the elected official personally come to grab me for the meeting. This may seem like a small thing—and it is—but it told me that Obama's huge celebrity had not gone to his head.

A group of mostly African American schoolkids on a field trip from Illinois were sitting in the lobby, waiting for a junior aide to give them a tour. They looked slack jawed at Obama. They didn't react to him like a senator. Most kids couldn't give a shit who their senator is, but these kids were staring at Obama like a hero. It was clear that this African American man potentially becoming president meant something very powerful to them.

Obama excused himself from me to go over and talk to the kids—none of whom could vote in the upcoming presidential primary contests. This was before the age of selfies, but Obama took photos with each of the kids. This wasn't a perfunctory photo op. Obama did something very rare for a politician. He listened to them.

"This guy is either very good or very good at faking it," I thought to myself.

Obama sat me down on the couch in his surprisingly small and very dimly lit office—as a freshman senator low on the seniority list, he had one of the worst offices on Capitol Hill.

Obama started the interview by telling me that in a few weeks he would announce he was running for president. He didn't hedge in any way or give himself an out. Obama didn't know me or have any reason to trust me with this information.

I had done this awkward dance with soon-to-be candidates on a couple of prior occasions. The entire conversations were conducted in a way to ensure plausible deniability:

"If I were to run, how would you approach the campaign that I have not yet decided to launch…"

The politician knew what they were saying was BS and they knew that I knew what they were saying was BS, but we all had to play our assigned role in an absurd play. Obama didn't seem to have the time or the patience for this sort of game.

I took this as another positive sign.

Over the next forty-five minutes, Obama talked to me about why he wanted to run for president; what he wanted to do as president; and why he was not going to heed the advice of the old Washington hands who were telling him to wait.

Not once in the conversation did Obama mention poll numbers, campaign strategy, or political tactics. He didn't try to convince me why he would win or how his campaign was the best path to a plush White House job.

Obama made the case that the campaign was worth running because he had something to say that he felt was worth saying.

At the end of the conversation, Obama looked me right in the eye and asked, "How often do you get to put your shoulder against the wheel of history and push?"

I was in.

I walked out of Obama's office after the interview having accepted a job on the spot. The position that the Obama campaign offered me was traveling press secretary. This job meant that I would travel everywhere with Senator Obama and potentially be on the road, nearly nonstop, for two years. This was not my first-choice job. But the two other jobs I wanted—communications director and national press secretary—were filled, so it was this job or no job. And I wasn't missing this opportunity.

I had no idea what I was going to get paid. I am notoriously bad at asking this question, which is awkward in any employment context, but particularly in politics, where the whole point is that the cause is more important than the compensation. Yet this was a critical piece of information, considering that I had a mortgage in DC and was about to pick up a rent bill in Chicago. I didn't find out the answer until Robert Gibbs sent me and Bill Burton, another early hire, the first draft of the communications department budget.

Exactly two weeks after my interview/immediate job acceptance, I gathered with my new coworkers in a conference room in a downtown DC law firm for the first official strategy meeting of Obama for America.

As we waited for the candidate to arrive, we went around and introduced ourselves to one another and made small talk.

In addition to Hildebrand and Rouse, who had recruited me to this effort, seated around the very large wooden table were:

David Plouffe: A nearly forty-year-old fellow Delawarean and college dropout, who was going to manage the campaign. Plouffe had cut his teeth working in the Iowa presidential caucus and had a reputation as being a numbers whiz, incredibly disciplined, and tough as nails. Plouffe was also a bit of an enigma. When he detailed the tragic death of his dog in his memoir of the 2008 campaign, even his closest confidants on the campaign were taken by surprise. We had no idea his dog has died. In fact, we didn't even know he had a dog.

David Axelrod: Axe was Obama's longest-serving political advisor and one of the best-known and well-respected political consultants in the party. Unlike most of his colleagues in the mercenary-like profession, Axe had never lost his soul in the pursuit of power or money. He was the rare true believer in politics, and his idealism would fuel our campaign. In addition to his strategic acumen, Axe was equally well known for being a bit of a mess. He once famously broke his BlackBerry by getting donut glaze in the trackball, and in the White House on the back of his office door hung dozens of neckties that had not survived his breakfast.

Alyssa Mastromonaco: One secret about politics is that the most important person on the campaign is the director of scheduling and advance. On the Obama campaign, Alyssa was that person. She combined a huge, warm, uproariously funny personality with the ability to work miracles on any and all matters. Alyssa was a huge fan of the Grateful Dead, knew every episode of *Beverly Hills, 90210* by heart (as I did), and treated her staff and colleagues like family. Alyssa would also become my closest friend and would literally save my life in the years to come.[24]

Robert Gibbs and Bill Burton: Gibbs, Burton, and I at this point made up the entire Obama national communications team.[25] Gibbs, a former college soccer player from Alabama with a long career working on Democratic campaigns, was one of Obama's closest political advisors, with a sharp tongue and a penchant for Southern aphorisms like "busier than a one-legged man in a butt-kicking contest." Burton, like me, was new to Obama World and had just come off a very successful stint helping the Democrats win back Congress. He was super sharp, but also known for getting on your computer when you weren't looking and sending joke e-mails to others on the staff.

Jon Favreau: I was surprised by the presence of the twenty-five-year-old speechwriter in a strategy meeting like this, but I quickly learned two things: One, Obama, who considered himself a writer who entered politics as opposed to a politician who writes, had a unique relationship with his speechwriters. Two, Favreau was a supremely talented political strategist with a knack for knowing the exact right argument to make and the way to make it. He would soon become very famous as a wunderkind presidential aide and not the guy who directed *Iron Man*.

Eventually Barack Obama arrived and walked around the table and greeted each of us.

As he took the one remaining empty seat at the very crowded table, he declared:

"All right, folks, let's get to work."

---

24   Stay tuned.
25   Future *Pod Save America* cohost Tommy Vietor was already on his way to Iowa to help lead our efforts in the must-win Iowa caucus.

CHAPTER 2

HOW NOT TO LOSE A CAMPAIGN

In my career, I had worked on a presidential campaign, a gubernatorial campaign, two Senate campaigns, and a ballot initiative. I thought I had seen it all—or at least most of it—but what awaited me in Chicago was like no campaign I had ever seen.

This was not a typical Democratic campaign.[1]

I didn't fully grasp what was so different about it until years later.

In a dreary meeting room in a nondescript hotel in San Jose in 2013, President Barack Obama was meeting with some of the most important players in Silicon Valley. Around the table were founders and executives from the most important tech companies in the world. These were titans of industry meeting with the leader of the free world. It should have been riveting. But somehow it wasn't. The conversation was focused on reforms to federal government information technology procurement rules, not exactly the stuff *West Wing* episodes are made of.

This meeting, like many others, was a response to the catastrophic failure of Healthcare.gov, the website where people were supposed to sign up for the Affordable Care Act. When the fate of

---

1 I know this because it didn't do the thing Democratic campaigns typically do: lose.

your signature domestic policy accomplishment depends on a website and the website doesn't work, it's time to pay a visit to Silicon Valley.

I was "backbenching," which is a White House term for staff who are in meetings with the president but didn't make the cut for the table,[2] and I was buried in my BlackBerry[3] catching up on endless e-mails.

At one point, one of the attendees told the president that we needed to bring a "start-up" mentality to government. I perked up because I knew this would get a strong reaction from the president. He spent his life being lectured by business leaders, particularly those on Wall Street, who have little understanding of and even less experience with politics and government.

Instead of getting annoyed, the president declared: "You know, my 2008 campaign might have been the greatest start-up in history."

WINNING IS FUNDAMENTAL

It has become somewhat in vogue in recent years to draw comparisons between Silicon Valley start-ups and presidential campaigns. By the simplest definition, every campaign is a start-up. Start from zero, raise money, rapidly build a staff and operation, and then scale it to meet demand. But truth be told, presidential campaigns had been run the same way for the last forty years. Organized the same way, funded the same way, and run the same way. By 2008, we had moved into a digital world, yet campaigns (particularly Democratic ones) were analog anachronisms.

---

2   Being at the table is great, but if you need an opportunity to get work done, sit backbench. Some of my most productive hours in the White House were in National Economic Council policy discussions. (Apologies to the Econ Team.)

3   My addiction to my phone will be a running theme in this book as it is in my marriage.

The fact that Obama 2008 functioned as a start-up wasn't some specific choice we made. It was the only option available to us.

We had some top tech talent on the campaign, including Joe Rospars, who had been one of the leaders of Howard Dean's Internet-driven campaign, and Chris Hughes, Mark Zuckerberg's roommate from Harvard and a cofounder of Facebook.[4] Obama was more Internet savvy than most politicians, but he had no particular experience in the tech industry. David Plouffe, our campaign manager and the architect of our effort, had spent his career in politics, not tech. We were traditional political operatives, frustrated with traditional politics, working for a nontraditional candidate. We ended up adopting a nontraditional campaign strategy for a very simple reason: a traditional campaign strategy would fail for Obama.

Our competitors in 2008 ran a slightly updated version of the losing campaign that John Kerry had run four years prior, and Al Gore had run four years prior to that.

You get the point.

Instead of the top-down, hierarchical campaigns fueled by rubber chicken dinners and geriatric party activists that had led to a mounting series of losses for the Democratic Party, Barack Obama took a different approach. He melded decentralized grassroots organizing and Internet-based enthusiasm with the most advanced technological tools and sophisticated data available. Our campaign forever changed how campaigns are run in the modern world. Campaigns are now massive data-driven entities that raise and spend hundreds of millions of dollars in a short period of time. They set up tech-incubator-style engineering shops staffed by alumni of Google and Facebook. Along with all this firepower come huge logistical and organizational challenges that stress the management skills of the candidates and their senior teams.

---

4   There was something surreal during the campaign about getting personal tech support for our personal use of Facebook from one of the guys who started the company.

As Democrats try to figure out why we lost the most winnable election in history and how we will win the most important election in American history in a few years, it's worth going back to Obama's 2008 campaign to see what worked.

For all the sexy data and tech, the killer oppo and gut-punching negative ads, and the inspiring speeches, nothing matters more than the fundamentals. You can get the fundamentals right and still lose, but you can't get them wrong and win.

There are five building blocks for any successful campaign:

- Attitude
- Scaling
- Culture
- Strategy
- Branding

The Obama 2008 campaign got these right (maybe not on the first try every time, but we got there eventually). How we navigated these challenges not only helps explain the unlikely election of Barack Obama, but also paints a path forward for future campaigns as Democrats try to return from the wilderness.

The Start-Up Attitude

In that first interview, Obama told me, "I have a great life. I don't need this, and if I lose, I will just go back to my life in Chicago." At the time, I was struck by the confidence in Obama's voice and saw this sentiment as a real strength in an industry where the overly cautious tend to lose.

Before too long, I learned that what Obama told me wasn't entirely true. Obama does not like to lose at anything—golf, basketball, cards, Scrabble, and most certainly campaigns. The president's personal assistant or "body guy," Reggie Love, a former Duke basketball player, once brought a Nerf basketball hoop into the anteroom of the Oval Office and the president would challenge visitors to a shoot-off and not start the next meeting until he had won.

But there was an essential truth in that statement. Obama wanted to be president; he didn't need to be president. Many—actually most—people who seek the presidency do it out of a desire to fill some insatiable internal need for approval and adoration or to work out some deep-seated psychological issue dating back to childhood. Obama was different. He was incredibly comfortable in his own skin and had done the hard work of self-discovery and self-actualization as a young man grappling with his identity and the father he never really knew. He could afford to lose, and this gave us a strategic advantage over Clinton in 2008 (and Romney in 2012). The candidate least afraid of losing normally wins.

Obama's have-no-fear attitude infected all of our thinking and planning. Most people think that the motto of the 2008 campaign was "Yes, We Can" or "Hope and Change"; it was actually something we abbreviated to the family-friendly "WTF." This was our motto and our attitude. When faced with a choice between something safe with less upside or a higher-risk, higher-reward option, we always chose the latter.

We weren't supposed to be in the race to begin with, let alone have a chance to win, so we were willing to take big risks. To use a Plouffe-ism, we believed we were best when we were on the high wire.

We would often one-up each other trying to come up with the craziest ideas. We took risks, because we had great confidence in Obama and were too green not to have tremendous faith in ourselves.[5]

Should we put the president on *Meet the Press* the Sunday before the Iowa caucus with the notoriously tough interviewer Tim Russert? Yes.

---

5   Getting your ass kicked in DC for a few years can beat that attitude out of you, which is when you know it's time to leave the White House.

Should we do the first ever international campaign swing?[6] Yes. Should we stop in Israel? Definitely. How about going to the West Bank? Absolutely.

SCALING: BOLTING THE WINGS ON WHILE THE PLANE TOOK OFF

Presidential campaigns are massive organizational efforts, and the better you do, the bigger the campaign and the more complicated the task. This was probably truer for the Obama campaign than any in modern history. No campaign had to go from a standing start to fully operational more quickly or under greater scrutiny.

It's easy to look back on our historic victory and forget that we started from the bottom.[7] But there was nothing glamorous about the early days of the Obama campaign.

On Martin Luther King Day, 2007, I arrived at Obama's Senate office to meet Robert Gibbs and Bill Burton. As I walked from the Metro to the Hart Building, where Obama's office was, I tried to soak in the moment. It was hard not to notice the powerful symbolism of going to work to elect the first African American president on MLK Day.

In about twenty-four hours, we were going to release a video to the world announcing that Obama was launching a presidential exploratory committee. Technically, setting up an exploratory committee means that a candidate is taking a step toward a race, but has not made a decision. This was bullshit and everyone knew it. In 99 out of 100 cases, the candidates have already explored the race and are running. For all intents and purposes, we were about

---

6   Technically, Minnesota Governor Harold Stassen visited Europe during his 1948 campaign, but I refuse to acknowledge it despite the repeated entreaties of this book's fact-checkers.

7   Drake may be Canadian, but I quote him often in discussing American politics because in the Trump era anything goes.

to announce Obama's presidential campaign. That's certainly how the rest of the world would see it and how they would grade our performance. There's no such thing as opening off-Broadway when your name is Barack Obama and you just announced a challenge to the ruling Democratic political dynasty.

The media was in complete freak-out mode about a possible Obama run. Burton and I had spent the night before hiding from one of the Associated Press's most dogged reporters who was trying to confirm rumors that Obama was running and we had joined the campaign.

No serious candidate had ever had such a short runway between even contemplating running for president and actually running for president. All eyes were on us.

John Edwards had been running for president nonstop for four years; the people around Hillary Clinton had been building a presidential campaign apparatus for at least a decade. Obama had decided a few weeks earlier, had no national political apparatus or network, and a ragtag group of staffers willing to bet their careers by taking on the Clinton machine. We had done none of the work that normally happens before an announcement. We knew the announcement was going to create a massive tsunami of interest, and we did not have anything near the necessary infrastructure to handle that interest.

Why not wait until we had our shit together?

We couldn't afford to. There is nothing more valuable in a campaign than time. You can always raise more money, hire more people, or run more TV ads. But Election Day can't be moved, and every minute wasted is one you will never get back. We were less than a year from the Iowa caucus, which was going to be make or break for our campaign. After Hillary Clinton's losses in 2008 and 2016, it's easy to forget what a political juggernaut the Clinton machine was in January 2007. Every day they were sucking up some of the best political and fund-raising talent as well as endorsements from key political leaders. The longer we waited, the bigger head start we gave her. John Kerry was the other factor pushing us to a quick announcement. Kerry had yet to rule out running again in 2008, and many of his key supporters were waiting for him to make up his mind before committing to another candidate. We knew that many of those Kerry backers were skeptical of Clinton and interested in Obama, but if Obama wasn't in the race yet, a lot of those folks would end up in the Clinton campaign. So ready or not, we had to announce.

Plouffe described our situation as bolting the wings on the plane as it took off. It was terrifying and tremendously exhilarating.

The plan was to meet at the Senate and drive over together to the temporary office space we had rented to house our operations before the whole campaign moved to Chicago in a few months.

We hit some speed bumps right out of the gate.

First, because it was MLK Day, the Senate wasn't in session, and Burton and I were locked out of the building and couldn't get anyone on the phone to let us in. We decided to wait around the corner because we didn't want to be spotted by any reporters wandering around Capitol Hill. After freezing our asses off for a while, someone came down to let us in.

Finally inside, Gibbs, Burton, and I were joined by Tommy Vietor, Gibbs's deputy on the Senate staff, who was going to be heading to Iowa to work on the campaign, and Jon Favreau.[8]

We quickly realized that we were supposed to send the announcement video to the press via e-mail tomorrow, and we had neither a contact list of reporters to send it to nor a campaign e-mail account to send it from. We also had no staff to help us gather and input this information into a campaign database, so we slowly went name by name through our BlackBerry contacts, adding every reporter whose e-mail address we had to the list. This was far from perfect, and when we sent out the video making this historic announcement

---

8   This is where *Pod Save America* was born. Insert Praying Hands emoji here.

(from Gibbs's Hotmail account), we missed some of the most important reporters in politics.[9]

When we arrived at our new digs, which were essentially a windowless room with card tables for desks, there were a handful of other soon-to-be staffers setting up the office. Once we received the final version of the video, we decided to watch it and then do a test run of the process for sending it out. We plugged in the laptop and pulled up the video and...no Internet. We tried several different Ethernet cords—nothing. Pretty hard to e-mail out our big announcement video without the Internet. We sat there until Bill took matters into his own hands and went to Staples right before it closed and bought us a new router and somehow managed to install it.[10]

We got the video out the next day, and all of a sudden our small team of about twenty people was inundated with thousands of media requests, interviews, and résumés. There was nonstop global press interest in Obama's candidacy and yet we were still a team of about twenty people working in two tiny offices—the windowless office that I was in with the communications and scheduling staffs and another equally spartan office that was above a Subway sandwich shop and smelled strongly, consistently, nauseatingly of baking bread.[11]

Everyone was working around the clock to build the campaign infrastructure, plan a massively complicated announcement tour, and turn as much of the interest in Obama into assets as possible. People who would have senior roles on the campaign were doing the work of interns: answering phones that wouldn't stop ringing, data entering an endless flood of résumés and speaking invitations,

---

9   This did not go over well. Turns out reporters really don't like missing news.

10 To this day, Bill Burton cites this example to claim that without him Obama never could have run. He's not right, but he's also not wrong.

11 No one who spent a lot of time in that office has eaten a Subway sandwich in the past decade.

and building the sort of basic databases of supporter information that campaigns for class president had, but we didn't.

Despite our most valiant efforts, the enthusiasm for Obama greatly outpaced our own operation. A few weeks after the announcement video went out, the Democratic National Committee was holding its winter meeting in Washington and all of the prospective 2008 candidates were asked to speak. This invitation posed a couple of challenges for us. First, the other candidates had been honing their pitch on the trail for years, and Obama would be debuting his campaign message in front of all the party poohbahs. The expectations for his performance were through the roof. A poor performance could really damage his candidacy. Second, the core message of the campaign was going to be that change came from grassroots activism outside Washington. Obama's raison d' être was that change came from the outside in, not the inside out, and we were starting the campaign talking to the ultimate group of political insiders. Not to mention this was a roomful of people who had been close to the Clintons for decades but whom Obama had never met. This no-win situation was the first of what we would come to call "shitburgers" over the years.

Despite these concerns, skipping the event wasn't really an option. This would signal to the media and the party that we weren't ready for prime time, which would be bad for any candidate but particularly for an upstart freshman senator new to national politics.

To communicate our outsider message and lessen the focus on Obama's DNC remarks, we came up with what we thought was a brilliant idea. After the DNC meeting, we would hold a rally at George Mason University, which was in Virginia right outside DC. Our goal was to demonstrate the enthusiasm for Obama's candidacy particularly among the young people who had been forming Facebook groups for months, urging Obama to run. If he received tepid applause in the room, we would be able to show the world an alternative picture in the same news cycle. Our advance staff, which was the best in the business but tiny at the time, booked the atrium of a building on the university campus.

After Obama's speech to the DNC meeting (which went fine enough), we arrived on campus and hordes of students were in line waiting to get into the speech. They had apparently been waiting all day and were getting antsy. Inside the building, people were jammed into every inch of the floor and were basically hanging from the rafters. We could have easily filled an NBA arena. We had totally underestimated the demand to see Obama.

In rallies like that, the staff built a buffer between the audience and the stage, so that during the event, the media could go into the buffer to get close-up photos and video, and afterward, the candidate could go "work the ropeline" or shake hands with the audience. This was an important way to keep the speaker safe, and it was pretty standard for a rally of any size. In this instance, the setup broke down as excited and enthusiastic fans climbed over the fence into the buffer and were swarming Obama. It was pure chaos. The line between rally and riot had gotten dangerously blurry.[12]

This was before the Secret Service started protecting Obama. Security was being provided by George Mason. They were a group of very large and aggressive men with a style more akin to nightclub bouncers than security professionals, who started physically manhandling the audience.[13] I entered into the chaos in the buffer, not out of some heroic attempt to help Obama, but it happened to be the fastest way out and I was growing concerned I was going to be left behind without a car (and before Lyft) in suburban Virginia. This was also the first event I had ever staffed Obama at, and it was an absolute shitshow.

Several times I was accosted by security types as I tried to catch up to the senator and at one point came upon a near-physical

---

12   It's worth noting that the Obama advance team ended up being the best that ever was.

13   Political Pro-Tip: Physically harming your voters is a bad idea.

altercation between a news photographer trying to do his job, an Obama staffer, and a very large George Mason security official who could easily have been mistaken for an NFL linebacker suspended for steroid use. That photographer was Pete Souza, who would go on to be the White House photographer and chronicle all eight years of Obama's presidency from the inside. Pete did not back down or flinch under the threat of severe violence from this very large man. I would see this toughness many times over the years when foreign governments would try to curtail his access to Obama as we traveled the world with the president. Pete is one of the nicest guys on the planet, but one of the most dangerous places in the world is between Pete and the shot he wants.

There were two take-aways from this fiasco: One, the demand to see, hear, and be near Obama was more fervent than we had imagined. It was more like being on the road with a rock star than a political candidate. Two, we were far from ready to manage that demand. There are stories in the tech world about Facebook co-founders Mark Zuckerberg and Dustin Moskovitz working out of a small house in Palo Alto and staying up all night in the early days of their company trying to keep their servers from crashing because so many more people than anticipated were using Facebook. We were in a similar situation. Small operation, huge and rapidly growing demand. Zuckerberg believed at the time that if the servers crashed and people couldn't join or access Facebook, the company could fail. The Obama campaign was in a similar boat.

We were weeks away from a multistate "announcement tour,"[14] which would include massively complicated logistics and an event in front of the old State Capitol Building in Springfield, Illinois, which would have a crowd perhaps twenty times larger than the one that got out of control in Virginia.

---

14   Even though we had done an "announcement" video, we still needed to do an in-person "announcement" tour, even though we had already "announced." Politics is weird.

For all the excitement around Obama's candidacy, there was also massive skepticism from the media and the political establishment. By deciding to run as a freshman senator with no previous national political experience, Obama was putting his thumb in the eye of a lot of conventional political wisdom. This was a precocious decision, and as much as the media loved writing about his rise, they were chomping at the bit to write about his fall. They were dying to pivot to the narrative that Obama had flown too close to the sun. A single mistake on the announcement tour could end the campaign before it started.[15]

In order to successfully scale an enterprise like a presidential campaign or a tech start-up, you've also got to build a culture.

BUILDING A CULTURE: NO ASSHOLES ALLOWED

As the Obama campaign became the Obama phenomenon, we needed people and we needed them really fast. A number of our staff were veterans of the Kerry campaign, which was known for a poisonous culture of leaks, backstabbing, and jockeying for power and access. This was not something we could risk repeating. We didn't.

Our team eventually became known as "No Drama Obama." Loyal to one another, total commitment to a cause, empowerment and inclusion, and no leaks. People who didn't adhere to these principles didn't get through the door, and the few that did ended up working a backwater field office in a noncompetitive state.[16]

If you ask anyone involved from President Obama on down to a field organizer in Story County, Iowa, they will tell you that our culture was one of the things of which they were proudest. The mar-

15   The announcement tour went off without a hitch although President
       Obama believes to this day that we tried to kill him by making someone
       born in Hawaii speak outside in 17-degree weather.
16   The message was not subtle.

gin of error for our campaign was so small and the odds of beating Clinton so steep that we couldn't afford to fight her and ourselves at the same time.

So how did we build this culture, and what lessons can be learned from it?

First and most important, our culture was a reflection of the man we served. Obama is at his core a really chill guy and I mean that in the most presidential way. He is a nice guy who expects his team to be nice to one another. This trait comes from how he was brought up. Obama may have been born in Hawaii, but he is "Midwestern Nice," which comes from his grandparents and their Kansas roots. He engendered loyalty to him and our cause by being loyal to his team. There were many times in the campaign where people, including some of our top donors, wanted the lot of us fired and replaced by people with more "DC experience," and every time, Obama stood by his team. We didn't know if we were going to win or lose, but we were going to do it together. If the person at the top of any organization does not reflect the values you want in the culture of that organization, it won't work.[17]

Second, our culture was not an accident. Obama, Plouffe, and Axelrod set out to build a very specific kind of campaign culture. It was as important as how much money we raised or how good our press coverage was. We measured our success and failure by whether we adhered to some of the rules we set out in the beginning.

- **No assholes allowed.** Our campaign grew quickly, which meant hiring people en masse. We had one rule that came from the top: No assholes. We didn't care about your pedigree or your ability—if you were an asshole, you weren't getting a job. We were proud of the camaraderie and culture of the early team, and we wanted to do everything to preserve it. We felt it

---

17   The fact that Obama had no preexisting political network was a hidden advantage. When we made a decision, he didn't get endless calls from unaccountable "advisors" trying to undo or question the strategic decision.

was critical to our success. Perhaps no one embodied this rule more than David Axelrod. Axe was the chief strategist on our campaign. This made him our Karl Rove or Steve Bannon.[18] Every campaign has a chief strategist, and nearly every one of them is an asshole. It just comes with the job. Axe wasn't an asshole. He was a good-hearted mensch with a propensity for puns. Axelrod would treat everyone at the campaign with the same respect, from the volunteers who answered the phone to the senior staff. This set the example for everyone on the campaign. If the most likely asshole wasn't an asshole, then no one got to be one.

- **You were all in or you were out.** Obama wanted our campaign to be run out of Chicago. This was partially a measure of convenience for him. Michelle and the girls had stayed in Chicago, and Obama came home every weekend the minute the Senate went out of session. A Chicago-based campaign meant he could squeeze out a little more family time in what was going to be a brutal travel schedule. Being in Chicago was also consistent with our anti-Washington message.[19] Besides, Chicago was key to our culture. Since most of the hires (myself included) were living in Washington, DC, taking a job on the Obama campaign meant making a major commitment. Plouffe would not allow folks to commute or work from Washington a few days a week. You were either 100 percent committing to this campaign over anything and everything else or you weren't joining, and don't even try negotiating your salary—we had specific salary bands and no one got paid a cent more than anyone else at the same level. Only true believers need apply.
- **Don't fuck the structure.** Jen O'Malley Dillon, who eventually became the field general of the '08 and '12 Obama campaigns,

---

18   Or Olivia Pope from *Scandal* or Kent from *Veep*, depending on your pop culture tastes.
19   Hard to run against Washington from Washington.

worked with me on a couple of Senate races early in our careers and she used to tell her team that Rule No. 1 was "Don't fuck the structure." What she meant by this colorful turn of phrase was that organizations function properly only if there is a clear hierarchical structure and everyone abides by it. If you had a concern or an idea, you were obligated to go through the chain of command. This was a core principle of the management of the campaign. If someone went into Plouffe's office with a complaint or concern without going through the proper channels, they were ushered out and not welcomed back. And never, ever under any circumstances consider taking your concerns directly to the candidate without sharing with the team first. This sounds overly strict and harsh, but what made it work was that we had a culture of trust where information was shared widely; therefore, you weren't afraid about what was being said in the meeting you weren't in and you knew your bosses would tell you what you needed to know.[20]

- **No leaks.** Our 2008 campaign was famously leak-free. So leak-free that no one, not even David Plouffe or David Axelrod, spoke to reporters without the communications department knowing about it in advance. I can think of only one time in the entire campaign that I read an anonymous quote from an Obama campaign official in a story and couldn't identify the person who had said it. And we found that person, and even then, it was an innocent mistake.

Barack Obama famously hates leaks. The press has twisted this into something more sinister than it is. There are very legitimate issues around the ways in which the Department of Justice pursued leak investigations, but the leaks Obama

---

20   Two exceptions were the choice of Joe Biden as VP nominee and our quarterly fund-raising numbers. Plouffe held those secrets so tightly I am confident that no amount of enhanced interrogation techniques could have pried them loose.

truly hates are not those leaks; it's the everyday leaks that fuel much of political journalism. Let me give you a sense of how those reporter-source conversations go:

Reporter: Hi, Anonymous White House/Campaign Official, I am writing a story about the president's decision-making process on issue X. I don't know if you were in the room for the conversation...

Source: I'm so glad you asked. *Of course* I was in the room. The president relies on me in these sorts of situations. Let me tell you about the advice I gave the president...

These aren't leaks out of malice—trying to stick a knife in an internal adversary—like the ones that have been so prevalent in the Trump White House. These aren't leaks of principle trying to bring some government malfeasance to light. They are leaks of vanity.

Whenever there was a leak of a pending policy decision or a detailed readout of some internal deliberations, Obama would ask some version of the question: "Can you imagine being so insecure that you need to call a reporter to show them how influential you are?"

We didn't need or want those people.

Now compare that work environment with the Trump White House, whose leaky ship has been a stimulus package for legacy media organizations. There have been leaks about the most sensitive conversations in the Oval Office and mundane but malicious leaks about White House intrigue. In my life in politics, I have never seen a group less loyal to the boss or one another. The fish rots from the head. Trump had never demonstrated loyalty to anyone other than himself, and, therefore, his staff feel they could be fired and publicly embarrassed at any minute so they are playing a version of the *Game of Thrones*. If Sean Spicer (reputation RIP) thinks Steve Bannon (dignity RIP) is leaking about him without consequences, he is going to leak about Steve Bannon to protect himself. It spirals from there.

Over the years, people—even those within the Obama campaign and White House—wondered why we took the no-leaking thing so seriously.

This is why.

STRATEGIC PLANNING: PLAYING CHESS

The greatest campaign or company cannot succeed without a well-thought-out and well-executed strategy. Strategic planning and execution is the hardest part of any endeavor, and this is particularly true in politics, where we have so many people with the title "strategist" and so few people who deserve that title.

In the early days of the Obama presidency, at one of those moments when the Washington insiders were kvetching about their new president, David Plouffe told the media that Barack Obama is a "Chess Player in a city of Checkers Players."[21] I have come back to or repurposed this quote many times over the years when describing why Obama was so successful as a candidate and a president.[22]

In politics, coming up with the strategy is a lot easier than having the discipline to stick to it. Especially in our currently insane media environment, it's easy to find yourself chasing the news of the day or the latest shiny object or switching to a new strategy because the pundits and insiders say you should. Avoiding this was referred to as playing the "long game."

Barack Obama's decision to run (and our belief that he could

---

21   For the generation raised on the PlayStation, chess is more complicated than checkers.
22   Another way to put it (in another tortured chess metaphor), he sees the whole board, or several moves ahead (I can't be stopped).

win) was not capricious. It was a leap of faith, of course, but we had theories about the political landscape heading into the election that combined with Obama's tremendous political talent to give us a level of optimism far exceeding that of the pundits or what our meager standing in the polls told us.

Like my new colleagues, I had learned much more about what works in politics from the many campaigns I'd lost than from the handful I'd had a part in winning. When I did my pro-con list to hone my thinking about working for Obama in 2008, I laid out my best case for why he could win:

1. **Enthusiasm matters.** Voting is a much bigger pain in the ass than it should be. People won't vote, let alone do the door knocking and phone calling that fuels campaigns, if they aren't enthusiastic. For whatever else you want to say about George W. Bush's policies and misguided Middle Eastern wars of choice, he had an enthusiastic following among his base, particularly evangelical Christians. This is one of the main reasons that he won. Al Gore and John Kerry, great Americans who would have been good presidents, did not generate as much enthusiasm among their bases and they lost.

   There was massive, grassroots enthusiasm for Obama. I had seen that firsthand on that fateful trip to New Hampshire for Evan Bayh.

   After eight years of Bush, a disastrous war in Iraq, Katrina-style incompetence across government, and a cynical politics of fear, people were desperate for change. People were channeling that desire for change into a freshman senator from Illinois. He was young, cool, and represented something different from the usual politics. Perhaps most important, unlike almost every other Democratic politician of consequence, he had proudly opposed the Iraq War and accurately predicted the consequences of this ill-considered policy decision. The question was how to channel that enthusiasm into actual votes.

2. **Organization matters more.** The specter of the Howard Dean campaign haunted our dreams. Dean had all the enthusiasm, the online organizing, and the big rallies that were the hallmark of the Obama campaign. And all that enthusiasm added up to a third-place finish in Iowa, a second-place finish in New Hampshire, and an early exit. The orange ski cap was the symbol of Dean's failure. In the run-up to the 2004 Iowa caucus, Dean's campaign organized a get-out-the-vote push by bringing volunteers from around the country to Iowa. They gave all the volunteers distinctive orange ski caps to wear as they courted Iowa caucus-goers. The Dean campaign called this effort the "Perfect Storm," and it worked out for the campaign about as well as the movie *The Perfect Storm* worked out for the *Andrea Gail*. The lesson we were all supposed to take away from this failure was that enthusiasm was great, but absent a professional political organization, you were going to lose.

The blowhards on Fox News loved to use "community organizer" to diminish Obama's qualifications for the Oval Office, but his years as a community organizer advocating for social and economic justice on the streets of the South Side of Chicago were a huge asset. Obama intuitively understood the importance of political organizing. While most candidates I'd worked for were more interested in what TV ad the campaign was airing or what the polling said, Obama always wanted to know what the organizers were hearing at the doors or on the phones. He got it.

That's why Barack Obama's first move was to hire David Plouffe to run the campaign. Plouffe's background was in political field organizing, and he had deep respect and affection for the organizers who knock on doors, make phone calls, and register voters. He cut his teeth as an organizer in Iowa for Senator Tom Harkin's 1992 presidential campaign. Plouffe's first move was to hire three of the best organizers in the Democratic Party, each of whom had deep ties to Iowa—Hildebrand, Mitch Stewart, and Paul Tewes. The four of us had worked together in two Senate races in South Dakota, and I knew they were the best in the business. This was not going to be an orange hat–type campaign.

3. **The Internet was changing the rules.** The 2004 election was the first time the Internet had a major effect on a campaign. The aforementioned Dean campaign had pioneered a new era of politics by utilizing e-mail to raise millions online and using the Internet to organize its supporters all over the country. In the end, the more traditional campaign tactics had prevailed. We believed the Dean folks were ahead of their time. The world was changing a lot faster than folks realized. Since that campaign, Facebook had dominated college campuses, the Internet had gotten faster and more readily available, and you could watch and post videos online via YouTube. The Internet was democratizing politics and erasing the structural advantages of institutional actors. Hillary Clinton was coming into this race with a massive fund-raising and political network, as well as a huge advantage in name identification with voters. In an earlier era, these advantages would have been insurmountable. But that was changing. There were already thousands of college kids using Facebook to create groups to urge Obama to run for president. People were uploading videos of Obama's speeches to YouTube and then sharing them via e-mails and blogs. The Internet was

pushing power down into the hands of the people, making it possible to run the insurgent grassroots campaign we needed to have a shot.

These factors allowed us to develop an overall strategic plan that was so simple and clear that every member of the campaign team—whether they sat in senior staff meetings at HQ or worked in a field office in rural New Hampshire—could recite in their sleep.

A Strategy You Can Believe In

> Win Iowa, come in at least second in New Hampshire, survive Nevada, win South Carolina, and get launched into Super Tuesday with momentum.[23]

The simplicity of the strategy—in conception, if not execution—made it easier to make strategic decisions. We knew it was win Iowa or go home, so every day for every decision, we asked ourselves, "Does this help us win Iowa?" If the answer was no, we didn't do it.

Strategy, organization, and culture are all great, but there is still nothing more important than the message.

THE MESSAGE: STORY > SOUND BITES

The perfect message is the holy grail of politics. People obsess over it, millions are spent to find it, and almost no one ever nails it.

There was an exchange at the initial strategy meeting that explains Obama's success in 2008 and beyond. Over mediocre

---

23   History will show it didn't work out exactly this way, but pretty damn close.

sandwiches and diet sodas, we started plotting out the campaign in detail. We talked about fund-raising strategy, a possible announcement tour, and which politicians we should target for early endorsements. At one point we started talking about message. There was some discussion of the key policy issues, about positioning the race as a battle between change and the status quo, polling, and so on. Pretty much par for the course in a political strategy meeting like this one.

In mid-discussion, Obama cut us off:

"There are only two campaigns that I can think of where the message really worked. My Senate campaign and Deval's race. They worked because the campaign was the message."

This caused some confusion among the people at the large conference room table. How could the campaign be the message? This ran counter to how a lot of us thought about political messaging. The rule of thumb was that you shouldn't talk about the campaign; you needed to talk about issues and policy positions in poll-tested, made-for-TV sound bites.

Obama tried to explain that the message of his 2004 campaign was about people coming together (Yes, We Can) to work for change. Newly elected Massachusetts governor Deval Patrick had run a similar race and, like Obama, upset a more favored, established candidate. As our collection of political consultants and pollsters debated the merits of Obama's point, it became clear that people still didn't get it.

At that point, Cornell Belcher, a well-respected pollster who was new to Team Obama, decided to speak up:

The Blueprint

> "It's like Jay-Z said. I'm not a businessman, I'm a business, man. You're not the message man, you're the message, man."

I would like to say that everyone in the room recognized Jay-Z's famous line from the remix of the Kanye West song "Diamonds from Sierra Leone," but that wasn't close to the case. I mean, one of our pollsters with a confused look on his face was wearing a calculator watch. What more do you need to know?

Obama, who is a true hip-hop fan, looked around the room and laughed and proceeded to explain Jay-Z/Cornell's point. Obama and his movement represented two things: Hope and Change, and that would be the message. I am confident the guy with the calculator watch is still confused about why Jay-Z helped explain our message strategy.

Cool Jay-Z anecdote aside, Barack Obama had recognized something about how political messaging was changing. Political messaging in a presidential campaign, especially in the age of social media, is about more than the words that come out of the candidate's mouth or adorn a bumper sticker. The message is the story of who the candidate is and why they do what they do.

The mistake most politicians make is that they start with the focus-group-tested sound bite instead of the larger story.

Hillary Clinton struggled with this throughout her 2008 campaign. Her campaign changed messages like most people change socks. It was the worst of what I call lowest common denominator campaign strategy. No one on the team can agree, so you take a little from column A and a little from column B, meld it together, so people will stop fighting, and the meeting can end. This was most comically evident in Hillary Clinton's final tour of Iowa in late 2007.

If she won Iowa, she would knock Obama and Edwards from the race and essentially clinch the nomination.[24] The importance of this moment should've focused the collective minds of the Clinton

---

24   And the White House, because whoever ended up becoming the Democratic nominee would be favored to win, since the incumbent Republican president was about as popular as the Ebola virus.

campaign to produce their best work. And what message did they come up with to meet this monumental moment?

"The Big Challenges, Real Solutions: Time to Pick a President Tour"

Each of those words individually means something (I think); together they are pure pabulum. This slogan was so laughably long that it barely fit on the side of the bus Clinton was using to travel around Iowa in the days before the caucus.

Obama (and Jay-Z) put us in the neighborhood of where we needed to be, but in the summer of 2007, we were struggling in the race. Clinton had stolen our early momentum, and our scrappy young campaign team was at times struggling to compete with the Clinton political machine. We were down by twenty to thirty points in some of the national polls.[25] At the end of August, Obama was headed to Martha's Vineyard for a little family vacation to rest up for the final sprint to the Iowa caucus. Our grand plan was to take the time while he was on vacation and prepare to hit the reset button on Labor Day. The plan was to hold a big rally in New Hampshire on Labor Day Weekend, where we would debut a new slogan.

The brain trust got together to bounce ideas off one another to find a way to pithily condense our argument for Obama and against Clinton[26] into something that would fit on a placard. It didn't go well.

The pollsters and ad guys formed a working group to figure something out, while the rest of us focused on putting together the New Hampshire trip and the rollout plan. We were under an onerous deadline for such a big decision. It was a holiday weekend, and if we didn't get the slogan figured out by Friday morning at the lat-

---

25 National polls are irrelevant to everyone other than donors and pundits, who feel about them the same way Sean Hannity Feels about Trump.

26 By this point, Edwards had faded and the race was seen as Obama versus Clinton.

est, we wouldn't be able to get the signs printed in time. As the clock ticked down, Alyssa Mastromonaco, whose team was responsible for ensuring that signs got printed, was getting more nervous, repeatedly poking her head into Plouffe's office to see if he could light a fire under the process.

The word around the campaign was that the process was not going well. This was confirmed a few hours before the deadline, when Plouffe's assistant sent out an e-mail to the whole staff—hundreds of people in HQ and in all the primary states—asking everyone for suggestions for a slogan.

It would have been hilarious if it wasn't so damn alarming. Eventually the team settled on something like "Better Together." It's unclear if this came from the brain trust or the suggestion box. Either way it was terrible and was soundly rejected by Obama, who said, "Is that the best we can do?" The reboot was put on hold and those signs never saw the light of day.

A couple of weeks later at a meeting in the same conference room in DC where we had the Jay-Z conversation, we settled on "Change We Can Believe In"[27] as the campaign slogan that would become synonymous with Obama in the coming months. That slogan worked because it was closely connected with our Change message and contained a subtle contrast with Clinton, who had a trust problem with voters, particularly compared with Obama.

The lesson here is that you can't fabricate a message. It can't be inorganic or forced; it has to flow directly from the candidate. Polling and focus groups can help you understand how the voters will receive your message. They can help you choose which words work best, but they can't create your message. The sound bite comes from the story, not the other way around.

All of our messaging was designed to address the fact that people

---

27   It ended up being perfect, but at the time there was no "Aha" moment. It felt like the best choice from a mediocre menu.

wanted change, and our job was to convince them that Obama was the right vehicle for that change—that he had the values, smarts, experience, and strength to bring that change.

Our success and Hillary's failure in having a resonant campaign message would be a harbinger of things to come in 2016.

I LOVE IT WHEN A PLAN COMES TOGETHER

I spent Election Day 2008 holed up in the "Boiler Room" a few floors above our campaign headquarters in a skyscraper in Chicago, monitoring reports on turnout and anecdotes from polling locations in the handful of states that would decide the election. I was cautiously confident. The night before, I had buttonholed our data and field people and made them tell me that we were going to win, primarily so I could get some sleep.[28] But even their certainty based on polling and early voting data was not enough to give me 100 percent confidence.

Most campaigns fail. Barack Obama is arguably the best politician in recent history, but if we reran the 2008 campaign 100 times, Obama would probably lose at least 90 times.

Campaigns are often victims of circumstances beyond their control. This is often referred to as an October Surprise. The final stretch of the 2008 campaign was rocked by a historic financial crisis sparked by the collapse of major banks such as Lehman Brothers. In 2012, the attack on a US diplomatic facility in Benghazi and Hurricane Sandy upended the final days of the campaign, and in 2016, FBI Director James Comey's letter to Congress about Clinton's e-mails may have tipped the race to Trump.

A campaign's ability to survive these events depends on how well they have tended to the things they can control, and ultimately

---

28 It didn't work.

that's the lesson for campaigns and start-ups. The only way to seize your moment is to take care of the things you can control. We did so in 2008, and that was the difference.

Everything went right for Obama on election night. We were winning by more than we'd expected, but I wasn't going to relax until we got the magic number of 270 electoral votes. As the night went on, I got an e-mail from someone at one of the major television networks saying that the network had seen enough in the exit polls in the state of Ohio to declare Barack Obama the next president of the United States at 10:00 p.m. I had to read the e-mail a couple of times. It was hard to process the words "Barack Obama, the next president of the United States."

As the clock ticked toward ten, Axelrod, Plouffe, and I gathered with a few others around the TV in the boiler room. As ABC Anchor Charles Gibson declared Barack Obama the winner, we shouted, high-fived, and awkwardly hugged. Then we just stood there and looked at one another. Not sure what to do next, we hugged again. This time it was even more awkward.

By the old rules of the game, Obama never should have won. But he—and we—had changed the way the game was played.

The Obama campaign had the most improbable of journeys— one I had almost missed. My life would never be the same. I will never forget the joy and pride we all felt as we gathered in Grant Park on an unseasonably warm night to hear Obama's first words as president-elect of the United States. The possibilities seemed endless.

Little did I know what would await us.

The easy part was over.

CHAPTER 3

TELLING THE COUNTRY AND OTHER TALES OF PRESIDENTIAL COMMUNICATIONS

Early one morning during the first week of the Obama presidency, I was sitting in my unpacked office in the West Wing.

Most of the desks in the area where the communications team sat were still vacant, and I was the only person in the office. I was deep into reading the morning papers when I was startled by a familiar baritone voice.

"Hey," said the president, who was standing in the doorway to my office.

I belatedly and clumsily scrambled to my feet. I was not yet used to the new protocol of standing every time the guy I used to call Barack walked into a room.

"Is this your office?" he asked rhetorically. "Not bad."

I couldn't tell if he was kidding since my office was only slightly larger than a decent-size broom closet, but then again it was in the West Wing and less than a hundred feet from his oval-shaped one. So yeah, "not bad" was a pretty good way to put it.

"I just banned torture. That's pretty cool, huh," Obama said.

Obama was referring to the executive order he had signed a few minutes earlier in the Oval Office banning the use of the enhanced interrogation techniques such as waterboarding, which were employed during the Bush administration. This was a core campaign promise and morally the right thing to do.

He was playing it very cool, but I knew this meant a lot to him. He'd clearly gone wandering in his new home looking for someone to bask in the moment with, and ended up stumbling upon me in an empty office suite. I will always remember the look on his face that morning—a mix of awe at the power he now had and pride at what he was able to accomplish with that power.

As the president turned to leave, he ran smack-dab into Ron Fournier, a longtime Associated Press reporter who had covered the White House since the early nineties. Ron, to his great credit, didn't bombard the new president with pointed questions about the news of the day. He asked Obama how he and his family were adjusting to life in their new digs. The conversation then moved to a friendly discussion of playing pickup basketball around DC, something the two weekend warriors had talked about in prior encounters on the campaign trail.

After Ron left, Obama asked me: "Does the press really have free rein up here by your office?"

I explained that traditionally the press could come up here anytime they wanted so that they could visit the office of the press secretary and the other staffers whose job it was to interact with the horde of well-meaning jackals better known as the White House Press Corps.[1]

"Fun," Obama responded.[2]

As he walked out the door of the office suite, he turned around and said, "I guess we better figure out how to tell the country about what I just did."

After Obama left, I mulled over what had just happened. The whole thing was pretty surreal. I was in the West Wing (the building, not the show, but sort of both). Barack Obama was president. This was pretty awesome.

---

1   (Mostly) well-meaning.
2   It's worth noting that upon learning that he could be cornered by reporters in our office suite, Obama didn't return to visit for months.

My foray into self-congratulatory reflection was cut short once I remembered the marching order that the president had given me.

"Tell the country."

That was the first time I realized what my new job entailed—telling the country.

Over the six years I worked in the White House, I learned that how presidents communicate with the public can be the difference between success and failure; between a president getting reelected or sent to premature retirement.

WHAT'S YOUR JOB AND WHICH *WEST WING* CHARACTER ARE YOU?

Deputy communications director is a great job. It's one most people in Washington would kill for, but it's not the one I wanted. I wanted to be communications director.

That was the job I had on the campaign, and that was the job I had on the presidential transition. I was only thirty-three at the time and had never done more than make copies and file documents in the White House, so I knew it was certainly not a guarantee that I would get the top communications job, but I thought I had a shot.

After the election, the *New York Times* had written a story that said I was the leading contender for the role.

The only problem was, no one had talked to me about the job, and no one—certainly not the president-elect—had interviewed me for it. Every time I asked someone about the job, I was told Obama hadn't yet gotten to the communications department in his staffing process. This seemed plausible since he had an entire government to staff in just a few weeks.

I assumed that I would get a chance to interview for the job, so I spent a lot of time thinking about how I would make the case even if the odds were long.

But I was wrong.

During this period on the transition, we were making daily announcements of various hires for the administration-in-waiting. Every morning, someone in the personnel department would send me an e-mail with the names and titles of the people we were going to announce that day. My job was to read over the list, make sure there was no major conflict with our message of the day, and then assign someone to write the press release.

I was about to hit Forward on the e-mail when I was taken aback by what I saw.

One of the jobs being announced that day was "White House communications director." The job I wanted. Not only did I not get it, but this was the professional equivalent of being broken up with via a Post-it note.

This was messed up.

Not only was I not interviewed or notified, but the job went to someone who, while well known in Democratic circles, had never worked for Barack Obama. I went into a blind rage. I sent several tirades masquerading as e-mails to the people well above me on the food chain. I was frankly more pissed about the process than the result. I wasn't owed the job—far from it—but I was owed a shot at the job, or at least a conversation.

My phone began ringing with sheepish apologies from the Obama high command about how this had gone down. Everyone thought that someone else was going to talk to me about the decision. Pete Rouse and Jim Messina, who was slated to be deputy chief of staff in the White House, sprang into action and I was immediately offered the deputy communications director job.

Barack Obama, who had heard about the misstep (and apparently my reaction to it), called to check on me later that day.[3] I

---

3   Obama is good like this. He cares a lot about the people who work for him. Seems obvious but worth pointing out that we once had a president who wasn't an incontrovertible narcissist.

appreciated the call, especially given everything else he was doing at the time. But I didn't feel much better.

White House deputy communications director was an important job and, in hindsight, the right one for me at the time.[4] The way the whole thing went down had put me in a shitty mood. I didn't really want to talk to anyone, so I walked to a bar nearby to watch some basketball, eat some food, and drink beer. I walked into Clyde's, a pretty generic and tourist-heavy bar a few blocks from the office and a place where I was unlikely to see anyone I knew. Immediately upon grabbing a seat at the bar, I realized I was sitting next to a guy I used to play basketball with around DC before I moved to Chicago for the campaign. We exchanged some awkward small talk about some of the other people we knew from the gym until his dinner companion arrived.

"Hey, this is Dan Pfeiffer, we used to play hoops together back in the day. Now he is going to be White House communications director."

I asked for the check and called it a night.

DROPPED IN THE DEEP END OF THE POOL

A few weeks later, I was on a bus headed from the inauguration to the West Wing to start my new job. I was equal parts excited and afraid. This was going to be only the third time in my life I'd set foot in the West Wing.

I had no idea what I was supposed to do when I got there, but still stinging from my job disappointment, I knew I was going to work my ass off to prove myself. This was Georgetown all over again. I walked into the doors of the White House with a chip on my shoulder and a desire to prove I belonged.

---

4   I wouldn't have made it three months as White House communications director. I was far from ready.

The transition of power in our country is so abrupt that it's a testimony to the strength of our institutions that the country doesn't fall apart for a few months every four or eight years. The process is as follows:

- The new president takes the oath of office.
- The old president gets into a helicopter and heads out of town.
- The new president and their new staff head to the White House, where they walk into an entirely empty building most of them have stepped foot in approximately one time before.
- The new staff wanders through the halls, each looking for the office that has a Post-it note with their name on it.
- The new staff members sit down at their new desks and are now responsible for the country even though they still don't know where the bathroom is.
- If a terrorist attack or a natural disaster happens one minute after the transfer of power, the new president and their new staff are on their own.

When you add in the fact that the country was teetering on the brink of financial collapse, it felt a little like we were Wile E. Coyote and had just looked down to realize we had run right off the cliff.[5]

While it took me almost two weeks to find the third bathroom in the West Wing,[6] I quickly learned there were three main parts of the job of the communications staff:

- Managing the press
- Getting the message out
- Responding to the crisis du jour

Now I just had to figure out how to do them.

---

5   If you don't get the reference, Google the GIF.
6   There are five total, but one is for the president and the other is technically for the vice president, but not everyone adheres to that rule.

OBAMA MEETS THE PRESS

Every White House is engaged in a low-intensity conflict with the reporters who show up every day to report on its happenings. Ours was no different.

This is the nature of the beast—the White House wants to get its chosen message out on any given day, and the press wants to report on the things it believes its readers and viewers are most interested in. The White House reporters want as much access as possible; the White House wants to find the amount of access that is minimally acceptable without getting in the way of doing their job. Conflict is inevitable, especially when you add to the mix huge amounts of stress, tight deadlines, and consistent sleep deprivation on both sides. Tempers could flare—especially mine. I was known to fire off overly hot e-mails about stories way too early in the morning.

The fact that this conflict existed at all may be a surprise to anyone who watched the 2008 campaign. The press loved Barack Obama in 2008—a sentiment best embodied by MSNBC host Chris Matthews's statement that a Barack Obama speech sent a "thrill up his leg." Part of the media love for Obama came from the fact that most journalists are liberal-minded, but the true bias of the media is not ideological; it's a bias for a good story, and Barack Obama's candidacy was a great story.

Like Trump, Obama was a boon for ratings and clicks. The media's crush on Obama didn't mean they didn't scrutinize every minute of his life. The Republicans loved to say that Obama wasn't "vetted," which was nothing more than a crypto-racist attempt to raise questions about his birthplace and religious affiliation.

This notion was ridiculous.

In 2008, the media gave Obama a journalistic colonoscopy. Every few days on the campaign, I would get an e-mail from someone in Obama's distant past saying some reporter had called them raising questions about some aspect of Obama's story.

My favorite of this genre was the *New York Times* digging deep into Obama's drug use in high school, something he fully admitted in his memoir. After weeks of interviewing everyone they could find in his native Hawaii, the *Times* ran a story saying that they couldn't find definitive evidence that Obama had used cocaine as much as he claimed in his own memoir. We laughed our asses off about this one at campaign headquarters. The media was so hellbent on playing "gotcha" that they went after Obama for *not* doing enough cocaine.

No question the media's love for Obama was an advantage that we benefited from through that first campaign, particularly in the primary against Hillary Clinton, whom the media viscerally disliked.

But once we got to the White House, Obama and the media broke up.

In the first week in the White House, President Obama stuck his head into White House Chief of Staff Rahm Emanuel's office with an idea.

He wanted to make a surprise visit to the White House briefing room to introduce himself to the White House Press Corps—many of whom he had never met before. And he wanted to do it right now.

"Ummm, sir. I'm not sure that's a great idea," I replied, joining the chorus of concerns from the staff that had been assembled in Rahm's office.

"Come on, guys, I'm just saying hi. It's not that big of a deal," said Obama as he headed down the hall.

After a beat, we realized that he was actually headed to the briefing room. Gibbs took off running after him.

Well, this nice gesture was not appreciated for long, and some in the press corps decided to turn his courtesy visit into an impromptu and aggressive press conference. Before too long, Obama turned tail and ran out of there.

Lesson learned. The White House briefing room was their territory. They made the rules. Their job was to hold the president accountable for his or her actions and to be watchdogs against malfeasance and corruption. They took this job seriously—as they should.

It was a common belief among the White House Press Corps that Barack Obama hated the press. This belief was wrong. Obama didn't hate the press; he really likes reporters. Seriously.[7]

He finds them to be incredibly interesting people who are smart, curious, and trying to contribute to democracy. Obama is a vociferous consumer of journalism in every form. The national papers at the breakfast table, digital media sites like *Vox* on his iPad, and every magazine from the *New Yorker* to *Sports Illustrated* whenever he flew on *Air Force One*.

Obama also kept very close tabs on the news, often finding articles on the *New York Times* website before anyone else.

One Saturday night, I was sitting on the couch watching TV when my BlackBerry made a sound like an abbreviated police siren from across the room, where it was charging.

I groaned. This couldn't be good news.

I had set up a special alert for e-mails from the president after missing a critical one a few months prior.

Not answering presidential e-mails is a big mistake. Due to Secret Service restrictions, Obama could e-mail only a small handful of senior aides and close friends so he noticed if you didn't respond.

And what was the subject of presidential concern on a weekend night?

He wanted me to get a correction in a *New York Times* article that misstated an administration policy position.

I had no idea what he was talking about. I did a quick search of my e-mail to see if I could find the article he was referring to. Nothing.

I went to the website, embarrassed that I had somehow missed this story.

When I found it, I realized why I had missed it.

---

7   That sound you hear right now is every White House reporter spitting out their milk.

Obama's e-mail was sent to me at 9:03 p.m. The story had been posted at 9:00 p.m. The movie studios traditionally send presidents movies to watch in the White House theater before they are released; for a while I was convinced Obama had struck a similar deal with the *New York Times*.

In contrast to Trump's addiction to cable news and Twitter, Obama had a much healthier (and thoughtful) media diet. If Obama read something interesting in a magazine, he would tab it and ask his personal assistant to share it with the relevant members of the senior staff. Sometimes these were stories that highlighted an interesting policy problem that he wanted the staff to address, and other times they were just interesting stories he thought we should read, such as a piece by historian Taylor Branch in the *Atlantic* criticizing college athletics and a piece in the *New Yorker* about the possible extinction of bees.[8]

Now, liking journalists and appreciating good journalism did not mean that he didn't get frustrated with the press coverage of his presidency. This was not unique to Obama. Presidential frustration with the media has been around as long as we have had presidents and a press. Some presidents vent to their aides; others angrily tweet that journalists are the enemies of the American people.

Here's another shocker: Obama also enjoyed press conferences. To me, that's like declaring that someone really enjoys root canals. But to each their own.

A White House reporter reading this book might ask, "If Obama loved press conferences so much, why did he do so few of them?"

The answer is simple.

For at least the six years I was there: me.

---

8   During a speech, Obama once ad-libbed an anecdote about the cost difference between men's and women's dry cleaning. The staff had no idea where it came from and was afraid that he'd passed along an urban myth. When the crack White House Research team went looking, they discovered it was from an article in *Marie Claire* from a few weeks prior that the president had clearly read.

As I said before (and will say again), I hate press conferences. My job was to get the president's message out. And press conferences are just about the worst possible way to do that.

First, you give up control. The reporters set the agenda based on the questions they want to ask—Obama wants to talk about his jobs proposal, the media may want to ask him about a legitimate policy area that we don't want to be the message of the day, but too often they devolve into trivia designed to get traffic for click-thirsty media outlets.

Second, there is often a performance aspect, especially from the TV correspondents, who are as interested in how their question will sound on the evening news as they are in what the president's answer to that question will be. Once during a press conference at the end of a long foreign trip, the president called on a TV correspondent, who stood up but didn't address the president. He just stood there looking at Obama.

"What is he doing?" I thought to myself.

This was not someone who usually covered Obama, so maybe he just got nervous on the big stage. This happens sometimes.

All of a sudden, there was a lot of commotion in the back as a cameraman came running to the front of the stage.

Instead of facing the camera toward the president—who was ostensibly the "news" in this news conference—the cameraman turned his back to the president.

He wasn't trying to get a better shot of Obama answering the question. Instead he turned his back to the president so he could get a better shot of his correspondent asking Obama a question. This highlighted the main problem with press conferences—some reporters were more interested in their own question than the president's answer.

Press conferences are important—even I can admit that[9]—and most reporters tried to use their rare moments to ask a president a question to inform the public. Reporters were right to push to do

---

9 I don't like admitting it, though.

more press conferences—that was their job.[10] However, the exalted status that press conferences hold in the minds of the media is a vestige of an era long past.

Ultimately, I learned a few lessons on how to best manage that dynamic between the press and the president.

The press isn't your friend, but it isn't your enemy either. Liberals tend to make common cause with reporters. We think that we have similar worldviews, and liberals do believe—or at least used to believe before 2016—that the media was a fundamental part of what makes democracy work. Because we like the media—in part to defend them from unfair attacks from conservatives—we are caught off guard when they turn on us like a pack of hungry hyenas. My reaction to this was to fight every story like the future of the Republic depended on it. In addition to being emotionally unhealthy for me, it was also counterproductive for the president. Not every journalistic sin is a mortal one. Reporters make mistakes like everyone else, and we all have to live to fight another day. This is a two-way street, though: the media as a whole presumes that all politicians are somewhat corrupt, and when something goes wrong, they assume the worst motives, but like reporters, politicians and their aides are human, too. Sometimes a mistake is just a mistake, and a misstatement is just a misstatement. The whole relationship would work better if there was a mutual assumption of good faith.

Trump—on the other hand—has forfeited the benefit of the doubt, because he is a deeply dishonest person who lied more than a thousand times in the first year of his presidency, according to independent fact-checkers. More on this later, but it's not just that Trump lies. He is waging a war on the very idea of

---

10   I would note that reporters complained vociferously when Obama went a few weeks without a formal press conference, whereas Trump held *one* formal press conference in his entire first year in office. So maybe we weren't so bad.

the media as arbiters of truth and checkers of facts. The ultimate goal of this war is to defeat the idea of objective truth. Trump says climate change is fake even though 97 percent of all scientists agree it's real. Trump claims his tax bill is popular even though it's the least popular piece of legislation passed in modern history. He calls stories that say he is wrong "fake news." This tactic sadly devolves us into a world where even the most patently true things are treated as "He said, she said" disagreements—despite the fact that the "he" is a known liar and the "she" is backed up by all the evidence.

One day (hopefully soon) we will have a new president, though, and that person deserves the benefit of the doubt (until they forfeit it).

The definition of a reporter has changed. For decades, the White House briefing room was filled with people who met the common understanding of what a reporter was—an independent, objective, just-the-facts type who worked for putatively nonideological entities designed to cover the news for a city, a town, a state, and in some cases, the nation. Each of these entities was a business, but making money was a secondary concern to the ideal of journalism. They didn't have to worry about the business because journalism was a good business.

That's still true, but just much less so. By the time I left the White House, the briefing room was populated by dozens of reporters from digital media entities such as BuzzFeed and VICE, which had barely existed when Obama arrived at 1600 Pennsylvania Avenue. These outlets operated differently than reporters from legacy outlets with different incentives and required a different strategy for engagement.

A more troubling trend was the emergence of "reporters" for right-wing political entities masquerading as media companies. I'm, of course, referring to Breitbart, but also the Daily Caller, the Free Beacon, and others. In 2017, when Alabama Republican Senate candidate Roy Moore was accused by multiple women of sexually assaulting them when they were teenagers, Breitbart—like most outlets—sent several reporters to Alabama to check out the story. But unlike most outlets, Breitbart's reporters weren't sent to Alabama to find the truth. They went there to discredit the women in an effort to help elect Moore, who was Breitbart's chosen candidate in the race. These "reporters" were not reporters in the common definition of the term. They were more like political operatives disguised under the banner of journalism. The White House would never grant media access to an event to an opposition researcher from the Republican or the Democratic National Committee, and there is an argument to be made that Breitbart and its brethren don't deserve that access either.

White Houses shouldn't be the ones to make this determination, however, because it would create a slippery slope. Trump had already banned several outlets from his campaign events for coverage he didn't like. This is an issue the White House Correspondents' Association, which makes decisions on access, is going to have to grapple with sooner rather than later.

More important, citizens can now play the role of journalist. All they needed was a scoop and the ability to post something on the Internet. You didn't have to have a White House press pass to be a journalist, but having a White House press pass also didn't mean you were a journalist—at least in the traditional sense.

All these changes are on the balance good (I think), but they disrupted the order and turned White House communications strategies on their head. During the run-up to the 2015 State of the Union, Obama took time out of his schedule to do more than an hour's worth of interviews, but he didn't sit down with CNN, NBC, ABC, or CBS. He didn't meet with local journalists from around the country. He sat down for interviews with YouTube stars—some of whom were eccentric to say the least. But they had audiences several times the size of cable staples such as *Morning Joe*. The new reality of the media was that to reach the American people, these nontraditional folks needed to be part of the strategy.

Honesty is the best policy. Trump's presence in the White House may belie this point, but hear me out. The relationship between the media and the White House depends on both sides adhering to long-established norms. Honesty is what keeps that relationship functional. The one piece of advice I got from alumni of both Republican and Democratic White Houses was "Never lie." You can spin, you can refuse to answer, but if you ever get caught in an obvious lie, that's the ball game. If the media can't trust you, then you will never be valuable to the president again.

Not lying in politics is actually easier than most people think. Only once in my time in the White House was I confronted with the possibility of lying.

In late 2014, I was participating in a Washington tradition called the *Christian Science Monitor* breakfast, where politicians and newsmakers field questions from a group of reporters from all of the major outlets.[11] I was in a zone, answering question after question about politics and the next items on the presidential agenda, when I got a question I had not prepared for: The reporter asked if the president was considering "a review of Cuba policy and any reach out to Cuba?"

"Oh shit," I thought to myself. The reporter had stumbled onto one of the nation's most tightly held secrets. The Obama administration had been working for eighteen months on a top secret rapprochement with Cuba that centered around the release of Alan Gross, an American in a Cuban prison whose health was deteriorating by the day. These negotiations were

---

11   The food served at this event was from a time before we knew we had to worry about cholesterol. Your HDL levels went up just by being in the same room with this breakfast meat-a-palooza.

so secret that only a small handful of people knew about them.

I was one of those people.

Normally, when a reporter asks a question about something that is true but not yet announced, the strategy is to be coy with something like, "I have no news to make today." The reporters know they have hit on something real, but the aide is able to avoid getting ahead of an official announcement.

I started with that approach by saying, "I don't—I don't have any, you know, news as to a new approach to Cuba policy to make today or any day." But halfway through, I panicked. I had been in a meeting in the Situation Room on this very topic just a couple of days earlier and the takeaway was that if the negotiations leaked, the Cubans could walk away from the table and Alan Gross, the American with rapidly deteriorating health being held captive and whose release was critical to any deal, would likely die in a Cuban prison. If I gave the press any reason to believe that a new approach to Cuba was afoot, it could lead to a premature end to the negotiations.

Do I lie (or come close to lying) or risk a historic diplomatic initiative and potentially the life of an American?

I chose the former.

I responded to a follow-up question by claiming, "There's not a new specific initiative undertaking." Now, I could argue this political-ese was technically true because the question was in the context of a postelection revisiting of Cuba policy and the revisiting had actually happened preelection, but that was dancing on the head of a pin. I tried to mislead because I felt like I had to. I was fortunate to get away with a mild scolding from the media once the news was out.

For future White House staff, I would revise the rule to say, "Don't lie to the press unless a historic diplomatic effort and the lives of American citizens are at risk."

The main takeaway is that these issues are not always black

and white. But in the long run, preserving the relationship of trust is critical, which is why the Trump White House seems like such a dumpster fire. No one feels like they believe a word Trump or his staff says. The American people need to be able to believe their president—whether they voted for him or her or not. That starts from the bottom up.

New Media and Old Hands

The fundamental task for a White House communications operation is to get the president's message out to the public. Theoretically, if you and your candidate made it to the White House, you successfully completed this task during the campaign. You communicated well and you communicated better than your opponent.[12]

Here's the thing: despite having all the tools of the presidency at your disposal, the job is just harder in the White House than it is in a campaign.

You have to balance complicated, competing interests in everything you say and do:

If you attack Wall Street, which is great politics, it will spook the markets and hurt the economy, which is bad politics. If you talk about being tough on trade, which is good politics, it endangers a treaty being negotiated, denying your boss a key accomplishment, which is bad politics. If you talk about this absurd pork barrel project, which is good politics, it might upset the junior senator from such and such state, whose vote we need to pass a key piece of legislation, which is bad politics.[13]

There are almost no easy options. Everything is a 51–49 call with no clear indications of which choice is better.

A good campaign is a lean, mean machine (or at least Obama's

---

12 Or you ran a terrible campaign but the Russians helped you.
13 I swear to God these are real things that happened.

campaign was), it can turn on a dime, and it's willing to take real risks. The White House represents the entire federal government, with dozens of agencies across the country and the world—all of whom want a say in what the president says and how and when he or she says it. This dynamic can cause some turbulence as the campaign staff and the permanent members of the DC establishment come together as one team.

During a scheduling meeting in early 2009, this cultural clash manifested itself. Scheduling meetings are weekly get-togethers where the senior staff of the White House plan the president's schedule and fight over how he will use the very rare free minutes that he has left. There is no better way to draw attention to a policy proposal or issue than to have the president talk about it, so these meetings can devolve into proxy battles about the overall White House agenda. President Obama was headed out to California for his first visit as president. We were filling the schedule with visits to projects being funded by the recently passed Recovery Act, which aimed to bring the country back from the financial crisis. As a communications team, we, of course, wanted to show the president focused on jobs and the economy. We wanted images of Obama in factories, shaking hands with workers straight from central casting, plastered across every front page in America. There was unanimity on this point.

Toward the end of the meeting, White House Press Secretary Robert Gibbs brought up the fact that Obama had a pending invite to appear on *The Tonight Show with Jay Leno*, and we were going to be in Los Angeles, only a few miles from the studio where Leno taped his show. You would have thought that Gibbs had suggested Obama deliver the State of the Union with his pants down.

People were aghast:

"Obama can't go on a late-night comedy show."

"It's never been done before."

"It's not presidential."

"He will get killed."

The campaign folks, myself included, were aghast that people were aghast. It made complete sense to us. Obama had done the late-night circuit during the campaign, and he was great in this format. He was funny, relaxed, and came off like a normal human, which was appealing to us since he had spent the first few months of the presidency standing behind formal podiums in ornate rooms responding to grim economic news. This was a chance to remind people why they liked Barack Obama.

The other side of the argument was that a young, inexperienced president appearing on a comedy show during a time of economic crisis would look bad and offend the sensibilities of the Washington establishment. The unspoken point was that a young, black president had to go out of his way to meet the bar of presidential stature in the eyes of the public. Bill Clinton could talk about his choice of underwear on MTV and George W. Bush could yuck it up while clearing brush, but Obama couldn't get away with what others got away with.

It could not be more obvious to me that doing *Leno* was the right thing to do. The biggest challenge in presidential communications is reaching the people who don't consume political news every day. Leno's audience was filled with hard-to-reach passive news viewers. Obama being funny had the potential to be a viral moment that would be seen by an audience exponentially larger than the number of people who tuned in on that particular night.

I thought the idea that appearing on a comedy show was somehow beneath the presidency was asinine. Some sacred cows of Washington behavior are meant to be slain, and this was one of them. People were not moved by my arguments, and I was certainly not moved by theirs. Neither side would back down, and both were oddly passionate about their case.

We took the argument across the hall to resolve it the only way we knew how—by asking the president.

Axelrod, Gibbs, Rahm, and I marched into the Oval. Rahm was

representing the other side of the argument, even though he was not as passionate about it as some others.

Obama was seated at his desk working on a speech. He looked up at us with a mix of annoyance and concern. An unexpected drop-by from a quorum of the senior staff rarely meant something good and often meant something very bad. In this case, it meant something very trivial.

"What do you guys want?" he asked faux brusquely, which was his typical way of still being nice while making us aware that interrupting his work was not completely welcome.

Rahm laid out the decision before the president. Now that we were all in the Oval Office, where some of the most important decisions in American history have been made, the question of "To Leno, or not to Leno" seemed pretty trite.

Before Rahm could finish, Obama said, "Of course I'll do it. Why wouldn't I?" and returned to editing his speech as we stood awkwardly in front of his desk and looked at one another before sheepishly shuffling out with our tails between our legs, feeling foolish for bothering him.

The whole *Leno* debate played out the way both sides had expected. Obama went on, got incredible ratings, and reached members of the public he couldn't reach with the traditional communications tools available to a president.

On the other hand, there was some hand-wringing from members of the DC establishment. David Gergen, the Washington graybeard who has worked for multiple presidents of both parties and has made a career out of being the Emily Post of presidential etiquette, was, of course, disappointed, but it blew over quickly.

On another occasion in that first year, my desire to push the bounds of presidential communications didn't go as well. A few months after the *Leno* appearance, the White House was hosting an event for NASCAR drivers. I can't really remember why we did this, but I assume the thinking was something along the lines of: "Wouldn't NASCAR be a cool way for the African American president from Hawaii, Harvard, and the South Side of Chicago to reach out to rural voters?"[14] Not willing to leave well enough alone, I doubled down on the absurdity of this event and pushed to have President Obama do an interview with the ESPN show *NASCAR Now* from the White House grounds. My thinking was that ESPN, like *Leno*, was a phenomenal means to reach a broad swath of the public that we didn't normally reach—young people and more passive consumers of political information. During the campaign, we leaped at opportunities to do nontraditional things (not to mention I was also overly enthralled with our reputation as innovative communicators who didn't need the "mainstream media"). This ESPN interview would be a great opportunity to once again show Washington how smart Team Obama was.

At some point in the process, Alyssa Mastromonaco, who had the most common sense of anyone in the White House, pointed out to me in the nicest way possible that this seemed like maybe not the best plan. I was too dense and cocksure to pick up the obvious hint.[15]

When the interview happened, the stupidity of this idea became very clear, very quickly. Obama by his own admission knew very little about NASCAR. Obama had read the detailed briefing, which we had outsourced to the biggest NASCAR fan we could find on staff, which was hard to find—validating every stereotype about NASCAR and Democrats.

Most politicians would have pretended to be a fan even if they weren't, in a ham-handed attempt to appeal to the public. The finely tuned bullshit detector of the American people always sees through these attempts. Obama, who has a visceral dislike for artifice such as pretending to like a sport about which he knows next to nothing, started out the interview making it clear that he knew very little about NASCAR. And it got more awkward from there as

---

14   I'm sure (or at least I hope) no one actually verbalized those words, but people were definitely thinking them.
15   A mistake I would never make again, because she is never wrong about these things.

the NASCAR hosts and the NASCAR neophyte struggled to find enough to talk about to fill the ten minutes or so of this interview. Barack Obama may be the greatest communicator in modern political history, but even he couldn't save my failed attempt to be creative for creativity's sake.

When the president came looking to see "who thought this interview was a good idea,"[16] I had to raise my hand.

The take-away from the success of *Leno* and the failure of *NASCAR Now* was that communications and media were rapidly changing and that meant presidents needed to communicate in new ways using new tools. This required creativity and risk-taking, but there were boundaries. The cleverest idea in the world won't work unless it is authentic to the person. In pushing Obama to do the *NASCAR* interview, I was more concerned about making a point than delivering a message. He knew it, everyone who saw the interview knew it, and I should have known it, too.

There were new rules to politics and media, new rules that we understood better than anyone, but a lot of the old rules still mattered, too. Authenticity is critical, but so is humility.

THE CRISIS DU JOUR, EVERY JOUR

"No battle plan survives first contact with the enemy."

This is a quote from a German WWI general that Denis Mc-Donough, Obama's last and longest-serving chief of staff, regularly used to describe life in the White House. We walked in every day with a communications plan on what message we were trying to tell the country. Dozens of people worked to develop it—from the communications staff to the speechwriters to the schedulers and event

---

16 Props to Alyssa Mastromonaco, who identified this as *the* question that you don't want to be asked by Barack Obama and then wrote a kick-ass book with that title.

planners. And more often than not, we would be forced to rip up the plan midway through the first meeting of the morning to deal with some unexpected crisis that had popped up between the time we'd left the office the night before and when we arrived in the morning.

There's an inherent tension that plagues every White House between trying to tell the story you want told and giving in to the desire of the media and, frankly, of the public to hear the president narrate the news as it happens.

In the 2008 campaign, we prided ourselves on having the discipline not to overreact to the ups and downs of the news cycle.

One of the hallmarks of President Clinton's White House was the idea that you should "Win the News Cycle." At the end of every day, the staff would gather to watch the evening news to decide if they had won or lost the day.

Team Obama rejected this idea out of hand. The value of the "news cycle" was dramatically diminished as fewer Americans watched the news and subscribed to the local paper. Barack Obama's philosophy of communications is about telling a story over time, and chasing the latest headlines could often be a distraction from the larger—and more important—task. We refused to let the media dictate our message. But being a candidate for president and being president are two fundamentally different jobs with different expectations, a lesson I learned the hard way early on in the White House.

Christmas Day, 2009, was supposed to be our first real break in over a year. In the morning on Christmas Eve, the Senate passed their version of the Affordable Care Act. *Air Force One* was headed to Hawaii with the Obamas for their annual holiday trip. I had driven directly from the White House to Delaware to spend my Christmas Eve birthday and the holidays with my family.[17] After the holiday, the plan was to head to New York City for a few days

---

17 Yes, I get fewer presents. Back off.

of R & R with some friends whom I hadn't seen since starting on the campaign nearly three years earlier. I was planning—like most of the staff—to return to the White House after the New Year when Obama was due to get back from Hawaii. I had never wanted a vacation—and sleep—so badly.

About midway through the first day of the long-awaited vacation, events intervened. For the first time in nearly three years, I wasn't tied to my BlackBerry, furiously checking it every time the little red light flashed, causing my heart rate to accelerate.[18]

I was sitting in the kitchen talking to my mom as she worked on her traditional beef tenderloin Christmas dinner.[19]

"Something is ringing in the other room," my dad yelled from the den, where he was watching an NBA game.

"Ugh. This can't be good," I thought as I literally ran to the other room to get my phone before it stopped ringing.

"Mr. Pfeiffer. This is the White House Situation Room. The chief of staff has arranged a conference call. Can I put you through?"

"Sure, when is it?" I asked.

"Now," the Situation Room operator responded as he clicked through and I was greeted with hold music.

This had to be bad. I wouldn't put a Christmas Day check-in call past Rahm, who was known to call my phone a half-dozen times before noon on a Saturday, but a conference call organized by the Sit Room meant this was serious business and somehow related to national security.

As I waited for the call to start, I furiously scanned the news alerts on my phone to look for clues as to what this could be about.

And then I found it: a report about an incident on a flight to Detroit where a man reportedly attempted to detonate a bomb smuggled in his underwear before being stopped by some very alert and brave passengers.

---

18   I still have nightmares about that flashing red light.
19   Mom, it's really good!

Once the call began, we received a briefing from a National Security Council staffer on what we knew about the incident—which was not much more than the original news report. We didn't yet know about the lethality of the explosive device. Most important, we didn't yet know if this was part of a larger plot, connected to Al-Qaeda, or just a lone knucklehead.

The question on the table was whether Obama should go out and make a statement to the press about the attack.

Gibbs argued that he should make a statement. Someone had tried to blow a plane out of the sky above Detroit on Christmas Day. I was opposed to Obama making a statement until we knew more—having the president address the nation on Christmas Day without new information would potentially cause a panic in a country that had been on edge since September 11, 2001.

What if he went out to discuss this and then it turned out the guy was some crank who couldn't have done much more than light his pants on fire?

I thought that would make Obama look like a rookie. My view was the president should go out and speak only when he had something specific and new to say. And in this case he didn't.

My side won the argument. We decided to ask the secretary of Homeland Security to do the Sunday shows the following day to address the situation. Decision made, I opened a beer and went back to enjoying Christmas.[20]

I was dead wrong.

We learned the underwear bomb could have brought the whole plane down, killing hundreds in the air and even more on the ground, and the plot was hatched by Al-Qaeda's deadly affiliate in Yemen.

The Homeland Security secretary said on CNN that the fact that the bomb wasn't detonated was evidence that "the system worked."

---

20 No war on Christmas in my home.

This verbal misstep combined with the absence of the president created a torrent of criticism of the White House for fumbling the response to a terrorist attack.

What I didn't understand at the time, but quickly learned, is that the role of the president is more than to inform or even persuade; it is to comfort.[21] Axelrod referred to this as the president's "pastoral" duties. Even if they disagree with the president every other day of the year, when tragedy or crisis strikes, the American people want to hear from the president. They want to know that the government is on the case.

The decision not to make a statement on Christmas Day dogged the White House for weeks. I was in the middle of conducting, at Obama's request, a review of communications operations when the failed bombing attempt occurred.

When I presented my findings to the president during a Saturday meeting in the Roosevelt Room a few weeks later, I told him that not overreacting to the noise of politics was one of our strengths as a team, but the flip side of this coin was that we were also prone to underreaction.

One of the ironies of this moment was that the media developed a narrative about Obama as being too aloof to be the comforter in chief. He was repeatedly compared unfavorably to Clinton, who was famous for "feeling people's pain," and George W. Bush's standing on the rubble of the World Trade Center with a bullhorn. Of all the dumb media narratives about Obama, the idea of him as aloof was perhaps the most absurd. He is a truly decent and empathetic human who genuinely liked being around people (less so politicians angling for a photo and a pork barrel project). It took years to shed this label, but by the end of his eight years, Obama was known for finding the perfect words to console the nation after such tragedies as the Boston

---

21 Donald Trump has made no effort to comfort the nation, but that may be because he has the empathy of a banana slug.

bombing; the shooting in Newtown, and countless hurricanes and other natural disasters.

Just as Obama found his words, we were able to find the right balance between responding to a crisis, keeping the calm in the country, and staying focused on issues like the economy that were at the top of the public's agenda.

THE TRUMP AT THE (ROSE) GARDEN PARTY

Much of American history is centered around moments of great presidential oratory. It's the touchstone by which we remember moments of triumph and tragedy. Kennedy on going to the moon; Reagan after the *Challenger* exploded; Bill Clinton healing the nation after the Oklahoma City bombing; Obama singing "Amazing Grace" after someone shot up a church in Charleston, South Carolina.

Of course, my loyalty was to Obama, and helping him achieve his place in history was my priority. But I also felt a deep sense of duty to the office itself. The new communications tools we were developing and the innovations we were making would serve not just my president but the presidency itself. I believed when I walked out of the office for the last time that the forums and formats of presidential communications would change as technology evolved. Just as we went from Roosevelt's fireside radio chats to Kennedy's televised press conferences to Obama's Twitter town halls and interviews with YouTube stars.

But I assumed that the job of White House communications director would stay fundamentally the same. That my successors would also show up to work every day trying to find the right balance between serving the person and the nation. That they would take the job of communicating the president's words with the seriousness such a task deserves.

I was wrong.

Now we have a president who tweets absurd, typo-ridden missives,[22] does interviews only with sycophantic propagandists, and lies through his teeth at every opportunity. Former White House communications officials of both parties watch with horror on a daily basis as our former jobs are debased by the Trump administration.

Some argue that Trump has fundamentally changed presidential communication and has proven there are few, if any, consequences for lies and absurdities. But Trump represents an aberration, not the new normal of how a president operates. If Democrats want to return to power, we should look not at how Trump communicates, but how Obama communicated, and project forward.

---

22   In fairness, my missives are often typo-ridden, but I am not the president.

INTERLUDE 1

SOMETHING PANTS-SPLITTINGLY FUNNY

One day in 2011, I walked into the Oval Office for a meeting to help the president prepare for a press conference where he was going to push the new Republican majority in Congress to come to the bargaining table to hammer out a budget deal.

A couple of things to know about press conference prep as we called it:

First, Obama hated press conference prep. He religiously read the briefings filled with hypothetical questions and suggested answers. And since he had read the answers, he found it tedious to go over the Q&A again with the staff. He found prep to be like going to the dentist—it had value, but he didn't enjoy it.

Second, it was always my job to lead the prep session, which meant walking the president through strategic objectives for the press conference and organizing the discussion. Obama liked my doing this because I knew how to communicate with him in clear, concise points. His brain works in a very linear fashion similar to mine (but his brain is much bigger), and he liked his briefing to reflect that fact:

"Mr. President, there are three key goals for this press conference."

"Sir, there are four potential strategies to deal with this issue."

But there was another reason I had this job. After so many years of working for the man, I had a sixth sense for his moods. I could always tell when he was growing tired of the prep session and therefore knew we had to get the most important information out before he moved on to the next thing on his never-ending to-do list.

On this particular morning, I was chatting with Obama as we walked over to the seating area in the Oval Office. He proceeded to his chair and I went to my usual seat on the couch closest to him.

I plopped down on the couch.

RIIPPPPP.

"Oh, shit," I thought. "That didn't just happen."

The sound of fabric ripping could mean only one thing—I had just split my pants. I quickly looked around the room to see if anyone else had heard the sound, but everyone was making small talk as we were waiting for Obama to start the meeting.

My mind started racing with some pressing questions:

What underwear was I wearing? I had taken to buying my boxers out of the bargain bin at Banana Republic whenever I didn't have time to do laundry and I didn't optimize for fashion. There were some pretty loud patterns.

Did my boxers also rip? Was my bare ass on the couch in the Oval Office?

And most important, how was I going to get out of the Oval Office and back to my office without becoming a laughingstock?

As I was plotting my exit route from the Oval Office, Obama interrupted my planning.

"Pfeiffer. Are you running this show?"

"Ummm, yes, sir."

I took a second to gather my thoughts and started prep. I tried to keep my mind off my bare posterior and run the prep session. During long explanations from some of my colleagues, I tried to reach behind me to see if I could divine the extent of the damage. We were packed on the couch like sardines and I was sitting about four feet from the president, and I couldn't really accomplish the task without looking like I was aggressively scratching my ass.

I wouldn't know anything until I stood up and then everyone else would know, too.

It wasn't my best work, but I managed to keep it moving and get the president the information he needed.

As the meeting wrapped, I girded myself to become the literal butt of the joke for the president and the ten or so aides who had been in the prep session. Everyone else stood up, but I stayed seated, pretending to write in the binder that held my briefing book for the day. I was paralyzed with potential embarrassment.

But then I saw an opportunity. A bunch of folks gathered around the president as he stood behind his desk. I might be able to slip out without anyone noticing me.

I awkwardly walked with my ass facing the wall toward the doorway into the anteroom to the Oval Office, and my plan was to sprint to my office, close the door, and then figure it out. I was on the cusp of getting out of the Oval when I heard my name.

"Is Dan still here?" I heard someone say from the group gathered around POTUS. I stopped in my tracks.

"Pfeiffer, come over here."

I took a deep breath and put my hands behind my back, draping my binder over the gaping hole in my pants, and walked back into the middle of the office to help hammer out one last answer.

Somehow no one noticed the weird way I was standing. Eventually everyone exited and I lagged behind, walking out last.

I had escaped, or so I thought.

Once back in my office, I closed the door and called Alyssa at her desk.

"AM. You won't believe this but I just busted my pants."

Once she was done laughing, Alyssa responded: "Oh, buddy. Wait right there. I will try to find some safety pins."

A few minutes later, she knocked on my door.

"Let me see it," she said.

I turned around with some trepidation and she busted out laughing.

"We're going to need more safety pins."

Alyssa went out and talked to Lauren Thorbjornsen, my assistant since 2008, and then went around looking for more safety pins. I made the first attempt to fix the pants while I was wearing them but it was a disaster.

By this point, everyone in the communications office knew what was going on and having a good laugh at my expense. I eventually took my pants off and handed them through the door as Alyssa and Lauren tried to fix them.

Behind closed doors, I was sitting at my desk in my underwear when the phone rang.

"Dan, the president wants you to walk over to the press conference with him," said the president's personal assistant.

What was I going to do? You can't say no to the president, and the only reason he would want me to walk with him was so we could go over an answer or two. This was my job.

I stuck my head out the door.

"I need my pants."

Everyone laughed hysterically.

I put my pants on, took two steps to the Oval, and they promptly split again.

Everyone laughed even more hysterically.

I was at a loss. I couldn't go back in the Oval Office with a giant and growing hole in my pants. Then I had what might have been my best idea in six years in the White House. I saw my coat hanging on the coat rack. It had been there since the past winter. It was not winter coat weather, we were pretty far into spring at this point and it was a nice day, but it would definitely cover my ass. I put it on and walked to the Oval to meet Obama.

The president was making some final notes on the opening remarks at his personal assistant's desk. He noticed my presence but didn't look up.

"Hey, I wanted to ask you about this line in the remarks about our demands."

I walked over to see what line he was talking about.

"Are you cold? Why are you wearing a coat?"

"Sir, that's a long story that we don't have time for."

And we didn't until now.

CHAPTER 4

THE NEW MEDIA WASTELAND

On the day President Obama promoted me to White House communications director, I was sitting in my office feeling pretty good about myself and replying to congratulatory e-mails. Martha Joynt Kumar, a professor who studies how presidents interact with the media, poked her head into my small office.[1]

Martha had stopped in to congratulate me and ask if I would follow the decades-long tradition of White House communications directors periodically meeting with her to help with her research. Everyone who watches the news knows the famous TV correspondents and *New York Times* reporters who interrogate the press secretary, but the briefing room is filled with a lot of people from outlets no one has heard of and in some cases people who have held on to their White House press passes even though their outlets have gone out of business years ago. At times, it's more like the bar scene from *Star Wars* than a scene from *All the President's Men*.

Martha is one of these lesser-known denizens of the White House briefing room, but her work is unquestionably valuable. I agreed

---

1 My promotion meant that I was going to get to move to the office next
   door, which was approximately two square feet larger.

to keep the tradition going and carve out time to talk to her every month or so for the next several years.

After Martha shared her latest research with me and asked me some questions about communications strategy, she got up to leave. As she was walking out the door, she turned back toward me:

"Did you know that historically White House communications directors get fired and go to jail more often than any position other than the White House counsel?"

I laughed until I realized she wasn't kidding. After an awkward pause, she left. I immediately Googled "White House Communications Director Fired."[2] Based on the Internet, which has never been wrong, the communications director is often the first head to roll when the shit hits the fan. While I (spoiler alert) managed to avoid this fate, President Trump's first communications director, Mike Dubke, lasted approximately two months before being put out of his misery.

Who could forget Anthony Scaramucci? The "Mooch" lasted all of ten days as communications director before being shown the door after he called up a reporter and accused Steve Bannon of a particularly limber form of self-gratification.[3]

As of early 2018, Hope Hicks, who replaced the "Mooch" as communications director, has done more interviews with the FBI than the media.[4]

In addition to being in a historically precarious position, I had the sense that I was in this position at a particularly precarious time. The White House communications director has a number of ever-changing and often amorphous duties, but ultimately it comes down to telling the country about the president's plans, accomplishments, and vision. For all of modern history, that meant communicating through the news media—speeches covered by the

---

2   I wasn't super worried about jail since, unlike Trump, Obama wasn't running a low-rent criminal conspiracy out of the West Wing.
3   My White House tenure lasted for approximately 220 "Scaramuccis."
4   She soon quit, presumably to have more time to meet with the grand jury.

TV networks, interviews with newspapers and magazines, and press conferences covered by all of them. The president had the largest megaphone in the world.

Barack Obama had the misfortune to become president—and I the misfortune to become his communications director—at the exact time when the mainstream media was going through an existential crisis that would diminish the power of the presidential bully pulpit and the media's capacity to be an independent arbiter of truth for the public.

As I was absorbing Martha's warning, my elation turned to worry. My natural tendency is to find the dark lining in any silver clouds. Getting the job was great; getting fired and publicly humiliated was worse than not getting it. One of the worst parts of political Washington is the ravenous blood lust the town has for someone—anyone—to get fired when a president hits a rough patch. And when someone is finally sacrificed to appease the pundit gods, the streets of Washington are flooded with collective schadenfreude. I could see the Politico headline regaling my firing: "Pfeiffer Pfired: White House Comms Director Out After Latest Mishap."

The media was in the midst of a massive, rapid, disruptive transformation that was rewriting all the rules of politics and presidential communications. Trying to stay ahead of this transformation was one of the main themes of the Obama era. When we were ahead of the curve, we succeeded, and when we fell behind, we didn't.[5] And beyond the Obama White House, the changes in journalism upended politics and created an environment where someone like Donald Trump could win.

It's impossible to understand Trump, his victory, and how to beat him without understanding the rapidly changing media ecosystem that Obama battled and eventually conquered.

---

5   That's the sort of axiomatic cliché that punditry is made of.

HOW WE GOT HERE

In early 2011, David Plouffe, who had just replaced David Axelrod as White House senior advisor, and I were interviewing candidates for press secretary to replace Robert Gibbs, who had decided to leave the White House. Late one afternoon, we were meeting with Jay Carney in Gibbs's spacious office while he was on the road with Obama. Jay was a well-known and well-liked former bureau chief for *Time*, who had left journalism to become Vice President Biden's communications director. Unlike most who make the transition from press to politics, Jay had done it seamlessly. He was probably the sixth or seventh candidate Plouffe and I had interviewed, and we had our routine pretty much down pat. The last question we asked every candidate was: "What piece of advice would you give us to improve our communications strategy?"

This is usually a good question to see if a candidate has the courage to tell you something you don't want to hear, and at bare minimum, if you are going to spend hours interviewing people, all but one of whom you aren't going to hire, you might as well get some free advice out of it.

"You guys pioneered ways of using the Internet to communicate directly with the public without going through the press," Jay said about our 2008 campaign. "You should keep doing all those things, but maybe don't rub the press's face in it so much. You have to understand, reporters are going through an existential crisis where they don't know if their job or industry is going to be around for that much longer."

Jay's comment summed up media in America, which was in a state of massive transition and turmoil with regular announcements of layoffs and legacy media outlets shuttering their doors. Plouffe and I both took what Jay said to heart.[6]

---

6   Most of the time.

Soon after this meeting, the president hired Jay as White House press secretary.

The existential crisis that Jay referred to was a long time in the making, but when it happened, it happened fast. Someone (not me) could write a very long book on this topic, but let me do the Cliff's Notes version:[7]

First, the Internet made it so people could get information without paying for it, which was not good for the newspaper business, which sold ads based on the number of subscribers.

Second, the Internet and the smartphone made it so people could get info whenever they wanted wherever they wanted it on their phone, which was not good for the television industry, which sold ads based on the number of people who sat down to watch TV at an appointed time.

Third, the 2008 financial crisis crushed the very businesses that bought the ads that funded the media industry. Newspapers were laying off people or closing altogether. The more experienced reporters were being offered buyouts so outlets could replace them with cheaper, younger reporters. You now had fewer reporters with less experience and fewer editors writing more often to meet the never-ending deadline of the Internet.

Fourth, while media was weakened by technology and economics, it was also losing its sacred place in American democracy in the eyes of many Americans. By the time Barack Obama had started running for president, the halcyon days of journalism were a distant memory. Public trust in the media declined precipitously, and by the time Trump won the 2016 election, the media was about as popular as Trump himself.[8]

Some of this decline is part of a general trend of greater skepticism of institutions, but the media is not blameless either. Several high-profile incidents have given the public legitimate reasons to be

---

7   In other words, *The Unraveling of Democracy for Idiots.*
8   Being as popular as Trump is not very popular.

more skeptical. Foremost among these is the coverage of the run-up to the Iraq War, where the media—and the *New York Times* in particular—parroted the Bush administration's false claims about the presence of weapons of mass destruction in Iraq.

Finally, the Republican Party and the right-wing media had been running a decades-long effort to convince their voters that the media was their enemy and to create an alternative version of reality. Fox News, the Republican propaganda outlet, which marketed itself under the banner of being "Fair and Balanced,"[9] was the embodiment of the effort to nullify news that ran counter to the political wishes of the Republican Party and conservative activists.

All of this meant that Barack Obama was entering office at a time when it was harder than ever to reach people through the news media and people were more skeptical than ever before about anything they learned from the media. Not exactly a recipe for success for a new president (and his communications director) trying to tell the country about his agenda. These changes created several media dynamics that defined daily life in the Obama White House and set the stage for the election of President Trump.

THE PULPIT GETS BULLIED

Reagan mythology aside, Obama is the greatest communicator of the modern political era.[10] He delivers speeches of oratorical brilliance. In interviews, he manages to seem extraordinarily talented and ordinarily grounded at the same time. No president has been able to hold a crowd so rapt, whether it was a boisterous political rally or a somber memorial service, like Obama.

Yet despite all of this talent, one of Barack Obama's greatest frus-

---

9   To quote Lionel Hutz from *The Simpsons*, Fox News being "Fair and Balanced" is "the most blatant case of fraudulent advertising since the film *The NeverEnding Story*."

10   I am most certainly biased. I am also most certainly correct.

trations during his time in the White House was his inability to use rhetoric and reason to better tell the story of his presidency.

After the Democrats lost the House of Representatives in 2010 in a rebuke to Obama's agenda, I was standing along the wall of the East Room during the president's traditional postelection press conference when he explained that his greatest failure was the inability to tell his story.

I felt like someone had just punched me in the stomach. Obama was talking about himself, but he was also talking about me. It was my job to help him tell his story. I had failed him. And he had just told the world.

I struggled to keep my emotions off my face since I was in full view of the media and was standing with Gibbs and Axelrod, the other two individuals who shared responsibility for this object of immense presidential frustration. I could feel the collective gaze of the assembled press corps turn toward us like a pack of vultures to the fresh carcass of our professional reputations.

Before long, pundits and columnists were calling on the president to fire his campaign communications team and hire some seasoned Washington hands to do our jobs.[11] I spent a lot of sleepless nights wondering what I did wrong and what I could do better. This was the first time I asked myself the existential question about whether I had what it took to play at this level of the game. I have always been extremely hard on myself when things don't go well. I was known to sulk for days after my high school basketball team lost a game, and we weren't that good so I spent most of my teenage years sulking.

I spent the Thanksgiving break preparing to be fired. In Washington, there is a ritual of sacrifice when elections do not go well. In order to appease the angry hordes of the chattering class, someone is usually sent packing as a symbol that the president "got it." If

---

11 As a "seasoned Washington hand," I can tell you that hiring a "seasoned Washington hand" is almost never the correct answer.

Obama went that route, I was sure I was near the top of the list of sacrificial lambs.

After a few days of gloom and doom, the president sat us all down in the Oval Office and said we were his team, we had been loyal to him, and he would always be loyal to us. We all got to the White House together after everyone had written us off more times than we could count, and we were going to get out of this mess together. But we had to do better. I was dispatched to write a memo about all that went wrong in our communications strategy in the first two years and how we could start to fix it.

The memo was filled with self-criticism of the past and ideas for the future, but it also addressed an essential truth about modern political communication that we all had to accept:

The presidential bully pulpit was dead.

President Teddy Roosevelt coined the term "bully pulpit" to describe his ability to move the public to enact his agenda. It has taken on legendary status in the decades since, creating the mythology that a president could bend the public to his or her will through the sheer power of persuasion.

The mythology of the bully pulpit certainly overshot the reality in hagiographic memoirs of Kennedy and Reagan and pop culture renditions of politics like *The West Wing*. But one thing is sadly true: the presidential megaphone has gotten much smaller over time.

Ronald Reagan mastered the communications tools of his presidency. He would speak to the nation so frequently through televised addresses that he spurred me to take my first act of political activism. When my second-grade teacher assigned each student to write a letter to President Reagan as homework, I scanned the waterfront of pressing issues and decided to write to my president about an issue that affected my life directly. I passionately complained that his too-often televised speeches frequently preempted *The A-Team*, my favorite show and the only one my dad would let me stay up past my bedtime to watch. And thus my life in politics was born.

Other than annoying eight-year-old *A-Team* fans across America, Reagan delivered these frequent addresses because they worked. Americans had access to only a few television channels, so if Reagan got the networks to preempt their programming to air him, every single person in America had a choice: watch Reagan or turn off the TV.

Compare that to the Obama era, where there are more cable channels than one can count, countless on-demand streaming services, and smartphones and tablets that provide endless alternative sources of entertainment and information. If you are tuning in to watch *Scandal* and suddenly an Obama speech comes on, you can change the channel or turn on Netflix or watch YouTube videos. Presidential addresses are no longer required viewing for the masses; they are optional viewing for the already committed. The audience for nationally televised addresses has been declining precipitously for years.

And this goes beyond the periodic presidential address. Americans have steadily moved away from the traditional sources of news that were the vehicles for presidents to inform the public.

These changes in media meant that Barack Obama had to work harder and smarter to communicate his message than any of his predecessors. And future Democrats are going to have to work even harder and smarter than that.

THE *SPORTSCENTER* EFFECT

As *Pod Save America* listeners know, I relish my role as a self-appointed media critic. This was particularly true during the 2016 campaign when I thought the press was giving Hillary Clinton a raw deal (they were).[12] I am motivated by my own partisan bias, a desire to work the referees for a better result, and an itchy Twitter

---

12   See what I mean?

finger. Even though it is rarely constructive, I can't help myself. I know the media is as interested in my opinion on their job performance as I am interested in their opinion on how I ran the Obama communications shop.

But, and this is a big but, I love great journalism and want more of it. I decided to go into politics in large part because on my first day at Georgetown University, someone stopped by my dorm room offering a great deal on a *Washington Post* subscription. I was immediately hooked. I soaked up every detail about what was happening on Capitol Hill and in the White House, each just a few miles away. I have been a news addict ever since. What follows may read as a harsh critique of journalism, but that is not how it is intended; instead, it is my analysis of how the media environment has changed. Many of those changes inadvertently advantaged Trump in 2016 and Democrats must first understand the new world before we can conquer it.

There was a lot of excellent journalism during the Obama presidency. Incredible reporting from the front lines of wars, probing investigative pieces that revealed fraud and abuse in government, and masterful feature articles that told the stories of the people who make up the cultural mosaic of our country. While some of these stories made my job harder, we as a country are all the better for them. More importantly, there is even better journalism happening in the Trump presidency. Trump's attacks on the press that border on the cyber-bullying that his wife has laughingly pledged to stomp out have reignited an appreciation for great journalism among the non-MAGA hat-wearing populace. The *New York Times* and the *Washington Post* have entered a new golden era, one-upping each with critical scoops on a daily basis.

It is also true, however, that too much of political journalism is about the horse race of campaigns rather than the policy of governing. Polls are like crack to reporters because they love to write about who's up and who's down. Coverage tends to conform to the chosen narrative of the moment, which lasts up until the moment the press gets tired of the narrative and looks for the first excuse to shift to a new, more interesting narrative. It's almost always style over substance. There are great informative pieces of political journalism that tell us about the players involved and the issues, but those are the exceptions, not the rule.

Too much of political coverage is glorified sports coverage. No different than what we see on ESPN.

Who's winning? What were the highlights? What were the bloopers?

This is not inherently a bad thing. Our system works better when people are interested, and the dismal viewership of C-SPAN suggests people are not interested in the daily grind of the legislative process.[13] And media outlets are businesses with shareholders, earnings statements, and payrolls to meet. We think of journalism as an endeavor of public service, and there is certainly a nobility in it relative to other industries, but the business model is no different than any other media industry. If people don't watch, advertisers don't buy ads, so media outlets have an obligation to produce content that causes people to tune in, subscribe, and click. If I were in their shoes, I would do the exact same thing.

With that undeniably fair caveat, let me be very clear—the way politics is being covered, consumed, tweeted, and Facebooked is royally fucking up America. Full Stop. This is not just the media's fault. Voters and politicians are also to blame because they willingly participate in and consume the spectacle.

Politics is covered like a game, but politics is not a game. It's a noble pursuit, even if it is sometimes pursued ignobly. The decisions made by politicians have dramatic—and sometimes life-and-death—consequences for the public. Those decisions and the process to pick the decision makers deserve coverage worthy of the stakes.

Covering politics like sports has created a self-reinforcing incentive structure that is not dissimilar to the one that ESPN's

---

13 Who could blame them?

SportsCenter has on the fundamentals of basketball. There is a long-running concern from basketball purists that the fundamentals of the game—passing, defense, and footwork—are eroding. The theory goes that players want to be like the stars they see on *Sports-Center*. You don't get on *SportsCenter* by doing the nitty-gritty work of winning basketball games. The more extreme the play, the more dramatic the showboating and celebrating, the more likely to be a featured in a coveted highlight segment. The reward system benefits the opposite behavior most basketball coaches would like to see in their players.

This is the *SportsCenter* Effect.

The exact same thing is true in politics. In fact, it may be even truer in politics, because the incentives are stronger. Media attention is the lifeblood for any politician. Steph Curry doesn't need media attention to be a great basketball player; politicians need media attention like oxygen. It's how they get known by the public; it's how they build up their ranks of engaged supporters that make up the donor and volunteer bases of their perpetual campaigns.

How do you get booked on cable news or get a lot of retweets and followers? Say something and do something more outrageous than everyone else. Push the envelope on decency. Throw a temper tantrum on the floor of the Senate.

Here's what won't get you attention: thoughtful public policy, bipartisan compromise, or basic governing. This has been true since the advent of cable news, but Twitter has made this situation exponentially worse, which shortens the acceptable length of any idea from an already unacceptably short 30-second TV sound bite to a 280-character tweet. The more attention you can generate on Twitter, the more likely you are to be booked on cable and vice versa.

Few will admit this, but political strategists spend an undue amount of time trying to create moments that may go viral. I know I certainly did.

We would often spend some of our morning communications meeting in the White House thinking of how to create "moments" that would get more attention than the usual presidential pronouncement. Instead of yet another speech on the need for more spending to repair America's infrastructure, let's give the speech in front of the crumbling bridge that spans Kentucky and Ohio, the states that just happen to be home to the Republican leaders of the Senate and the House of Representatives.

The media that ignored almost every other Obama speech on infrastructure spending covered this one like it was the State of the Union simply because of the obvious pugnacity. The lesson was clear—if you want attention, you better punch someone in the mouth.

This is how President Obama ended up going Christmas shopping with his dog in the car in the run-up to the 2012 election. Romney had been dogged (literally) by a story about how he had once strapped the family dog to the roof of his car for a family road trip.[14] For good reason, this story bothered a lot of people—especially dog lovers. So we had the White House release a photo of Obama traveling with his dog *in* the car. The subtlety was not lost on anyone, and a viral moment was born.

It's not surprising that the political discourse has become coarser and less serious over time, and it's not surprising[15] that we ended up with a reality TV star with his notoriously twitchy Twitter finger on the nuclear button.

The *SportsCenter* Effect took on a different dynamic in the 2016 presidential race. Trump was a master of the game. Whether it was intellectual or instinctual, he was an expert at saying and tweeting the things that would dominate the conversation on Twitter and then across the media landscape.

Trump's utterances got the best ratings and the best traffic. The best way for any of the other candidates to get the media attention

---

14   This is such a weird thing to do that it is basically disqualifying for any
       job, let alone president of the United States.
15   OK, maybe it is still surprising.

they so desperately needed was to talk about Trump—not their own stories or policy plans. Those got ignored. Trump came to define the four corners of the political conversation. He blocked out the sun.

WHAT ABOUT YOUR GAFFES?

The signature image of the 2012 campaign is the viral video of Phil Rucker, a very talented young reporter for the *Washington Post*, screaming "What about your gaffes?" at Mitt Romney during Romney's gaffe-filled campaign trip to Europe and the Middle East.

Even more famously, Romney's campaign suffered a mortal wound when he was caught on video writing off 47 percent of the American people.

The media's obsession with gaffes was a perpetual challenge and frustration that symbolized much of the dumbing down of political discourse. Gaffes aren't new to politics, but they have gotten much more attention in an era where media outlets are monetizing clicks and political campaigns are looking for reasons to manufacture outrage to motivate their supporters.

When the media is focused more on the misstatements of politicians than the actual statements, it damages the discourse and denies the voters the discussion of the issues they deserve.

There was one moment in the 2012 campaign that exemplified the inanity of political coverage focused on catching politicians making gaffes.

During that campaign, Europe found itself on the verge of a financial crisis that could have devastating effects on the US economy. Most of the public and the reporters covering the White House knew very little about this looming disaster, so we decided to send President Obama to the briefing room one Friday to educate the press and the public and put pressure on Republicans in Congress not to make the situation worse (which is their natural instinct). The goal was to get ahead of a potential economic and political disaster.

While a policy explanation without a specific announcement would rarely get enough coverage to merit asking the president to walk down the hall to deliver it, I hoped that the context of the campaign and the tradition of "equal time" would force the media to cover it.

All was going swimmingly when Obama responded to a question about the state of the economy and said the words "the private sector is doing fine."

In context, this statement made complete sense and was completely noncontroversial. Obama was accurately stating that American businesses had recovered faster from the financial crisis than American families. But my political antennae went up. This was ripe for being exploited by Republicans desperate to show Obama as out of touch with an economy that was still recovering. I was seated along the wall in the briefing room in full view of the reporters.

I tried to keep a poker face, but anyone who plays cards with me knows that is not my strong suit.[16] Plouffe was seated next to me and heard me utter some unintelligible curse word under my breath and looked at me quizzically. The reporters perked up because the press conference had just got more interesting. They were licking their chops at the opportunity to cover something other than the United States' efforts to work with the European Union.

Why write about the potential collapse of the European economy, which would cause a global recession affecting billions of people, when you can cover a good ole political fight?

After the presser ended, I walked Obama back to the Oval and mentioned casually that his remark might be an issue.

"Really? I was pretty clear about the context," he said with some annoyance.

---

16   The first time I played poker with Obama, he took all my money in record time.

"It's campaign season. Context doesn't matter. Romney is going to make this an issue and then it's off to the races."

By the time I got to my desk, the *New York Times* had already published a story about Obama's faux gaffe, which was all over the *Drudge Report* and blowing up on Twitter. I got the author of the offending story on the phone, and seething with unbridled rage, I started arguing why the story was both inaccurate and untrue. While this was more madness than method, I knew my only chance to keep this from being a days-long controversy was to kill it immediately. Every minute that story was online, it was spreading like wildfire across the Internet.

The story didn't include the very clear context of the president's statement. The conversation quickly devolved into a yelling match that got more profane by the minute.

I knew the argument had escalated quickly when a colleague walked over to my office with a look of great trepidation on her face and closed my office door.[17] I learned later that people standing in the hallway waiting to go into the Oval Office could hear me yelling. The reporter knew what Obama meant, but that was irrelevant. It had to be written about because the Romney campaign was likely to make it an issue. This sort of circular logic said more about journalism than it did about this particular journalist, who was one of the good ones.

The reporter eventually hung up on me with a vague promise to take my concerns under consideration and a less vague request that I stick my head up my ass. Needless to say, the story did not get sufficiently fixed and the Internet and media were in a feeding frenzy, incorrectly representing what Obama said to create an incorrect perception of him. The campaign spent the next couple of days trying to right the ship.

The possible collapse of the European economy and its impact

---

17   This "colleague" would eventually become my wife, whom I probably shouldn't have introduced via footnote.

on the United States was a deadly serious issue, but that wasn't a conversation that could happen in our modern media environment.

The next day was the annual party the vice president throws for the media at his house. This is a wonderful event with rides and games for the media and their families.

As I was waiting in the security line to enter the event, I thought I heard a familiar voice behind me, so I turned around to see who it was.

It was the reporter I had screamed at the day before, standing there with his wife and young children.

It was awkward to say the least.

"Ummm. Hi, I'm Dan Pfeiffer, I sorta...umm...work with your dad," I stammered before faking a phone call to get away.

THE INSATIABLE CONTENT MONSTER

During the '08 campaign, our press strategy was geared toward the idea of always being on offense. This was a simple concept: we wanted to make news early in the day to push the political conversation, which in those days occurred primarily on cable TV, in our preferred direction. We wanted the media and our opponents to react to our news throughout the day as opposed to forcing us to react to theirs.

Therefore, we would get up before 5:00 a.m. most days to make announcements of new endorsements, new television ads, or new policy proposals.[18] Nick Shapiro, who was a deputy press secretary on the campaign, was assigned the task of getting up every morning to send out our news of the day at 5:30 a.m. for the network morning shows. Nick did this task without fail or complaint for months. It wasn't till a year after the campaign when we were both working

---

18 I loved that our campaign was in Chicago, but if your strategy depends on early morning news announcements, think twice about putting your campaign in the central time zone.

in the White House that I learned that Nick didn't have Internet in his apartment, so he was getting up every morning and going to a nearby hotel to steal their Wi-Fi to send out our press releases seated among a group of prostitutes who gathered in the lobby of the hotel at the crack of dawn.[19]

That strategy now feels like a relic of a bygone age before Facebook and especially Twitter became the arenas in which political combat occurred. By 2012, the news cycle moved so voraciously fast that we stopped making announcements early in the morning, because it would be old news by lunchtime. The political media machine—which was made up of an ever-growing collection of media outlets, cable channels, websites, bloggers, and tweeters (so many fucking tweeters)—now had an insatiable appetite for content.

The news cycle is dead; long live the content monster.

As with most things, the Internet is to blame for this.

First, the news cycle is dead in the eyes of the consumers; they want news immediately on demand. They don't want to wait for the 6:00 p.m. news or the next morning's paper to be delivered to get the latest news; they want to look at the news on their phone at any hour of the day while killing time in line at the grocery store or sitting on a city bus. This means that reporters are basically working 24/7, updating stories posted earlier and writing new stories as soon as events dictate. Second, digital advertising—the revenue source for most media in the modern era—is a volume game. The more content you create, the more ads you can sell, and with declining print ad sales, you need to make up the difference somewhere.

This means we live in a never-ending, always accelerating news cycle, which makes the brutal White House lifestyle more brutal than it has ever been. When we first arrived at the White House, the press staff was informed by the outgoing Bush staff of something

---

19   The fact that Nick never shared this fact with me makes more sense now that I know he would eventually become a top aide to CIA Director John Brennan.

called "pager duty," where one member of the press staff was on duty to take press calls that came in through the White House switchboard while the rest of the team got a little time off. The fact that this was called "pager duty" in the era of the smartphone was a sign this was an outdated tradition. After a few weeks of the person on call getting inundated with queries and e-mails well beyond the capacity of a single human to handle, we gave in to the new media reality and conceded that everyone would be on call every weekend.

My daily routine, particularly in the early years of the White House, was as follows:

4:50 a.m.	Alarm goes off.
4:50–5:00 a.m.	Read e-mails on BlackBerry that came in over the five hours or so I was asleep.
5:00–5:30 a.m.	Shower, get dressed, read e-mails that start to come that morning from reporters.
5:30–5:45 a.m.	E-mail the morning tip sheets to ask them to include articles from the papers that fit our message and vigorously (sometimes overvigorously) argue against the inclusion of articles that did not fit our message.
5:45–6:45 a.m.	Talk on the phone with White House correspondents preparing to go on the network morning shows while I drive to work and eat breakfast at my desk in the White House.[20]

---

20 Long before she was the world-famous host of the *Today Show*, Savannah Guthrie and I used to have an energetic, but respectful, debate every morning about the news of the day while I ate my breakfast. Now she interviews the likes of George Clooney and Beyoncé, and I record a podcast at my kitchen table. So we both won.

7:30 a.m.–7:30 p.m.	Attend endless series of meetings (scheduled and impromptu) and take nonstop phone calls while careening from crisis to crisis (real and manufactured).
8:00–10:00 p.m.	Clean up desk, work on to-do list for the next day, drive home, and eat an unhealthy dinner at an hour later than any doctor would recommend.
10:00 p.m.	Log on to the *Washington Post* and *New York Times* websites to read the next day's stories that just got posted, begin e-mailing with other colleagues to craft responses to any problems or e-mail reporters to fight for changes to any inaccurate or unappealing parts of those stories. Eventually go to bed, rinse, repeat.

On Christmas Eve in 2009, right after the Senate passed the latest version of the Affordable Care Act, I stopped by the office of White House Chief of Staff Rahm Emanuel. I was about to head out of town for my first days off since Barack Obama had won the nomination. I wanted to check in before heading for the train station. Rahm was a top advisor in the famously chaotic Clinton White House for more than six years, where he dealt with countless calamities, including the effort to impeach the president.[21]

As I was bidding him farewell, Rahm looked up from his BlackBerry, rubbed his eyes, and said, "This year felt longer than all my years in the Clinton White House combined."

The reason: Everything was moving faster than ever before.

---

21   Impeachment is really the ultimate political calamity; it's hard to top that one.

Politics and government were now operating at the speed of the never-ending news cycle. What used to take weeks now happened in a matter of hours. When you used to have a day to respond, you now had minutes—if you were lucky.

And it's only got worse since then. Much, much worse.

THE TRUMP MEDIA ENVIRONMENT EMERGES

Late in 2014, after a particularly rough period politically for the president, Obama called me into the Oval Office for a "chat."

He was, rightly, frustrated about the state of our communications operation.

"In 2008, we were so far ahead of the curve. Governing is harder than campaigning, but for most of our time here, we have at least kept pace with the change. Lately, it feels like we have fallen behind."

I had been anticipating this chat, because the president was correct. We had been on the defensive for the last eighteen months. Every time we would get a little momentum, something would knock us back on our heels. And we paid the price at the ballot box, losing the Senate and handing full control of Congress over to the Republicans.

The old tricks weren't working anymore.

I hatched a plan with Denis McDonough. In the past, our challenges had been execution related and we could address them with the usual tools available to us. This felt like a more existential challenge. Something fundamental had changed in the media environment. I needed to figure out what had changed and what we should do about it. I needed help.

For most of my time working for Obama, whenever we encountered some Beltway political crisis that dominated cable news, we would ask focus groups of voters if they had heard anything about it. Almost every single time, they had no idea what we were talking about. There were things Washington got worked up about and things the American people cared about and rarely did those things overlap.

But something had changed. Suddenly, focus groups knew all about the trivial things that Washington would get worked up over, and they knew about them in great detail. Often reading back to the moderator what sounded just like Republican talking points or a Fox News story—which are actually the same thing.

When the moderator asked them where they'd learned this information, the answer was almost always the same: Facebook.

By 2016, the media ecosystem of 2008 was impossible to recognize. It was the perfect petri dish for a fungus like Trumpism to grow.

Trump understood that there were no rules and referees and that a good story was much more valuable than an accurate one. Trump's main media experiences are the absurdity of reality television and the no-holds-barred world of Big Apple tabloid journalism. Sadly, these were the perfect experiences to compete for president in 2016.

In hindsight, it seems obvious that Trump would thrive in this environment. The hints were there all along, going back way before he even ran.

To grapple with these changes, I proposed going to Silicon Valley and New York to pick the brains of the smartest people in tech and media to better understand the current state of affairs and where things might be going. I went to Google, Twitter, YouTube, LinkedIn, and everywhere in between. I met with the venture capitalists who were looking for the next Google and Facebook.

The gravity of the challenge before us came in a meeting in Silicon Valley when I explained the difficulty in getting our message out in the fragmented media environment, and one of the executives from a Silicon Valley giant responded:

"We have been wondering the same thing and hoped you had some good ideas."

CHAPTER 5

FIGHTING FAKE NEWS

On a dreary morning in April 2011, I found myself facing sleep-addled reporters in a half-empty White House briefing room. From the earliest days of my career, I had dreamed about standing at this very spot.

The "Podium," as it's known to everyone in Washington, is the top of the game. It's like the mound at Fenway for a ballplayer. If you are standing there, then you have made it. The White House briefing room is one of the most famous rooms in the world.[1] History has been made in this room more times than one can count.

I had long thought about what it would mean to be in this exact spot as a senior White House aide. This was supposed to be a big moment for me. But as I walked up to the podium, I thought to myself:

Was I there to announce important new government policy?

Nope.

Was I there to joust with the media about the issues that mattered?

Nah.

Was I there to respond to the mad ravings of a conspiracy theory–spreading reality television star?

---

1   It's also a shithole, but you can't see that on camera.

Bingo.

I had walked into the briefing room that morning with fifty copies of Barack Obama's birth certificate, so we could prove once and for all that the man who was in his third year as president after winning a historic electoral landslide was an American citizen eligible to be president.

The term "fake news" was not yet part of the political lexicon, but this might very well have been the moment when it rose from something that elicited an eye roll to something that necessitated a full-throated response from the White House.

The era of #FakeNews was born.

WHAT IS #FAKENEWS?

"Fake news" may now be on the tip of everyone's tongue—especially President Trump's—but it didn't just magically appear in 2016. The battle against fake news was a defining element of the Obama era. We dealt with it, worried about it, and were disheartened by it from the very beginning of the campaign. It's something Donald Trump played a large role in perpetuating long before he was a candidate for president, and it just may have cost Hillary Clinton the White House.

But what is fake news? Like so much in politics these days, it's way more confusing than it should be since it has several meanings.

In the months before the 2016 election, the following stories went viral:

- Pope Francis shocks the world, endorses Donald Trump for president.
- Wikileaks confirms that Hillary sent weapons to ISIS.
- FBI director received millions from the Clinton Foundation.
- ISIS leader calls for American Muslims to support Hillary Clinton.

- Hillary Clinton in 2013: "I would like to see people like Donald Trump run for office; they're honest and can't be bought."

Each of these stories received more than 500,000 engagements on Facebook—much greater than factual articles from the *New York Times*, *Washington Post*, and other outlets during the same period. And they were all complete, unadulterated bullshit. In these cases, the stories were completely made up by outside actors, including the Russians, and then spread on Facebook to influence the election.

There is also the screaming of "fake news" at any piece of information that one doesn't like, even (and often) when it is undeniably true. This is in some ways a defense mechanism for our infantile and insecure president, but it has an even more alarming purpose. The point is to signal to Trump's most diehard supporters to dismiss any piece of news that is bad for Trump, even if it is objectively and obviously true. When it was revealed that Donald Trump Jr., Trump's oldest son and the Fredo of the Trump clan, was corresponding with someone representing the Russian government about their efforts to help Trump win, Trump's supporters refused to believe the story and questioned the authenticity of the e-mails, even though they were released by Fredo himself.

However one chooses to define it, the fake news phenomenon is about the country moving into an era of post-truth politics, and 2016 was the tipping point.

In the past, even the slipperiest politicians adhered to a plausible deniability of dishonesty. Instead of outright lying, they put some measure of spin on a set of facts. Sometimes the spin was so absurd that it was hard to distinguish it from a lie, but at the end of the day, it was rooted in some truth, even if it perverted that truth beyond recognition.

Trump was a wholly different entity. He was unburdened by the shame that keeps most people from outright lying. The media and the Clinton campaign were entirely unprepared to deal with something like this. Trump didn't play by the rules. He couldn't be chastened by criticism or persuaded by facts.

In 2016, Trump and his team (foreign and domestic) were able to take this one step further and used Facebook to weaponize his lies and spread the fake news far and wide.

But like so much with Trump, it's easy to forget that Trump is a symptom, not the disease that affects the body politic. The underlying causes of the fake news phenomenon have been building for years and they were a defining element of the Obama era. Even if we didn't use the term "fake news," we dealt with the seeds of the "post-truth" era from the very beginning of Obama's first campaign.

THE BATTLE AGAINST BIRTHERISM

When I pictured my debut in the White House briefing room, I did not imagine that it would be for such an absurd reason.

Serious things were happening in the world. We had two active wars, Europe was on the brink of a financial crisis that could collapse the US economy, and we were headed into a major legislative showdown with the new Republican majority in Congress that had massive implications for the future of the country. Yet nearly every time the president or any White House official took questions from the media, they were asked to respond to whatever absurdity had come out of Trump's mouth in his latest appearance on the *Today Show* or *Fox & Friends*.[2]

In all fairness, most of the time the reporters were sheepish when they asked the question. These were (mostly) serious people who had joined a serious profession to cover serious issues being forced to ask an unserious question because of the never-ending search for ratings, clicks, and retweets. But nonetheless, the president of the

---

2   These two shows did the most to aid and abet Trump's efforts.

United States was being forced to respond to a reality star less relevant than the Real Housewives.[3]

Beyond the abject absurdity of the messenger, the claim that the president wasn't born in the United States, which came to be known as birtherism, was a particularly kooky conspiracy theory.

Birtherism wasn't new when Trump turned it into a crusade. It had been around since the early days of the campaign. It was the subject of a series of malicious e-mail chains that were being forwarded around the Internet. These e-mails contained a wide array of false and particularly ridiculous information about Obama including:

- Obama was born in Kenya.
- Obama was educated in a madrassa during his time living in Indonesia as a small child.
- Obama was sworn into office in the Senate using a Koran instead of a Bible.
- Obama was not the son of Barack Obama Sr., but was the son of African American activist and socialist Frank Marshall Davis.

This was the era of journalism before social media, so the media mostly responsibly refused to cover the e-mails. They would check out the rumors, find them to be ridiculous, and then refuse to amplify them.

Despite this mainstream media blackout, birtherism was gaining a disturbing amount of traction among some of the voters in rural Iowa—which hosted the critical first-in-the-nation caucus. Our field organizers were getting questions from the voters they were contacting. Most of the questions were well intentioned. Democratic primary voters were scarred from consecutive losses and were viewing this information through the prism of Obama's electability. If we nominate Obama and this info comes out, will the Republicans

---

3   This is admittedly deeply unfair to the Real Housewives, all of whom would have been a better president (especially Bethenny Frankel).

win again? Our field staff would tell people it's not true, but they wanted proof to soothe their own concerns but also to share with their friends and family.

So we made the decision to post Obama's "Certificate of Live Birth" on the Internet. This was not an easy decision. It ran counter to one of the cardinal rules of political communications: Don't give oxygen to malicious rumors. It's better to ignore them than dignify them with a response that would catapult rumors from the dark corners of the Internet to the front pages of the *New York Times*. But that rule—like most of the rules that governed public relations strategy—was written before the Internet.

To a certain extent this tactic worked—the voters who wanted to support Obama were mollified by this information. Like all campaigns, we focused all our energy and resources on the people who might support our candidate. These are the people on whose doors our organizers knocked and whose phones they called. It's one of the realities of campaigns that you cannot afford to spend any energy talking to voters or campaigning in states that will never support your candidate. Therefore, we didn't have any insight into how the Far Right of the Republican base was feeling about Obama's citizenship. As far as I was concerned, the issue had been put to bed.

Once we got to the White House, we were inundated with the more serious issues that come with running the world and I didn't think about those old campaign rumors. Every once in a while, I would get called up to the White House counsel's office to get a briefing because a collection of crackpots had sued the president to challenge the legitimacy of the election over the birther issue. The lawyers told us not to worry about it, and I didn't.

While we were focused on things like saving the economy and passing a health care bill, however, the right-wing fringe was in overdrive. They had become convinced that the "Certificate of Live Birth" we'd released during the campaign was a forgery. A major part of the conspiracy centered on the difference between the

"Certificate of Live Birth" we released and his "long-form birth certificate," which was on file with the state of Hawaii. It's hard to overstate how dumb a discrepancy this is, but it is also hard to overstate how dumb the Far Right of the Republican Party can be.

And then Donald Trump, a man whose depraved desire for attention would make a Kardashian blush, latched on to the cause. Trump was embarking on a press tour to promote the next season of *The Celebrity Apprentice* and was looking for ways to juice up the middling ratings of the show. He was even floating a presidential run, which is an old PR tactic for tricking the media into covering you. Almost no one took the idea that Trump was going to run seriously, he had employed this gambit before, but all the media needed was an excuse to put Trump on the air to say absurd things. And he certainly obliged again and again. Early on in this effort, he realized that he could get even more attention if he brought up the birther conspiracy.

All of a sudden, the media could talk only about Donald Trump and the president's birth certificate (or the lack thereof). Jay Carney, the White House press secretary, was being asked to respond to Trump almost daily. It was coming up in Obama's press interviews. It was becoming clear we had a problem.

One day I was walking back to the Oval Office with Obama after yet another encounter with the press where he was asked to respond to questions about his birthplace.

"Maybe we should put the birth certificate out and be done with this," Obama said half in jest or so I thought.

"That would show them. But you know we can't do that, right?" I responded also half in jest.

Obama said he agreed with me, but I could tell he didn't really mean it. I had seen this before, when he was working his way to a certain position. I made a mental note to warn Plouffe so that he could head it off at the pass.

A few weeks later, we were on a fund-raising trip to Chicago. Whenever we spent the night in Chicago, the president would stay at his house. He would often say that his Chicago home was frozen in time from the moment right before he took office. On his desk was the mail that came in January 2009 before they moved to DC. Whenever he was home, often alone, he would root through all his stuff. On this particular trip, he was going through a box and found what he believed was his birth certificate. To this day, it isn't clear whether he stumbled upon this document or went looking for it. I have always suspected the latter.

The president was excited about his find. He brought it back to the White House and showed it to Plouffe and Bob Bauer, the White House counsel. He told them that he wanted to release the birth certificate and put the issue to rest. Bauer took one look at what Obama had in his hand and knew that it wasn't his actual birth certificate. Instead, the president had found a ceremonial document that is sold in hospital gift shops. This is the document that families often frame, but you can't use it to get a passport or debunk a racist conspiracy theory burning up the Internet.

Obama was clearly disappointed by this fact, but was not deterred. He directed Bauer to begin the process of acquiring his official or long-form birth certificate from the state of Hawaii. He didn't commit to releasing it, but he told Bauer and Plouffe to get it so we had it in our back pocket just in case.

During this period, I was living in blissful ignorance of these machinations even though I knew the president was interested in releasing his birth certificate. This was a classic Barack Obama move. He had a natural tendency to want to address the elephant in the room, even if it took him off whatever we thought was the best message. His instinct was usually right, but in this instance, I couldn't bring myself to give in to Donald Trump and the band of racist nutjobs that he represented.

In late April, I got a call to head up to Bauer's office. When Lauren Thorbjornsen, my assistant, asked about the topic of the meeting, she couldn't get an answer. Being called to the White House counsel's office was a lot like getting sent to the principal's office in high school. If you were there, there was a good chance you were in trouble. This was a particularly anxious time to be summoned by the White House counsel, since the Republicans had taken over Congress and were launching politicized investigations into Obama administration activities in the hopes of finding wrong-doing somewhere.[4] We all lived in fear of being subjected to a congressional subpoena, having our e-mails and other documents released to the world, and amassing tens of thousands of dollars in legal bills that we couldn't afford.

I walked into Bauer's wood-paneled office with more than a little trepidation. Plouffe was sitting on Bauer's couch. This was another alarming sign. My boss, the lawyer, and me; this can't be good.

"Am I going to jail?" I asked to break the ice.

"Almost certainly, but that's not the purpose of this meeting," Bauer responded with trademark sarcasm.[5]

As I sat down on the couch, Bauer started explaining how he'd ended up requesting the president's long-form birth certificate from the state of Hawaii and how the president was intent on releasing it to the public. As I processed this piece of information, Plouffe chimed in to say that the president wanted to go into the White House briefing room and release it himself.

"Well, that's fucking crazy," I said.

Plouffe explained that the president wanted to use this opportunity to take the conversation to a bigger idea beyond the birth certificate. He wanted to talk about the danger of the political conversation getting diverted by these side issues. This was a better idea than simply going before the nation and saying, "Hey, look, I am American. Deal with it." But I was still horrified by the thought of the president being forced to go before the nation to defend his own legitimacy. It felt beneath him. It felt beneath the Office.

---

4   They didn't find anything.
5   They probably don't make this joke in the Trump White House since some of them are undoubtedly going to transition from the White House to the Big House.

I could already read all the headlines and tweets to come about how this made Obama look weak. I tried to make my case, but I could tell by the look on his face that Plouffe had made these points to the president and had not prevailed. The basic message was: Take your case to the big guy.

"And, oh yeah, he wants to release the birth certificate in the next two days," Plouffe added.

Later that day, I went into the Oval Office loaded for bear. The president was seated behind his desk reading some memos. Before I could get my first sentence out, Obama said without even looking up from his papers, "I bet you don't love my idea."

I knew I had lost the argument. Obama had already played out all the scenarios in his head and come to a conclusion. I wasn't going to tell him some angle that he hadn't already thought of. I beat a strategic retreat. Instead of trying to convince the president not to release the birth certificate, I focused my energy on two things:

First, separating him from the actual release. I proposed that Bauer and I provide it to the media at a briefing and then later that morning Obama could deliver his message to the world in a speech. This would hardly address my major political concerns, but it would at least keep Obama from having to answer a bunch of logistical questions about how we got the birth certificate.

Second, I argued that the release should be a surprise. If we announced it in advance, the press would lose its collective shit and there would be a CNN countdown clock ticking down to the second of release. In the age of the Internet, where a million things are happening at the same time and everything is dissected and analyzed before it even happens, one of the only ways to break through is to catch the world by surprise. He agreed with my recommendations, and I headed back to my office to plot out how to execute this newly hatched plan. My desire for surprise meant we had to avoid leaks at all costs, which meant we would have a very tight circle for this plan. The president's top advisors and a couple of members of the press staff would need to pull it off without letting anyone else know.

On that sleepy morning, I walked into a nearly empty briefing room. It seemed that many reporters had assumed it would be a typical newsless briefing and decided to skip it. Even many of the reporters who had decided to come to work that day couldn't be bothered to walk the hundred feet from their work space to listen in.

Then one of the press assistants started handing out copies of the birth certificate. All hell broke loose.

There were audible gasps. People immediately started e-mailing their news desks to tell them that "real news" was being made. The reporters, who had planned on skipping the briefing, were tripping over one another as they sprinted to their seats to get in on the action. After everyone was in place, I read a statement that explained the difference between the document we'd released in 2008 and the one we were releasing today. The reporters assembled before me were equal parts shocked, amused, and ashamed at the spectacle that was unfolding.

The media's reaction was not different from my own. I couldn't help but laugh at the absurdity of the whole thing, but I was also embarrassed by the state of my chosen field. In the back of my mind I wondered if I was standing there due to some failure on my part. Was there something I could have done that would have prevented the president from having to try to convince a decent part of the country of his American citizenship?

The media responded to the release of the birth certificate with the professionalism of a pack of rabid hyenas. All the cable news switched to nonstop coverage. Trump was coincidentally headed to New Hampshire that morning for a speech, which added to the drama. We had turned a quiet day into a major news event.

A couple of hours later, the president came to the briefing room to lay out his case.

"Now, normally I would not comment on something like this...But two weeks ago, when the Republican House had put forward a budget that will have huge consequences potentially to the country, and when I gave a speech about my budget and how

I felt that we needed to invest in education and infrastructure and making sure that we had a strong safety net for our seniors even as we were closing the deficit, during that entire week the dominant news story wasn't about these huge, monumental choices that we're going to have to make as a nation. It was about my birth certificate... But we're not going to be able to do it if we are distracted. We're not going to be able to do it if we spend time vilifying each other. We're not going to be able to do it if we just make stuff up and pretend that facts are not facts. We're not going to be able to solve our problems if we get distracted by sideshows and carnival barkers."

As I sat in one of the chairs on the side of the briefing room reserved for staff to watch the spectacle, I knew the president had been right and I had been wrong. He was making an important point. This was not the first and wouldn't be the last time that Obama's unconventional approach to politics had proven to be more prescient than my own.

The release of the birth certificate shut up Trump to the extent that was possible. The reporters covering his faux campaign visit peppered him with questions about how wrong he was regarding Obama's birthplace. The media that had been party to Trump's absurdity turned on him with a vengeance. While there were some who thought we had made a strategic error, the bulk of the coverage applauded Obama for how he'd handled a less than ideal situation.

A few nights later was the White House Correspondents' Dinner, where the president gives an annual comedic speech, and Trump was going to be in attendance. We had been planning to make a number of jokes about Trump and the birth certificate issue before the decision was made to release the document.

My first stop after the president gave me my marching orders was Favreau's office. He had been working on the speech for weeks with Jon Lovett, Axelrod, and a collection of comedians and joke writers. The speech was almost done. Then I showed up with the information that would upend the whole process.

Favreau's first reaction was to curse me for fucking up his process about forty-eight hours before he owed a draft to the president, but he quickly realized the golden comedic opportunity it presented.

It was an open question if releasing the birth certificate would forever demean the Office of the President and hurt our chances for reelection, but there was no question we were going to have an epic Correspondents' Dinner speech.

During the dinner, the president brought the house down with joke after joke about Trump, who sat in his seat refusing to laugh. He reportedly got up to leave not long after this joke, which went to the abject absurdity of Trump's credentials as a potential president:

Now, I know that he's taken some flak lately but no one is prouder to put this birth certificate matter to rest than The Donald. And that's because he can finally get back to focusing on the issues that matter, like, did we fake the moon landing? What really happened in Roswell? And where are Biggie and Tupac? All kidding aside, we all know about your credentials, and your breadth of experience. For example, on a recent episode of *The Celebrity Apprentice*, at the steakhouse, the men's cooking team did not impress the men from Omaha Steaks. There was lots of blame to go around, but you, Mr. Trump, recognized that the real problem was a lack of leadership. Ultimately, you didn't blame [rapper] Lil Jon or [singer] Meat Loaf; you fired Gary Busey. These are the kinds of decisions that keep me up at night. Well handled, sir! Well handled.[6]

And then the night after the dinner, President Obama stood in the East Room of the White House and announced that a unit of Navy SEALs had killed Osama Bin Laden on his order. Trump had been ushered off the national stage in humiliation. His foray into politics forever ended (or so we thought).

---

6   This joke is even funnier now.

Here's the bad news: years later, four in ten Republican voters still believed that Barack Obama was not born in the United States. And it's not that they didn't know about the birth certificate that was released; it's that they refused to believe it. They thought it was a forgery. If the mainstream media said it was real, then the mainstream media was lying to cover up for Obama. We had shamed the media into stopping their nonstop, uncritical coverage of Trump's claims,[7] but we hadn't convinced a lot of people about the truth. They couldn't hear what Obama was saying because Obama was saying it. And therein lay the problem.

The birth certificate imbroglio was Obama's highest-profile battle with fake news, but it wasn't the only one. Over the years, we faced several conspiracy theories propagated by conservative media figures who were believed by an alarmingly significant portion of the populace.

The rumors about Obama's legitimacy were mostly advanced by figures on the fringes of the Republican Party.[8] Notably, establishment figures refused to disavow these conspiracy theories for fear of upsetting their base, but they wanted to avoid being labeled "birthers." In other words, they wanted weaponized racial animus stoked by people like Trump without being called a racist. In 2012, Mitt Romney made the pilgrimage to Trump Tower to beg for the endorsement of the birther in chief.

This was a sign of things to come.

THE REPUBLICANS MOVE THEIR HQ TO THE GRASSY KNOLL

In 2009, during the battle to pass the Affordable Care Act, better known as "Obamacare," we saw the first example of mainstream

---

7   This was a temporary victory at best.
8   We can debate whether Trump was on the fringes of the Republican Party.

figures utilizing fake news or a false conspiracy theory to advance a specific policy goal.

In a 2009 meeting in the Roosevelt Room prior to kicking off the effort to pass health care reform, David Axelrod presented President Obama with his political analysis of the issue. David made it very clear that even in the most ideal scenario, where we passed the bill quickly and without a lot of fuss, the president would take a big hit—with consequences for the midterm elections the next year and potentially Obama's reelection in 2012.

David was not trying to convince Obama not to take on health care. As the father of a daughter with epilepsy, he believed passionately in fixing the injustices in our health care system that denied needed health care to people like his daughter. David wanted the president and the rest of the senior White House team to know what we were getting into.

Obama's response was pretty simple: "What's the point of amassing political capital if you aren't willing to use it to help people?" He pointed out to us that if he didn't try to pass a law to give access to health care to the uninsured on the heels of a landslide election win with huge majorities in Congress, then it would never get done.

"If not now, when?" Obama asked. There was only one answer to that question.

We knew from the failed efforts that came before that health care policy was uniquely susceptible to demagoguery. Fear of the unknown greatly exceeded the public's concerns about the present system. This factor was the one that was most concerning to me.

We prepared for some of the obvious criticisms of any health care bill: Is it a government takeover of health care? Will it raise your taxes? Will it raise your premiums? Etc. Here's one we didn't prepare for: Obamacare will kill you.

I was sitting in my office during a quiet day in August when I received a forwarded e-mail from someone in the White House

Legislative Affairs Office asking for talking points to respond to Sarah Palin's allegation about "death panels" in our health care bill.

Congress had just left town for their monthlong August break, and as far as I could tell, the only people working in Washington were in the West Wing with me. It was also the habit of our Leg Affairs staff, as we called them, to treat any request from Congress, whether it was a request for a bill signing, a White House tour, or talking points from an intern, as if it were a five-alarm fire.

Do I really need to drop what I am doing because some junior staffer for a no-name member of Congress thought it was cool to call the White House? And to top it all off, it was Sarah Palin, who had gone from sensation as Alaska governor and GOP vice presidential candidate to national joke in record time. Palin was last seen delivering her annual Thanksgiving turkey-pardoning speech while behind her a farmer was putting turkeys one by one into the slaughter machine.

Included in the e-mail was the text of something Palin had posted on Facebook earlier in the day:

> The Democrats promise that a government health care system will reduce the cost of health care, but as the economist Thomas Sowell has pointed out, government health care will not reduce the cost; it will simply refuse to pay the cost. And who will suffer the most when they ration care? The sick, the elderly, and the disabled, of course. The America I know and love is not one in which my parents or my baby with Down Syndrome will have to stand in front of Obama's "death panel" so his bureaucrats can decide, based on a subjective judgment of their "level of productivity in society," whether they are worthy of health care. Such a system is downright evil.

While no one in the media took Palin seriously, she still had a devoted following on the Far Right. Her post had caused a stir, and members of Congress had started to get calls. I had a decent handle on the details of the health care bill making its way through Congress, and I had no clue what Palin was talking about. I dismissed it as gibberish, forwarded the e-mail to someone on the research staff, and went home for the weekend.

Although I didn't realize it at the time, Palin was referring to a provision in the law that provided Medicare funding for voluntary consultations with doctors about hospice and other "end of life" care options. This was an innocuous policy that had previously received bipartisan support. Now, in hindsight, using the term "end of life" was a terrible idea, but in a world where facts and truth reigned supreme, it would be impossible to turn this into forced euthanasia for the elderly. But alas, we did not live in that world.

Because Congress was on recess, the members were spending time back in their districts. More and more people were coming to their events and asking about these "death panels." The idea took off like wildfire. People believed it and were scared.

Unlike the birther controversy, Republicans leaders didn't stay away. They jumped at the opportunity to score political points. The Republican leader of the House, John Boehner, issued a statement a few weeks later that said, "This provision may start us down a treacherous path toward government-encouraged euthanasia if enacted into law."

Boehner knew that what he was saying was complete bullshit. He just didn't care. He saw an opportunity to cynically exploit people's fears and went for it.

In August, Iowa senator Chuck Grassley, who was the top Republican on the Senate Finance Committee, which was helping write the Senate version of the health bill and had been discussing a potential compromise with Obama, was confronted by a constituent sincerely concerned about the rumored death panels in the health care bill.

Grassley, who was intimately familiar with health care policy and certainly knew the truth, had two options at that moment: Tell his constituent the truth and reassure them, or try to score political points. Grassley chose the latter, telling the constituent that "you have every right to fear...[We] should not have a government run plan to decide when to pull the plug on grandma."

Obama wanting to pull the plug on Granny became a common GOP talking point amplified 24/7 on conservative talk radio and Fox News. One day Sarah Palin posts on Facebook, and before we know it, we have a full-blown political crisis on our hands.

I was the deputy communications director at the White House at the time and auditioning for the top job. Once the death panel rumors started and our political prospects had started to go south, Rahm and Anita Dunn, who had become the interim White House communications director, asked me to oversee the communications regarding health care. My charge was to "bring some Obama campaign style rapid response tactics" to the fight for health care.

Step 1 was to set up a website specifically dedicated to responding to these false attacks. Obamacare as a not-so-secret strategy to kill old people was the highest-profile and most pernicious attack, but it was far from the only one. The Republicans would repeat ad nauseam that our plan would increase the deficit, even though it was completely paid for through a combination of tax increases and spending cuts. They alleged that it would cut the Medicare benefits that seniors depend on. Also completely false. We needed a one-stop shop where people could come for the truth and our allies could easily find the talking points and other information that they needed to respond to questions.

We started using the work done by fact-checking sites such as PolitiFact and Factcheck.org to set the record straight and call out specific politicians for perpetuating this lie.

A major effort was made to shame the major news outlets into running stories that debunked the claim. We deployed surrogates to local TV stations via satellite.

We even had the president address the death panel accusation in a nationally televised address before Congress that was watched by 32 million Americans.

These efforts had an immediate impact. The media began to challenge Republicans who brought up death panels. Most important, we calmed the waters with the Democratic members who were afraid that we were marching them off to slaughter without a plan to fight back.

Here's the problem we didn't solve, though: a decent number of people still believed that our health care bill included death panels.

They had been presented with facts from independent arbiters—experts, the media, and other politicians. Yet they couldn't be convinced to stop believing something so obviously untrue. Every time President Obama or the *New York Times* told them the truth, Sean Hannity or Rush Limbaugh would tell them the opposite. For this part of the populace, President Obama and the mainstream media were disqualified as messengers.

Six years after the law was passed, 29 percent of voters (nearly all Republican) still believed that the law included death panels. One would have hoped that after the law was passed and no death panels had convened, people would come around to the truth. Not a chance.

THE PERFECT PETRI DISH

The eventual passage of health care and the short-term humiliation of Donald Trump over his birtherism were the beginning, not the end, of the phenomenon of fake news. The situation got much worse during the 2016 election and even worse in the early years of the Trump presidency.

We elected a conspiracy theorist as commander in chief. In the early days of his presidency, Trump falsely claimed that millions of illegal votes were cast in the 2016 elections and falsely claimed that Barack Obama had wiretapped his phones. In the campaign, he accused Senator Ted Cruz's father of being involved in the assassination of John F. Kennedy.

Snake oil salesmen like Donald Trump pushing conspiracy theories are nothing new in politics, but they have never been more powerful than they are now. It's not that America is getting dumber;[9] it's that changes in media and technology have weaponized the worst parts of our politics.

First, distrust in the media sowed by generations of Republican politicians screaming liberal bias has reduced the ability of the press to serve as referees in factual disputes. For many conservative voters, the *New York Times*, CNN, or the *Washington Post* stating a fact is actually proof positive that said fact is not true. They believe—as Donald Trump so disturbingly stated early in his presidency—that the press is the enemy of the American people. Theoretically, the conservative media could have stepped in and fought for the concept of objective truth. But led by Fox News, they decided to exploit this very belief for profit and partisan gain. We saw this time and time again in the 2016 election: Trump would be accused of everything from sexual assault to rank corruption to bald-faced lies with detailed, fact-based reporting. And he would slip the political noose every time because his voters believed the media was engaged in a conspiracy to bring down a conservative politician.

Second, the emergence of Facebook as the primary news source for so many Americans has made it easier for these conspiracy theories to spread across the country in a matter of seconds. Reading the news within Facebook makes it easy to confuse a credible news source with completely fake news or distorted partisan talking points. Facebook tends to promote the stories that draw the most controversy or elicit the most emotional response. The hucksters and political saboteurs pushing an agenda with stuff like birtherism are trying to push the emotional buttons that make stories go viral.

---

9   I may feel differently about this after a few more years of Trump.

Sarah Palin knew exactly what she was doing by posting the death panel theory on Facebook. She would have been laughed off the set if she had done it on *Meet the Press* or *Good Morning America*. But on Facebook, the outrageous is rewarded.

WINNING THE BATTLE AGAINST BULLSHIT

We have a plague affecting our democracy that is getting worse by the day; is there anything we can do about it?

There are no easy answers. The fact that one of our two political parties now openly traffics in false conspiracy theories as their primary political strategy poses a threat to our system of government. This may sound dramatic, but if anything, it understates the problem.

The American system of government operates on a set of norms, and if one party decides to regularly violate those norms in order to acquire more power, it cripples the ability to respond to disasters like hurricanes, threats like North Korea, and existential challenges like climate change. The Republican approach is one of immense cynicism and utter cowardice, but there is nothing I have seen in twenty years in politics that suggests Republicans are going to change their stripes anytime soon.

Russia clearly played a huge role in promoting the conspiracy theories that dominated the conversation in 2016 in order to help Trump win. All of our intelligence agencies agree with this assessment. Congressional Republicans agree with this assessment. Yet somehow this still seems up for debate. Why? Because there is one person in our government who doesn't agree, Donald Trump, which should tell you everything you need to know.

It's alarming that Russia was willing to be so aggressive, but it is even more alarming that such an absurd strategy worked. The Russians were pushing on an open door. Even if the government was able to stop the Russians from ever doing this again, we now have a conspiracy theorist in chief in the Oval Office. Pure propaganda is the official strategy of the Republican Party, and if Democrats don't figure out how to combat it, we will be relegated to the opposition for years to come while Republicans flush the country down the toilet.

Here are some lessons from Barack Obama's encounters with the purveyors of fake news that can be applied to the battles to come:

- **Nothing is too crazy not to believe.** It's easy to think some of the stuff circulating on the Right is too crazy for anyone other than the fringe to believe, but that's a huge mistake. I was wrong to dismiss the idea that anyone would believe that Obama wanted to pass a law to kill old people, and we paid a huge price for letting it fester. We live in a time when the president of the United States is willing to use his Twitter account to spread lies to millions of his supporters, who are willing to believe anything he says. Every conspiracy theory—no matter how ridiculous—must be taken seriously and responded to by the media and Democratic politicians before it takes off. The traditional calculus of being afraid of giving additional attention to the crazy stuff is an anachronism in the social media age.

- **If Fake News is the disease, Facebook is the carrier.** All of the fake stories mentioned earlier in this chapter spread across the populace through Facebook. For many Americans, Facebook is the Internet. It's how they keep up with friends, it's how they communicate, and it's how they get the vast majority of their news. The problem is that despite being the primary news source for a lot of people, Facebook is not a media company in the traditional sense. They don't have editors or fact-checkers. For financial reasons, Facebook values content that engages users over all else for the simple reason they want you to stay on Facebook for as long as possible so they can show you more ads. Facebook doesn't show you everything your Facebook friends post, they show only content the algorithm thinks you will engage with. In the most simplistic of terms, Facebook defines engagement as the sum total of shares, likes, and comments. In a reflection of our highly polarized political times, "holy shit" stories like "Pope Endorses Trump" generate a ton of engagement and are therefore shown to more people. The stories written by the mainstream media or the campaign-authored posts that debunk these stories receive exponentially less engagement and are therefore seen by exponentially fewer people. Facebook has pledged to fix this problem and I think they are very sincere in that pledge. But this is a little like the NFL's pledge to deal with concussions, when to do so would fundamentally change a very successful business. So, it's unlikely to happen anytime soon. Democrats cannot wait around for Mark Zuckerberg to fix their problems; we need to first monitor Facebook more closely to track the spread of these stories and memes, and second develop fact-checks and countermessaging that generates enough engagement to be seen by as many people as possible. The next election will be fought on Facebook.

- **Everyone is a fact-checker.** The "fake news" stories are spread through Facebook and Twitter, but those same platforms give agency to everyone to lead the fight for truth. People are scrolling through their Facebook feeds seeing posts about where Obama was or wasn't born or alleging some made-up act of corruption by the Clintons. They don't click on the post to see where the story is from or whether it's credible, and depending on the Facebook algorithm or the makeup of their social network, they may be seeing these same false stories multiple times a day. Absent Facebook hiring millions of fact-checkers to comb the platform, the only solution is to fight back. Multiple studies show that people are most likely to believe news if it comes from someone they personally know; therefore, there is great power in people sharing on social media the stories and fact-checks that debunk the lies being spread by Trump and his friends in the

Republican fringe media. Democratic politicians need to build tools to make this easier for their supporters, but there is no reason we have to wait for that.

- **Play a different game.** Ultimately the Right's strategy is to nullify the idea of objective truth. On issues such as climate change, health care, and tax policy, Republicans simply can't win an argument on the facts. So instead of changing their policy, they try to change the facts. Democrats could look at the (relative) success of Trump and decide to play his game. That would be a mistake. Cynical conspiracy theories are the Republicans' home turf, which we wouldn't be good at, and our supporters, who still trust objective news sources, wouldn't be fooled. Instead, we should swerve in the other direction and abandon normal political spin to ensure that our statements, positions, and analyses of the other sides are factually bulletproof. The smallest error will allow Republicans to call the truth "fake news," but we have the power to deny them that opportunity.

Whenever one opens up Twitter or turns on the TV and sees some Republican congressman screaming about some made-up scandal that they learned about on Fox News or denying the very idea of climate change as America is hammered by hurricanes, it's easy to feel despondent about the future of the country.

I feel that way sometimes, too, but then I catch myself. There are some very good reasons to be hopeful about the future.

It's easy to forget that it wasn't that long ago that we had a president and an administration that strove to tell the truth and make fact-based arguments. And the public rewarded that president with an overwhelming reelection and high approval ratings.

We are still at the beginning of the Internet age. The power and reach of new platforms like Facebook and Twitter are not yet fully understood, and savvy actors have the opportunity to exploit them with malicious activity. A good portion of Americans—particularly the older ones, who vote most often—did not grow up on the

Internet. Their experience is from a different era, where one had reason to trust the things they read in the news.

Most important, millennials are going to save us from ourselves.

The millennial generation is about to become the most powerful force in politics, and they are equal parts Internet savvy and skeptical. They were raised on the Internet. They have a natural and well-earned skepticism about what they read online, as well as the skills to verify or debunk anything. As millennials become a larger part of the electorate, the propaganda tactics of the Right are going to be less and less effective.

In the meantime, the Democrats must learn the lessons of Obama's battles with fake news, conspiracy theories, and con men. We cannot expect to win power again until we have figured out how to defeat the propaganda forces that created, elected, and are now propping up Donald Trump.

It's that simple.

No pressure, but the fate of the free world (or at least this part of it) is at stake.

INTERLUDE 2

MY BEAUTIFUL, DARK, TWISTED (WHITE HOUSE) FANTASY

One of the cool parts of working in the White House is that you get to meet the most interesting people in the world. My top three are as follows:

- The Queen of England
- The Pope (the cool one, not the other one)
- Kanye West

Kanye is the best story, so that's the one I will tell.

We were flying on *Air Force One* for a fund-raising trip to California in 2014, when Anita Breckenridge, President Obama's deputy chief of staff and longtime gatekeeper, got an e-mail from someone on the White House political staff.

"The host wants to bring Kanye West and Kim Kardashian to the event. They will write checks. Are we OK with this?"

Showing me the e-mail, Anita then said, "Are you OK with this?"

I was torn. Kanye, on paper, passes all our vetting tests. He says outrageous things, but hadn't been in legal trouble or been part of any sort of embarrassing scandal. I'm also a huge Kanye fan. He can be insufferable at times, no question, but Kanye is without a doubt a genius. I love his music. I've been to a half dozen of his concerts over the years and am generally just fascinated by someone who seems to be simultaneously the most and least self-aware person alive.

But the actual problem I was thinking about was that Obama and Kanye had had a blowup of sorts a few years before. Several days after Kanye famously interrupted Taylor Swift at the MTV Video Music Awards, Obama was chatting with John Harwood of CNBC before an interview when Harwood asked him if he had seen what Kanye had done.

"I thought that was really inappropriate," Obama responded offhandedly. "He's a jackass."

The cameras weren't on, but the microphones were, and the audio was being fed to the White House pool. An ABC reporter violating the off-the-record nature of the comments tweeted them out and the world went nuts.

Even though Kanye had been a big supporter of our 2008 campaign—flying across the country with Jay-Z to do concerts to encourage people to vote,[1] Obama and Kanye had not been in contact in the years since the jackass flare-up.

Kanye was as unpredictable as they came, and I was worried that he would use the fund-raiser to go after Obama, and if that exchange leaked out, it would dominate the media for days.

"Let's tell them no and see what happens," I told Anita.

The response was quick. The hosts said they would cancel if Kim and Kanye couldn't come. We gave in pretty quick. Kimye would be in attendance.

As a general rule, I hate fund-raising events. I would always prefer to sit in the staff office rather than mix and mingle with donors. But there was not a chance I was going to miss this one.

This event was a roundtable of about twenty-five people arrayed on deep leather couches and folding chairs in the wood-paneled library of a huge LA mansion. Kanye and Kim were seated on the

---

1   Our campaign was so good.

couch closest to Obama. I was seated with the staff in the back of the room. The format of these types of events was that Obama gave some brief opening remarks and then just took questions from the donors, who had paid a pretty penny to be there.

Leonardo DiCaprio went first, asking a substantive question about how to convince Americans about the reality and the severity of climate change.[2] For the next hour, the donors peppered Obama with questions about politics and policy.

"I have time for one more question," Obama said to the donors.

I had one eye on Kanye and one eye on my BlackBerry. The event was wrapping up and I was a little annoyed that I had sat in this painfully uncomfortable chair for an hour. I had hurt my back playing basketball, and sitting for long periods of time was incredibly painful. I was willing to endure the back pain for the great story of a Kanye rant, but time was running out.

Then it happened. Kanye's hand shot up. Obama's face was frozen in a look of alarm and amusement as he girded himself for whatever came next.

"Last question goes to Kanye," Obama said.

Kanye took a breath and started talking. Yeezy did not disappoint.

"You and I are a lot alike," Kanye said to Obama. "We are both from Chicago; when we first came on the scene, we got so much love. Now we got so many haters."

And it went on like that for nearly *a half hour*. Some highlights:

"Everyone has opponents. Coke has Pepsi. Adidas has Nike. I have Drake[3] and you have the Republicans.

"The only way to get things done is to get the best people together. Me and Jay on the mic. Mario Batali on the pasta and we need Elon Musk.

---

2   I went to a lot of fund-raisers with Leo and he consistently asked some of the smartest questions. Believe it or not, Ashton Kutcher is also on the "smartest questions from a celebrity" list.

3   Best day of Drake's life.

"I was drinking a fresh-pressed juice in Japan one day, when I realized that everything in Japan is designed perfectly. Japan is the Apple of countries.

"I was riding a bike in Shanghai when I had this thought."

I was mesmerized. Obama kept a seriously inquisitive look on his face the whole time.

Like all of Kanye's music, it seemed crazy at first, but before long I was nodding along as if it made complete sense.

Eventually, Kanye had to take a breath and Obama jumped in.

"Kanye, thank you for your thoughts. You make some really good points, especially about the value of meeting with smart people like Elon Musk. Thank you, everyone, for your support of the DNC. My staff is signaling from the back of the room that I'm late for my next event."

After the event, I jumped in the presidential limo with Obama, Anita, and Valerie.

We all looked at Obama and waited for his assessment.

What did he think of Kanye? Was he annoyed that we made him sit through it?

Obama had a serious look on his face. I prepared myself to try to explain how the president, who had very important work to do, had ended up in this room with rappers and movie stars. And then Obama broke into a huge grin.

"'That shit cray,'" Obama said in reference to a famous Kanye line, proving once again that he is and always will be our coolest president.

We all laughed and didn't really stop until we arrived back at the White House eight or so hours later.

CHAPTER 6

FOX (AND FRIENDS) IS DESTROYING AMERICA

"Oh, come the fuck on."

That was my response to the reporter who called my cell phone to earnestly ask if I had heard about a piece of blockbuster, campaign-altering news.

I had been working on Obama's campaign for less than two weeks when the phones started to ring off the hook. We were still operating out of a windowless temporary office in DC. My "desk" was a card table that was designed to fit two people, but had three people. The quarters were so tight that we had to take turns typing to avoid elbowing one another.

I turned to my office mates, Robert Gibbs and Bill Burton, to tell them what I had just heard.

"Guys..."

But they were both on the phone having the exact same exasperated, heated conversation that I had just had.

The source of this media firestorm was a report on *Fox & Friends*, the network's morning show. The hosts had discussed—with the palpable enthusiasm of kids on Christmas morning—a vaguely sourced report on an obscure right-wing news outlet that "researchers for Hillary Clinton had uncovered the fact that Obama had been educated in an Indonesian madrassa." One of the hosts, Steve Doocy,

who makes Brick Tamland look like Edward R. Murrow, declared
with clown-ish enthusiasm that "this is huuuge"[1] as he repeated the
false report without ever once questioning its veracity.

Doocy said that madrassas "teach this Wahhabism which pretty
much hates us," then declared, "The big question is, why was that
on the curriculum back then?" At one point a caller said of Obama,
"Maybe he doesn't consider terrorists the enemy." And how did the
hosts respond to the suggestion that a United States senator was
sympathetic to Al-Qaeda?

"Well, we'll see about that."

Gibbs, who unlike Tom Hagen in *The Godfather* is a wartime
consigliere that every candidate needs when the shit hits the fan,
sprang into action. Within minutes, he was on the phone with anyone and everyone at Fox News to raise holy hell. It's safe to say that
people two blocks away could hear Gibbs forcefully make his argument in his trademark Southern drawl.

The senior executive in charge of news at Fox eventually got back
to Tommy Vietor, Gibbs's deputy, with something more akin to an
excuse than an apology. He said that he couldn't control *Fox &
Friends*, one of their most watched shows, because it was "entertainment programming" and the normal editorial rules didn't apply
there.

It's worth taking a moment to absorb that statement: the morning show was entertainment, not news. He promised to take steps
to make sure this didn't happen again, which we took as seriously
as O. J. Simpson's pledge to find the "real killers."

Eventually the hosts submitted to public pressure and delivered
a particularly insincere and unenthusiastic clarification; everyone
moved on, but the damage had already been done. Fox News had
taken a scurrilous, racist, unsubstantiated rumor and injected it into
the middle of a presidential campaign. This was no garden-variety
journalistic mishap; it was part of an intentional strategy to hobble

---

1   Extra *u*'s added for effect and accuracy—watch the video.

a promising progressive voice, and this was the beginning of the "Obama is an un-American Muslim" smear campaign.

Thus began Obama's relationship with Fox News.

Fox News is one of the most insidious and dangerous forces in American politics, and much of what ails our civil discourse today can be traced back to Fox and its successors.

If you want to know why the Republican Party has become so far out of the mainstream, you have only to look to Fox News.

If you want to know why large portions of the Republican Party believe in debunked conspiracy theories about Barack Obama and refuse to believe accurate reports about Trump, look to Fox News.

If you want to know why so many Republicans yell "fake news" at information that challenges their point of view, look to Fox News.

If you want to know why nativism and racism are resurgent in the Republican Party, look to Fox News.

And if you want to know how we ended up with Trump as president, yet again look to Fox News.

WHAT IS FOX NEWS?

Fox News was launched in 1996 as the "Fair and Balanced" conservative alternative to the purportedly liberal mainstream media. On paper, this is not a terrible concept.

The long-running conservative critique of the mainstream media establishment as liberal is not an entirely incorrect one. Most journalists are socially progressive. They believe in climate change and support marriage equality, a woman's right to choose, and gun control.[2] Most reporters don't vote, but if they did, they would probably vote for a Democrat. There is no doubt that this ideologi-

---

2   It says a lot about the distorted reality that Fox has helped create that believing in the scientifically proven fact that the climate is changing can be seen as "ideological bias," but I digress.

cal bias bleeds into coverage and commentary. But it's important to separate the difference between ideological bias and political bias.

The mainstream media does not skew their reporting to help Democrats win, which is something conservatives have suggested for a long time. They are wrong about that—just ask Bill and Hillary Clinton. The "liberal media" has covered the Clintons with what is at best a ferocious skepticism and at worst a monomaniacal obsession to prove them guilty of something.

Despite the liberal leanings of individual reporters, the overriding bias in the mainstream media is not ideological; it's toward conflict, controversy, clicks, and ratings.

However, it would be naïve to think that there isn't some bias in which topics are covered. Most reporters, editors, and television executives live and work in New York City, Los Angeles, and Washington, DC—three of the most liberal cities in America. Their sensibilities are shaped by their surroundings. Democrats unwilling to admit this fairly obvious fact are actually proving the Right's point.

A TV network that would cover issues from a different perspective is a good idea and a healthy one for our democracy. That sort of network may have been what Rupert Murdoch and Roger Ailes had in mind when they started Fox News more than twenty years ago. But that's not what it is anymore (or ever was, really).[3]

Fox News isn't covering news from a perspective that is outside the elite media bubble; it is not even covering issues from a conservative perspective.

Simply put, Fox News is not a news outlet. It is a Republican propaganda machine masquerading as a news outlet that exists to elect Republican politicians and promote their positions—whatever they are at the time. This makes Fox News very different from tra-

---

3   I'm giving them too much credit. Let's dispel with the fiction that Roger Ailes and Rupert Murdoch didn't know exactly what they were doing (h/t Marco Rubio's most embarrassing and revealing moment).

ditional ideological outlets like the conservative *National Review* or the liberal *Mother Jones*.

When George W. Bush was president, Fox News was a primary booster of the Iraq War and the Bush administration's quasi-legal (and often illegal) antiterrorism strategies, often questioning the patriotism of those who disagreed. When Obama became president, Fox News became the loudest critic of Obama's strategies, but their criticism was not that he wasn't tough enough, but that his drone policy and surveillance activities were too tough. When Obama was president, Fox News almost never covered the good news in the economic recovery, but now that Trump is president, the same jobs and growth numbers that were ignored or dismissed under Obama are trumpeted from the rooftops. When Obama was president, the consistent theme was that Obama was not tough enough in his response to Russian aggression in Ukraine and Syria. Now that Trump is president, in part because Russia interfered with our election, Fox News is leading the defense of Trump's pro-Putin foreign policy.

Fox's defenders like to draw a distinction between the opinion shows with conservative personalities like Sean Hannity and Tucker Carlson and the news division. Some media types like to say that Fox News is the mirror image of MSNBC. News during the day and ideological opinion at night.

This argument is complete horseshit. Yes, there are "real journalists" at Fox News. Many are veterans of places like CNN and CBS, but they don't do journalism at Fox. Their work is used to serve the larger political goals of Fox News—they work on positive stories about Trump and negative stories about Democrats. They are nothing more than beards for the larger propaganda aims of the network. They sold their integrity to the highest bidder.

After a few beers in the hotel bar on a long presidential road trip, some of the Fox staff would admit that the fix was in but this was a job and they were trying to make the best of a bad situation. They suggested we come to them with complaints about the ideological tilt of the network. It was a nice gesture, but complaining about coverage of Obama to Fox News was a little like banging your head against a wall: it wasn't effective and you felt worse after doing it.

There were other journalists at Fox who would never under any circumstances admit that Fox was different from other outlets. They would swear up and down that they were as objective as the next journalist and that their bosses really wanted to live by their unintentionally ironic slogan "Fair and Balanced." I could never figure out whether these folks were brainwashed to believe the un-believable or they were afraid that Fox News honcho Roger Ailes was tapping their phones.[4]

During the Obama era, their story was largely about an effete and un-American president who failed to protect white people from an array of nonwhite forces, including but not limited to militant black activists, job-stealing undocumented Latinos, and Muslims both foreign and domestic. According to Fox News, Obama was leading America down a path of economic and cultural decline where (nonwhite) people who didn't work were taking from hard-working (white) Americans.

If this story sounds familiar, it's because it had been the message of the Republican Party since long before Barack Obama arrived on the scene.

The point was to appeal to and then exploit the legitimate anxi-ety of people who felt left behind by a rapidly changing America.

When Donald Trump famously came down the escalator in the garishly gold-plated Trump Tower to announce his presidential run, his announcement speech could have just as easily come out of the mouth of Sean Hannity.

Trump, like a significant portion of the Republican base, had been mainlining Fox News for years. Trump didn't have to turn

---

4   We learned in 2016 that Ailes did spy on his reporters, but after he was fired for being a serial sexual harasser and all-around horrible person, nothing changed in how the network operated.

to pollsters or experienced political strategists to figure out a message that would appeal to Republican voters; he just had to turn on the TV.

THE FOX WARS

In our 2008 campaign office in Chicago, the main wall in the section of our sprawling office that housed the communications staff was adorned with several flat-screen TVs. We used these TVs to monitor in real time what was happening in the news.[5] One day in June 2008 as I was walking past the TVs between meetings, I heard a loud commotion from people gathered by the desks of one of our media monitors. It was hard to make out the noise, but I could hear some very colorful cursing.

In campaigns, you spend every waking moment waiting for some unknown shoe to drop that will irreparably change the trajectory of the campaign.[6] I was a particularly paranoid campaign staffer, so I walked over to the group with great trepidation. Had the Republicans unveiled some devastating new ad campaign? Had a new piece of opposition research surfaced? Had Obama been caught making a terrible gaffe?

Nope.

Fox News was just being Fox News again.

The week prior, Barack Obama had finally secured the Democratic nomination after a long and brutal campaign against Hillary Clinton. As Obama came onstage to deliver his acceptance speech in Minneapolis, he greeted his wife, hugged her, kissed her, and then Michelle fist-bumped her husband. Most people saw this as a charming exchange between a loving and very cool couple.

---

5   And by "we," I mean an army of overworked, underpaid (and sometimes not paid) media monitors who watched cable TV eighteen hours a day. In other words, they had the same schedule as President Trump.

6   This used to be called the "October Surprise"; now just call it a "Comey."

Not Fox News.

During a midafternoon broadcast a few days later, the Fox anchor previewed an upcoming segment on the Obama fist bump analyzed by a body language expert with the following teaser: "A fist bump? A pound? A terrorist fist jab? The gesture everyone seems to interpret differently."[7]

A terrorist fist jab.

It was outrageous and patently racist that Fox would take something so benign and use it as an opportunity to once again attempt to portray Obama as unpatriotic and sympathetic to terrorists simply because he wasn't white and his middle name was Hussein. This wasn't a shock after the madrassa incident of the year before. Like before, we raised hell with the leadership of Fox News, and we received some sort of insincere apology followed by a halfhearted correction. It never mattered. A week after the anchor apologized for the fist-jab jibe, a Fox personality referred to Michelle Obama as Barack Obama's "Baby Mama," which has racist overtones to say the least.

Everyone makes mistakes. I've certainly made more than my fair share, but Fox tends to err only in ways that hurt Democrats and help Republicans. And more often than not, in ways that exacerbate racial animus. After a while, it becomes clear that these are not mistakes.

Despite these transgressions, I was not yet ready to cut off all our engagement with Fox.

First, 2008 was a very different era in that there were more independent voters who swung back and forth between parties, particularly in states like Ohio and Pennsylvania. Barack Obama was especially appealing to these voters, many of whom supported Bush in 2000 but were fed up with the Republican Party over the Iraq War and Katrina. Fox News was one way to reach them.

---

7   More than a decade or so later, I am still in awe of how ham-handedly racist Fox can be.

It seems quaint to think about now, but at the time, outreach to Republicans was a core part of our strategy, so much so that at one point I pitched Plouffe on hiring a disillusioned Republican staffer[8] to join the campaign to serve as a point of contact with the conservative media, including Fox News.

Plouffe loved the idea, and we went so far as to put together a list of possible names before the plan died on the vine. The fact that we even considered such an idea is a sign of how different politics was back then.

Second, Obama's willingness to go before hostile audiences to tell them "what they needed to hear, not what they wanted to hear," was a core part of his pitch to voters. His stump speech often included the story of when he went to speak before the National Education Association, the nation's largest teachers union, and pitched his idea for merit pay, an anathema to the union. In Obama's telling, you could "hear a pin drop" during his speech. Engaging with Fox was proof that Obama wasn't afraid of a hostile audience. The most high-profile example of this strategy was our decision to have Obama appear on Bill O'Reilly's show *The O'Reilly Factor* on the night of John McCain's acceptance speech during the Republican Convention. Traditionally a candidate stops campaigning during his or her opponent's convention, but Obama wasn't a traditional candidate, and we weren't running a traditional campaign. Besides, it's a dumb tradition. Campaigns had been a rhetorical blood sport for a while now, and we were long past the era of these sorts of niceties. This was an opportunity to step on McCain's thunder, and we knew that Fox would have a huge audience on the final night of the convention. The interview turned out to be at the time O'Reilly's second-highest-rated episode ever.[9]

---

8   Someone we would now call a "cuck."
9   I thoroughly enjoyed the irony of one of Fox's highest rated interviews ever being with a notorious terrorist fist jabber.

I appreciated the huge audience for the interview, no political operative would turn that down, but it was a secondary concern. What I really wanted was for all the media to cover the spectacle of Obama going into the lion's den with the notoriously belligerent conservative interviewer. O'Reilly is a buffoon and I had no doubt that Obama could easily handle him.[10]

The strategy worked. Every media outlet covered the fact that Obama was going to do the interview and then they covered the interview on the network morning shows, including clips of the interview during their coverage of McCain's speech.

The O'Reilly interview summarized our Fox strategy during the campaign: treat them as a useful tool for our own political goals. Fox seemed to feel the same way about Obama. Despite the various manufactured attacks, Fox News and Ailes didn't yet see Obama as some sort of mortal threat to their conservative agenda. Like the rest of the media, Fox was addicted to the Obama story. Back in 2008, an Obama appearance was guaranteed ratings gold for any network, even Fox. The Fox-Obama relationship was a cold war. We weren't allies, we didn't trust each other, and we often disagreed, but we weren't at war.

That all changed when we got to the White House.

Fox declared war on Barack Obama from the first day he was in office. Right from the outset, Fox made a strategic decision to position itself as the opposition to Obama. Its top talking heads—Sean Hannity, Megyn Kelly, Bill O'Reilly, and Glenn Beck—became the point of the spear in channeling the conservative angst over the new black president.

They promoted widely debunked conspiracy theories in order to raise questions about the integrity of Obama's victory. Most notable was the certifiably insane idea that the Obama administration was covering up an effort by a fledgling black militant group called the New Black Panthers, who had been dispatched to scare white voters away from the polls. This one hit all the right-wing erogenous

10   I was right.

zones: voter fraud, an illegitimate Democratic president, and scary black people threatening innocent white people.

Another favorite Fox fable was that a little-known housing advocacy group called ACORN had helped steal the election through various forms of voter fraud.

That same year, in response to the election of Obama and the financial crisis, the conservative antigovernment Tea Party was born. The grassroots movement named after the Revolutionary War–era Boston Tea Party rapidly became a cause célèbre on Fox. The movement was a real and powerful force in politics, shifting the ideological terrain of the Republican Party and the overall dynamics in Congress. It was an important news story worthy of coverage and scrutiny. But Fox didn't cover the Tea Party, they celebrated them—promoting their events and regaling them as heroes fighting back against an oppressive government.

In the Fox News version of reality, Barack Obama was King George III, raising their taxes and asking hardworking average "Americans" to pay for the misdeeds of the Wall Street banks, irresponsible homeowners who bought houses they couldn't afford, and poor people too lazy to get off the government dole. It didn't matter that Obama had cut their taxes and Bush was the one who had bailed out the Wall Street banks. Fox host Glenn Beck had taken to wearing a powdered wig as a form of colonial cosplay. Beck also held a large pro–Tea Party rally on the National Mall, to which Fox gave wall-to-wall coverage.

In the heat of the moment, it was easy to miss the larger significance of what Fox was doing. A national cable news network was encouraging, promoting, and nurturing the opposition to the US president. Their goal was to nullify the results of the election and get rich doing it.

This did not sit well with President Obama. Now to be clear, Obama avoided cable news and he certainly doesn't watch Fox. He is really more of an ESPN and prestige TV guy—think *Game of Thrones*, *The Wire*, and *The Americans*. But he knew what was happening on Fox. Because this was happening during the effort to pass health care, Obama was spending a lot of time with congressional Democrats from conservative districts who were very concerned about what was happening on the network. At town halls and other events in their districts, their constituents were reading back to them conspiracy theories they had heard on Fox and they were getting worried. In private meetings, Obama was increasingly venting his frustration to us and imploring us to see if there was anything we could do to change Fox's behavior.

In a June 2009 interview with John Harwood of CNBC, the frustration spilled out in public.

"I've got one television station that is entirely devoted to attacking my administration," said Obama in response to a question about his media coverage. "That's a pretty big megaphone. And you'd be hard pressed if you watched the entire day to find a positive story about me on that front."

Obama's response was 70 percent presidential venting and 30 percent a shot across the bow. With no shortage of crocodile tears, Fox played the victim card—how dare anyone question their credentials as objective journalists?

The relationship only got worse from there. Tensions mounted and our frustration grew with each passing day, particularly during the month of August, when Fox became a 24-hour-a-day false negative advertising campaign against Obama's health care bill.

The problem in my view wasn't so much what was on Fox's airwaves; I had long resigned myself to the fact that they viewed their job as screwing us and there was nothing we could do to change that fact. It was a simple business move; their ratings had gone up—a lot—during the Obama presidency as a direct result of positioning themselves as the place to go if Obama's election pissed you off. The bigger concern was that the rest of the media was treating Fox as if it were a normal news outlet. There was a disturbing trend of the

Washington Post, the *New York Times*, and others parroting some of the sketchy reporting on Fox News.

Around this time, Fox News reported that a senior White House staffer named Van Jones in the Council on Environmental Quality (CEQ) was a 9/11 truther. While he had at one point in time many years ago signed a petition without reading it, Van was not a 9/11 truther.

On top of that, the council is not even in the White House. It's outside the complex, about two blocks away. I didn't know who Van Jones was when the press called to ask us about the allegation. But the rest of the media followed Fox like a group of uncritical lemmings, treating this like a major scandal. Van was forced to resign and his reputation was temporarily smeared.[11] And Fox had helped advance their "Obama is anti-American" narrative.

Around that same time, Glenn Beck declared that Obama "had a deep-seated hatred for White people."

The frustration within the walls of the White House was boiling over.

We declared war on Fox. I would like to say that this was the product of some grand strategy, but it wasn't. There were cooler heads in the White House that counseled against this strategy.

I was not one of them. I was young and pissed and looking for a fight.

Just because the strategy arose from pique doesn't mean that it didn't have a purpose—we weren't trying to beat Fox or change their behavior.[12] But the press felt the need to respond to conservative anger that they had been too nice to Obama, so they wrote an endless number of stories trying to placate the Right. What the mainstream press didn't realize (yet) was that the Right's critique was born from a place of bottomless bad faith.

---

11 Van Jones has since gone on to become a leading progressive voice made famous by his impassioned anti-Trump critiques as a CNN commentator.
12 Although that would have been very enjoyable.

Instead, the goal was to shine a large public light on a fact that everyone knew, but no one admitted: Fox is not a news organization. They are a propaganda outlet with a specific political agenda and do not abide by the traditional norms of a news organization—even a conservative one. The hope was that we could convince the rest of the mainstream media to treat information on Fox with a more appropriate level of skepticism.

In my mind, it was absurd that we were forced by the norms of politics to pretend that Fox was like everyone else. When the president took questions at press conferences, we included Fox. When the president did a round-robin of network interviews, we included Fox. We dispatched White House officials to appear on Fox shows.

But why?

Their goal was not to inform their viewers of the truth; it was to convince their viewers that Obama and his policies were dangerous.

There is an old adage that you never pick a fight with someone who buys ink by the barrel. This is doubly true for picking a fight with a TV network, but we did it anyway.

David Axelrod and Rahm Emanuel went on Sunday shows to declare that Fox News would no longer be treated like everyone else. Rahm declared that Fox News was not "a news organization insomuch that it has a perspective."[13]

The White House Press Corps treated this as a massive story, and Fox News treated this as a massive opportunity.

Soon thereafter, Obama was going to do a round of interviews on the Sunday shows to pitch his health care bill. The long-standing rules for presidential interviews on Sunday shows is if you do more than one, you are supposed to do all of them.

We scheduled interviews with ABC, NBC, CNN, and CBS, but not Fox. We debated this decision among the staff for a long time. The argument was that skipping Fox would distract from the actual

---

13   Fact-check: true.

message about our health care bill, which was the whole point of the interviews. I aggressively took the other side of the argument. The brazenness of Fox's bullshit really bugged me. I wanted to inflict some measure of pain on them. Denying them an Obama interview and giving one to their competitors was the biggest card we had to play.[14]

Giving Fox an interview would be like waving the white flag of surrender in the early days of our newly declared war. Washington would interpret this as a sign that the new president and his team weren't tough enough for Washington politics. My side of the argument prevailed. But it shouldn't have.

First, Chris Wallace, the host of *Fox News Sunday* and son of legendary journalist Mike Wallace, is the exception to the rule when it comes to Fox. Unlike most of his counterparts, he will aggressively question Republicans and Democrats and at times has called out some of Fox's bullshit. Wallace was the wrong person to pick this fight with.

Second, the media's favorite thing to cover is itself. Obama versus Fox became the dominant story in politics. Every White House briefing, press conference, and interview devolved into a discussion about Fox News.

Finally, I underestimated the reaction of the rest of the press. The media felt that an attack on one of them was an attack on all of them, and they leaped to Fox's defense, peppering Robert Gibbs with questions at every White House briefing.

Fox loved every second of this. They covered the feud 24/7 and used it as validation of their role as the toughest critic of Obama.

The War on Fox was soon drowning out our message. It was time for a strategic retreat.

Obama, for all of his frustration and annoyance with Fox, was

---

14   This is the first piece of evidence that we misunderstood Fox. Their rival wasn't CNN; it was Obama.

never as enthusiastic as the rest of us about picking this fight. The president called a group of us into the Oval Office and told us to end it. We had made our point and it was time to get back to business.

Gibbs was sent to call the Fox bureau chief and broker peace. Axelrod went to break bread with Ailes, with whom he had a relationship that went back to the days when Ailes was a Republican political consultant.

Fox handled this rapprochement with the decorum of the immature frat boys we would later learn they were when much of the company resigned in multiple sexual harassment scandals. They immediately went out and declared victory.

In the end, picking this fight was a mistake of hubris, but there were two upsides. First, the rest of the media did begin to take the reporting of Fox News with more of a grain of salt. Many of the reporters who rose to Fox's defense now tell me that they regretted the way it played out because it gave Fox a veneer of objectivity that they didn't deserve. And years later when Trump declared war on all of the media except Fox, blacklisting some from campaign events and using the White House to attack networks by name, Fox did not reciprocate that loyalty. In fact, they reveled in their new role as the propaganda arm of the Trump White House.

Second, I heard a great story from someone who was in a meeting where Ailes discussed the fight with the White House. Ailes told this person that despite our battles, Axelrod and Gibbs were good guys, but "that Pfeiffer guy seems like a real dick."[15]

The following year we were making one final push to get health care across the finish line. The final vote to pass the bill was coming up and I was charged with putting together a communications plan to drive the media coverage. I included in the plan an interview with Bret Baier of Fox News. My logic was to

---

15 There's a 50 percent chance this will go on my tombstone.

show congressional Democrats, particularly the Democrats from Republican districts, that Obama wasn't scared to defend his bill in a conservative forum. There was a lot skepticism around the table in Rahm's office, but I pushed hard and eventually won the day.

In debates that happen in the White House, there is great risk in winning one where you are the only strong advocate, because even though everyone technically signs off on the idea and will gladly and publicly share in the success, the failure will be yours and yours alone.

The interview was a disaster. Brett Baier, who is ostensibly one of the "real journalists" at Fox News, used the interview to prove his bona fides with Fox's conservative viewers.

This was Baier's "Fair and Balanced" second question.

Let me insert this. We asked our viewers to e-mail in suggested questions. More than 18,000 people took time to e-mail us questions. These are regular people from all over the country. Lee Johnson, from Spring Valley, California: "If the bill is so good for all of us, why all the intimidation, arm twisting, seedy deals, and parliamentary trickery necessary to pass a bill, when you have an overwhelming majority in both houses and the presidency?"[16]

Sandy Moody in Chesterfield, Missouri: "If the health care bill is so wonderful, why do you have to bribe Congress to pass it?"

It went downhill from there.

Baier famously interrupted Obama sixteen separate times in a twenty-minute interview. Even Obama, who has a legendary

---

16 If you want to accuse the president of the United States of bribery, have the courage to do it yourself and don't hide behind a random e-mail from a citizen who believes this because your biased network told them to believe it.

amount of patience, couldn't take it anymore. He could barely finish a sentence without Baier interrupting and eventually snapped at him. Of course, the interruptions and Obama's response became the news of the interview, not health care. It had the exact opposite effect of what I'd intended.

I watched the interview on a monitor in an adjacent room. From the very first question, I knew I had fucked up and I knew it was my fuckup alone. With every question and interrupted answer, I sank farther into my seat. I kept hoping for some silver lining that I could point to so that I could argue it was time well spent. But it was a disaster on all fronts. I thought about making a quick exit and avoiding the long walk back to the Oval Office with the president but decided to take my medicine sooner rather than later.

I could tell from the moment I greeted Obama outside the Blue Room in the East Wing of the White House that he wasn't pleased—who wouldn't be annoyed if some guy accused you of bribery and then interrupted you whenever you tried to respond? After a few minutes of walking in interminable silence while Obama checked his BlackBerry, I could see the flash of anger in Obama's eyes. As he reholstered his BlackBerry on his belt, he looked at me and I steeled myself for a well-deserved ass kicking. But instead of yelling, Obama started laughing uproariously.

"Well, that went well," he joked.

I was so shocked that I didn't know what to say, so I just laughed awkwardly.[17]

"Don't get me wrong, I didn't enjoy that, but right now we need to figure out how to clean it up."

Like a man spared from the firing squad with a last-minute stay, I hustled back to my office to figure out what to do next. There was wall-to-wall coverage on Fox of the Baier interview. Not the

---

17   An unfortunate and frequent verbal tic that I have.

substance of the health care bill, of course, but the verbal fisticuffs between their anchor and Obama. Baier was treated like a returning war hero. He appeared on all of the Fox shows to recount how he and he alone was able to stand up to Obama. Implicit in all of this was that the rest of the media was too nice to the president. Fox saw this as a clear win for them and even I had to agree it was.

Looking back on that moment, I realize that I overcorrected from our battle with Fox the previous year. Back when we did the O'Reilly interview in 2008, Fox's incentives and ours were in alignment—we both wanted the spectacle and the ratings that came with an interview so big that it was considered a news event. In this instance, I wanted to use Fox to objectively communicate information to their viewers through an interview that I had expected to be tough, but fair. Fox had zero interest in that plan. They had become the anti-Obama network, and that role meant more ratings and more money. The Fox News stars, even the anchors like Baier, were the most liked and recognizable conservatives in the country, much more famous and better liked than Republican leaders like John Boehner and Mitch McConnell.

If I had thought through Fox's incentives in this situation, it would have been patently obvious to me that Fox had zero reason to treat this as a straight-up interview. The backlash from their viewers would have been brutal if Baier had been seen as too nice or not challenging enough in the interview.

In other words, I made the same mistake that I had warned others about a year earlier. I expected Fox to abide by the normal rules of journalism. But Fox isn't in the journalism business. Fox is not a conservative version of CNN or MSNBC. Fox is a Republican propaganda outlet with a specific political agenda.

My opinion of Baier's objectivity was cinched a few years later during the traditional lunch that the president holds with network anchors on the day of the State of the Union. These lunches are off the record and an opportunity for the anchors to hear directly from the president about the big speech coming later that night and ask questions. When it was Baier's turn, he reached into his suit pocket and pulled out his notebook. This gave me some pause since this was an off-the-record meeting, and while note taking was certainly permissible, it always gave some fear that those notes would be shared around the newsroom and leaked.[18] But Baier wasn't taking notes; he was reading them.

"Mr. President, I wanted to get your response to something. The Congressional Republican leadership today held a press conference to pre-but your State of the Union." Baier then read off a series of quotes from the likes of House Speaker John Boehner verbally assailing Obama.

The other anchors looked at one another with some measure of shock and embarrassment. Obama looked on with bemusement before making a joke to defuse the tension in the room.

Baier didn't get the joke.[19]

There is nothing technically wrong with what Baier did, but it was a window into his and Fox's worldview. Baier, whether he knows it or not, serves as a Republican Party operative with a press pass who pursues his agenda even if it's at an off-the-record lunch over an heirloom tomato salad in the White House.

FOX IN THE TRUMP ERA: FROM SHITTY TO DANGEROUSLY SHITTY

There is no better example of the intellectual and moral rot fostered by Fox News than Donald Trump.

Trump is the president of Fox's America. Without Fox, there is no Trump.

---

18   *New York Times* columnist Maureen Dowd seemed to have a knack for getting her hands on quotes from Obama from off-the-record meetings she didn't attend. But this wasn't even near the top of the list of things she did that annoyed Obama World.

19   Baier was the joke.

It's not just that they gave Trump a regular forum on *Fox &
Friends* to build his brand with the voters who would decide the
Republican nomination. But if giving Trump free airtime to spout
racist conspiracy theories about Barack Obama was the test, then
NBC, which broadcast *The Celebrity Apprentice*, would be as re-
sponsible as anyone.

Fox created Trump by creating the context for his rise over
many years. Fox News has created an alternative reality for
their viewers that has perverted politics in so many dangerous
ways, because it's not just Republican voters who get their news
and their worldview from Fox; it's Republican politicians and
their aides.

Fox News has created something I call the Cycle of Bullshit:

- A piece of false information, a misleading story, or a conspiracy theory shows up somewhere in the dark corners of the
  Internet.
- A Fox News show (and often a news show, not just one of the
  opinion ones) repeats the false story.
- A Republican politician (often Donald Trump) communicates
  the false information to the voting public, citing Fox News as
  the source.

Once Trump won, Fox News transitioned from an opposition
force to essentially a state-run propaganda outlet that carries his
chosen message of the day. It's not just the opinion programs; the
news department operates like an adjunct of the White House press
office—promoting good news for Trump, trying to sow discord
among his political adversaries, and attacking other media outlets
for not being sufficiently pro-Trump. The Fox News Twitter account is indistinguishable from that of the Republican National
Committee.

President Trump does the overwhelming majority of his media
interviews with Fox News personalities, who don't so much ask
questions as offer compliments with an inflection.

An excerpt from a 2017 interview by Sean Hannity exemplifies the Fox-Trump relationship:

> Hannity: The market is up 25 percent since you won. You tweeted this out that nobody in the media brings it up so I said, you know what, I am going to bring it up tonight. $5.2 trillion in wealth created. We have the lowest unemployment rate in sixteen years. We have the best labor participation rate in seven years and the best—the lowest number of people on food stamps in seven years.

And it's not just the opinion hosts. Maria Bartiromo, who was seen by many[20] as a serious financial journalist before selling her soul to Fox, told Trump once in the middle of the interview, "You definitely have an incredible connection to voters and to supporters—[and] the American people."

This ridiculous level of presidential pandering would be hilarious if it weren't an actual threat to the health of our democracy.

When Barack Obama was president, Fox refused to truly cover any good news, and now that Trump is president, they mostly refuse to cover any bad news. On the night of the 2017 elections, when Democrats won offices up and down the ballot in a clear repudiation of Trump, Fox barely acknowledged the result and spent most of the night dredging up debunked fake scandals about Hillary Clinton. For the Trump-loving Fox News viewer, it's as if the elections had never happened.

Fox News's affection for Trump is not unrequited. The president watches Fox News for hours a day. We know this from news reports, but also because he is constantly tweeting about Fox. Promoting stories he sees as favorable, thanking Fox personalities for praising him, and congratulating/taking credit for Fox's ratings.[21]

---

20   Not that many people.
21   Trump has invented the concept of the backhanded self-compliment.

Now, it's also worth noting that under no circumstances should a president have time to watch this much television during the day, given the pressing demands of running the free world.[22]

Fox & Friends is the worst of all the Fox shows because it pretends to be a news show like the *Today Show* or *Good Morning America*, yet it is pure unfiltered propaganda. And it's the program Trump watches most religiously—reportedly in his bathrobe.[23] Its influence is so great that the *New York Times* once referred to it as the "most powerful show in America."

Whenever Trump says something that seems totally out of context, factually inaccurate, or genuinely bizarre, it is almost certainly related to something that was broadcast on *Fox & Friends*. During his first year in the White House, Trump falsely accused Barack Obama of wiretapping him with the assistance of Great Britain—causing a massive political and diplomatic crisis—because of something that a random pundit appearing on Fox News said.

Amid the daily barrage of insanity and embarrassment that is American life in the Trump era, it's easy to miss the danger of the Fox News phenomenon. But just ponder the idea that the president of the United States—the person whose words can start wars and move markets—is taking at face value random things uttered by cable pundits and then repeating them to the world as fact. I don't know what's a more alarming prospect: Trump spreading absurd conspiracy theories that he doesn't believe in or Trump believing the absurd conspiracy theories he spreads. Either way, the idea that a major American television network with little to no journalistic standards that spreads false information is replacing the presidential daily intelligence briefing as the commander in chief's primary source of information is a terrifying prospect.

---

22 Trump apparently has time to watch four to eight hours of cable news a day.

23 I can never unsee that image and now neither can you.

DEFEATING THE TRUMP PROPAGANDA MACHINE

Fox News is notable as the most famous part of the pro-Trump propaganda army, but they are not alone. Fox proved that there was real money to be made in laundering Republican talking points through performance art masquerading as journalism. New outlets have been coming out of the woodwork in recent years. The new mini-Foxes are in some ways more dangerous. They are more radical, less responsible, and adeptly utilize social media to spread their messages far and wide. Most notable among these outlets is Breitbart, which was headed by Steve Bannon, Trump's former chief strategist. In addition to new media outlets, the right wing has developed an army of conservative provocateurs with hundreds of thousands of Twitter followers that spread Trump's message (and his debunked conspiracy theories). Trump uses the imprimatur of the White House and his powerful Twitter account to promote these new media forces.

Individually these folks are ridiculous con artists, unrepentant racists, and boorish clowns, but together they represent a massive propaganda operation that can be deployed to pull the wool over the eyes of a significant portion of Americans with a single tweet.

Our experience during the Obama White House with Fox and their ilk makes it clear that you can't beat them and you can't join them. What can or should be done to actually deal with Fox News and the right-wing propaganda machine?

Fox will never be your friend. Fox has no shame. They don't care about media or liberal critiques. Shaming them is not an option.

There has been some success in convincing advertisers to join boycotts of Fox, particularly around the sexual harassment allegations against Bill O'Reilly and Sean Hannity's promotion of a sick conspiracy about a DNC staffer murdered in 2016. But the last fifteen years have shown that major American brands want to sell to the Fox audience and are perfectly comfortable with the shenanigans that go on there. And if they aren't comfortable, they are too afraid to pull out because of the potential backlash from Fox's engaged audience.

At the end of the Obama era, our approach to Fox was one of strategic ambivalence. Our White House continued to provide them access to all the briefings and press conferences. The president would periodically take questions from their reporters. We did all this not because we thought they deserved this sort of respect and fair treatment. Well, I certainly didn't. Like any media outlet, they were able to cover the White House without interference, but we treated them like a normal media outlet because it was the path of least resistance. It wasn't worth the headache of making a martyr of Fox. Instead we mostly ignored them; we didn't get worked up about what was on Fox. We didn't respond to their silliness. This starved them of the reaction they so craved. Not worrying about Fox made our lives more efficient and certainly more pleasant. In the White House, you simply have too much shit to do to spend any energy on things you can't affect. Fox was one of those things.

Talk to Fox News viewers—just don't do it on Fox. The problem with ignoring Fox News, though, is that you end up ignoring Fox News viewers. Now there is no doubt that most Fox viewers are a lost cause for Democrats. They are hardcore conservative Republicans. But one of the reasons that Donald Trump is president and Hillary Clinton isn't is because a lot of voters from rural areas who supported Barack Obama in 2008 and 2012 chose Trump over Hillary in 2016. Many of these voters are Fox News viewers, and if they aren't, they live in communities where Fox is on in the bars and the waiting rooms. What is said on Fox affects the contours of the political conversation in these communities.[24] Electorally—and morally—Democrats cannot afford to cede these voters to the Republicans. I am resistant to any strategy that says we give up on a third of the country.

I have the scars to prove that Fox News will never give a

---

24   I call this ignorance by osmosis.

Democrat the opportunity to deliver their message in a fair way. Even if the individual interviewer is fair—which occasionally happens—the network will pluck out the most problematic part of the interview and use that on all of their shows to beat you over the head with it, much as they did with Obama's interview with Bret Baier.

We need to combat Fox News by going around Fox News to communicate with their viewers through interviews on local television and interactions on Facebook, and Democrats can and must campaign in those rural areas. Democrats need to give these voters a chance to see them in person instead of getting to know them only through the fun house mirror of Fox.

Barack Obama would often say that if he could just meet every person in America, much like how he was able to in Iowa in 2008, it would change the tone of politics. People would see that he is a good, honest person trying to do the right thing. Maybe he wouldn't get any more votes than he otherwise would have gotten, because there are legitimate, sincere differences of opinion on issues. But people would know the real Obama, not the Fox News caricature of a Muslim socialist intent on destroying American values.

Build out a progressive media. Ever since the nineties, Democratic politicians and donors have asked the question: "How do we get our own Fox News?"

It seems so appealing—a television network that would carry your message and savage your opponents beamed into the homes of millions of Americans.

Who wouldn't want that? I would have been willing to cut off several limbs for such a network when I worked in the White House.

Over the years, every effort to create a progressive version of Fox has failed and failed miserably. This is largely because Democrats have not spent decades trying to convince their voters that the mainstream media is terrible and therefore it's harder to get them to abandon the mainstream media for some alternative. The previous attempts at liberal television and radio networks also failed because they missed a key ingredient of Fox's success: entertainment. I personally would rather have a root canal than watch Fox News, but they hired horrible but entertaining personalities to deliver their propaganda.[25]

In the Trump era, we either adapt or lose. First, Democrats need to learn that the rules of the game have changed. The mainstream media plays an important role in our democracy, but it is a very different and smaller role than in the pre-Internet era. When I was communications director on the 2008 Obama campaign and in the White House, I spent 80 percent of my time thinking about the traditional media—thinking about what reporter Obama interviewed with, how to manage his relationships with the press corps writ large. I did this because the media was the primary way to get our message out. That is no longer true. If the communications director of the campaign of the 2020 Democratic nominee spends even a fraction of that amount of time focused on the traditional press, we will lose and lose badly. Modern political communications mean convincing the public through every means necessary—the press is now only one of those means.

Second, we are massively outgunned in the media space. Republicans have powerful weapons amplifying their message, parodying Democrats, and shaping the online conversation in ways that are bad for progressive causes. Trump is unique in his ability to dominate public discourse with outrageous utterances, but Trump could not have been this successful without the army of right-wing propaganda outlets that had sprung up in the shadow of the Obama presidency.

If Democrats do not close the gap soon, we will once again have our message drowned out. With the possible exception of Russian

---

25 I can't believe there are people who choose to watch Hannity and Jesse Watters, but some people do. There is no accounting for taste.

hacking, the right-wing media advantage is the greatest threat to progressivism.

Developing an activist, entertaining progressive media is an imperative. This is different from creating a Democratic Fox. We cannot and should not try to adopt the mirror image of their dishonest, divisive, and frankly racist approach. We should not try to pretend to be "fair and balanced" in order to pull the wool over people's eyes.

Unlike conservatives, progressives do not hate the mainstream media and are not looking for a replacement. But we do need a way to engage our supporters, amplify our message, and try to win the battle of social media conversation.

We cannot—and should not—get in the propaganda business, because that is about nullifying the idea of an objective media, and if we want to continue winning arguments based on facts, we need independent arbiters of truth.

Crooked Media, the media company started by my *Pod Save America* cohosts, is the model for how progressives can erase the Right's substantial media advantage. Jon, Jon, and Tommy started Crooked Media in the weeks after the 2016 election to inform, entertain, and engage. *Pod Save America* and the rest of the Crooked Media empire of podcasts are unique in the progressive media space because they are building an engaged audience and helping that audience find ways to channel their energy into action. Come for the witty banter; stay for the activism.

That's ultimately what *Pod Save America* is about:[26] trying to engage and channel the energy of the grassroots activists who have taken over the Democratic Party—many of whom are participating in politics for the first time.

During the battle to save the Affordable Care Act in 2017, *Pod Save America* and other Crooked Media podcasts used our platforms to encourage our listeners to get involved in the grassroots

---

26   In addition to helping us manage our own tortured emotions in the Trump era.

efforts to pressure Congress to do the right thing. Crooked Media worked hand in hand with groups like MoveOn, the Center for American Progress, and Indivisible to inform people about which protests to attend, which members of Congress to target with phone calls, and the best talking points to use.

Unlike Fox and Breitbart, this is not a command-and-control operation trying to manufacture outrage.[27] It's an ongoing, honest (no bullshit) conversation about where the country is headed and what we can do about it. We are as influenced by the conversations we have with our listeners as they are by us.

Crooked Media is the first bright spot for progressives in the fight against Fox and the pro-Trump propagandists.

Now we just need more Crooked Medias.

---

27   No need for that while Trump is president.

CHAPTER 7

THE REPUBLICANS GO OFF THE DEEP END

On a dark, dreary night in 2014, during a dark, dreary time in the Obama presidency, Barack Obama explained exactly how the Republican Party would become the Party of Trump.

We were on *Marine One*, headed back to the White House after a long day of campaigning in the midterm elections.

The president's poll numbers were near his lowest ever, and candidates weren't exactly beating down the door to get Obama to travel to their states. The White House had been buffeted by a series of disasters—real and media-created.

You couldn't turn on cable television without being afraid you would get Ebola if someone coughed on you at Costco. The Republican-controlled Congress was blocking all of our agenda. Every day, the Internet was filled with pundits declaring in columns and tweets that Barack Obama was a "lame duck," the kiss of death for a second-term president.

ISIS was on the march and the president had held a notorious press conference in which he said he didn't have a strategy to defeat ISIS (he did have a strategy; it just hadn't been finalized), wearing a tan suit that became an instant meme on the Internet.

Control of the Senate was at stake in this election, and the president really wanted to win. If the Republicans took over, they would block most of his nominations and all of his judicial appointments.

Barack Obama hates to lose and he really hates to lose to Mitch McConnell,[1] the Republican leader of the Senate. McConnell is smart, diabolical, and basically a robot sent from the future to destroy the progressive agenda. He is the most cynical person in politics and cares about nothing other than the accumulation of power.[2]

But despite our public talking points to the contrary, we knew were going to lose. You can just tell sometimes in a campaign. We wouldn't admit this publicly or even privately to one another. We grasped at every glimmer of hope in the polls. Every slight bit of movement or anecdote about voter registration was like a political Xanax. But we knew.

The candidates and their staffs had the smell of death. The rallies had all the enthusiasm of a funeral for that relative no one really liked that much.

This was the less than ideal backdrop to that fateful helicopter ride. Barack Obama is a particularly thoughtful guy. However, amid the endless crises and nonstop meetings, you rarely got to hear him reflect on the big picture.

But things were different on the road. Presidential travel is filled with downtime—time on the plane, in the Beast (the presidential limo), backstage while some elected official enters minute eleven of their proposed three-minute introduction of the president. This downtime was a chance to talk about more than what to expect in the next meeting. The "traveling crew" was usually made up of people the president had known the longest and felt the most comfortable with. He would say things to us on the road that you wouldn't hear in the regular meetings in the White House.

---

1   Everyone hates Mitch McConnell. He's terrible.
2   He's really bad. Like, really bad.

At the time, I was "senior advisor" to the president, which is an amorphous job that is some combination of general strategist, consigliere, and decoder of presidential moods and desires.

As we flew back to the White House, Obama was alternatively reading his BlackBerry, catching up on e-mails and news, and looking out the window as we passed by the monuments.[3] At this time, I was pretty close to deciding that I was going to leave the White House in a few months after the midterm elections. I was so exhausted, I couldn't see or think straight and knew down deep that it was time. Because of my impending departure, I was paying extra attention. I knew that I didn't have many more of these moments in front of me.

I was sitting across from the chair designated for the president. We were talking about whatever the latest crazy thing some Republican had done or said. The president looked up at us, laughed at whatever the Republican lunacy du jour was, and said: "You know, I was elected about a decade too soon."

The president said that it was inevitable that the country would have a president of color, but the unique circumstances of his candidacy caused this to happen much sooner than would have otherwise occurred.

He went on to explain that we were living in a period of massive, disruptive economic, cultural, and technological change. And that having a black president with the middle name Hussein as the face of that change had real political and cultural consequences.

In other words, Barack Obama drove the Republicans insane.

So insane that the Republicans nominated and America elected Donald Trump.

When I think about how the first African American president was replaced by a man whose election caused white supremacists to

---

3   This is a supremely obnoxious thing to say, but there really is no better way to see a monument than at night by presidential helicopter. The president once had us buzz the Statue of Liberty at night just to impress House Minority Leader Nancy Pelosi. Pretty sure it worked.

come out from behind their Pepe the Frog[4] Twitter avatars to dance in the street, I think back to this conversation with Obama on the helicopter. When I watch Paul Ryan and McConnell bend the knee to a man they know to be dangerously unfit for the presidency, I hear Obama's observation in my head.

The modern Republican Party is dead. It has no coherent ideology or policy agenda. It's a conglomerate of clowns, con men, and racists and those who enable the clowns, con men, and racists. American democracy depends on having two functioning political parties. We have only one (it's the Democrats, I swear).

The election of Obama in 2008 had felt like a cleansing moment for America, a proof point that our present was better than our past. People wanted so desperately to believe that we lived in a country that could elect an African American, and when that came to fruition, people wanted to believe that America had crossed the Rubicon and left our less than glorious past behind. There was some real truth in these hopes and dreams, but Obama's historic election and successful presidency also roused some sleeping demons and brought them from the fringes into the mainstream of the Republican Party.

It's possible the Republican Party was headed down this path anyway as their voters got older and whiter while the rest of the country was getting younger and more diverse. But there is no question that the election of a young African American president with the middle name Hussein catalyzed the craziness.

If you want to understand how and why the Republican Party stands by the daily moral and political outrages of Donald Trump, it begins with their response to the election of Barack Obama.

---

4 A cartoon frog becoming the mascot of white supremacists is very weird, but not even close to the weirdest thing that happened in 2016.

HOPE MEETS HATE

A few years after entering the White House, I returned to my desk after one of the endless series of meetings that defined my life to find an e-mail from Paul Begala, the renowned Democratic strategist and CNN pundit. This unsolicited, but not unwanted, e-mail came in response to some olive branch that President Obama had offered to the new Republican congressional majority.

The e-mail, which I later printed out and put in a drawer but have since lost, said something to the effect of:

> Pfeiffer: Sooner rather than later, the Republicans will try to destroy Obama. Don't be surprised if they try to impeach him. Trust me, I have seen this before.

I took Paul's note seriously because he is a smart guy, but I also thought his view was colored by his time working for Bill Clinton during impeachment. Obama was different from Clinton. He wouldn't put himself in the same position that Clinton did.

Paul was wrong on the impeachment, but that was only because Obama didn't give them an opportunity. I wish I had gotten Paul's note a few years earlier, though, because he was right about the rest. Stopping Obama at all costs became the only animating principle of the modern Republican Party.

Once we arrived in Washington after the 2008 election, the Obama transition was all about living up to the promise of restoring civility, unity, and bipartisanship to our politics. One of Barack Obama's first moves was to host John McCain for a meeting to seek his advice.

He also immediately reappointed Robert Gates, George W. Bush's secretary of defense and a longtime and well-respected Republican official. Not long after, Obama appointed Republican congressman Ray LaHood as secretary of transportation. Later on, Obama would announce the nomination of Republican senator

Judd Gregg as commerce secretary, only to have Gregg drop out a few days later when he realized that if he worked for Obama, he would have to support Obama's agenda. To this day, I have no idea what he possibly thought the job was and cite it as a piece of evidence that the Senate is not necessarily a Mensa meeting.

In the midst of the rapidly worsening economic crisis that Obama inherited, we wanted to work closely with the Republican minority in the Senate and the House to construct the economic package designed to rescue the economy. The hope was that at a time of nearly unprecedented crisis for the country, the Republicans would be willing to put politics aside.

The president instructed his economic team to reach out to Republicans and incorporate their ideas, which they did—making nearly half of the package tax cuts instead of the sort of government spending that was (wrongly) an anathema to Republicans (unless it was in their district).

The president-elect decided in an unusual gesture of bipartisan outreach to travel to Capitol Hill to pitch the Republicans on his plan and personally solicit their help in saving the economy. Usually Congress gets summoned to the White House, but Obama wanted to show them his desire to work with them in good faith.

The distance between our transition office and the Capitol was less than two miles. In the brief interim between when Obama got in the elevator to leave our office and when he arrived at the Capitol, John Boehner announced that the Republicans would not work with Obama and would to a person oppose the economic stimulus package. Watching this press conference on the TVs in the office with the other staff who weren't part of the large contingent of aides accompanying Obama, I was flabbergasted.

"What a dick," I thought to myself. "You do the right thing and they ratfuck you anyway."

Despite Boehner's announcement, we kept reaching out to Republicans in the hopes of picking some of them off.

On the day of the vote, we gathered in the anteroom to the chief of staff's office. With every passing day, we had revised down our estimate of the Republican votes the bill would get. The tension in the room was high because anything under ten votes or so would be seen as a loss for Obama and make it harder for the bill to pass the Senate.

As we watched the vote unfold on the small TV mounted near the ceiling, a sense of doom pervaded. With every additional Republican "nay," our list of possible votes got shorter and shorter. There was still a small handful of gettable votes left, but then one by one they all walked up and voted "no."

Zero "yea" votes from the Republican caucus.

Not a single House Republican was willing to work with the newly elected Democratic president to prevent the economy from careening into another Great Depression.

I would like to say this was the low point of our relations with Republicans, but it was not even close.[5]

- They shut down the government for weeks in a failed attempt to repeal the Affordable Care Act, because the only thing they hate more than Barack Obama is Barack Obama giving people needed access to health care.
- Not once—but twice—they walked up to the line of causing a collapse of the global economy by refusing to pay the nation's bills, roiling markets and hurting the economy.
- They repeatedly opposed legislation they had previously supported in order to deny Obama an accomplishment even though it hurt the country and their policy priorities.
- John Boehner disinvited Obama from an address to Congress in order to prevent him from speaking during prime time.
- And here are some of the things Republicans said about Obama:
  - Representative Doug Lamborn called Obama a "tar baby."
  - Senator David Perdue literally prayed for Obama to die, saying to applause, "Let his days be few."

---

5   You could argue it was the high point (seriously).

- ◦ Former Republican Speaker Newt Gingrich called Obama the "food stamp president."
- ◦ Gingrich also described Obama's worldview as influenced by a "Kenyan, anti-colonial" mind-set.
- ◦ Representative Steve King said of Obama's election, "The radical Islamists, the al Qaeda, the radical Islamists and their supporters, will be dancing in the streets in greater numbers than they did on September 11 because they will declare victory in this war on terror."
- ◦ And of course, there was Republican congressman Joe Wilson yelling, "You lie!" in the middle of Obama's joint address to Congress about health care.[6]

The Republicans not only wouldn't work with Obama, they wouldn't even be seen with him.

When the Republicans took over the House of Representatives in an electoral landslide, the media covered it as a rebuke to Obama and all of his policies.[7] In the aftermath of the election, one of us had the idea of Obama inviting the congressional leadership to dinner at the White House for a bipartisan discussion of how to move the country forward. I had no idea if this would be productive. I suspected not, but I loved the image of Obama bringing the parties together to try to bridge the ideological divide. This was straight out of the 2008 campaign playbook. Around the table in the chief of staff's office, there was tremendous enthusiasm for the idea, with one exception. Phil Schiliro, the president's point person for Congress who had worked on Capitol Hill since I was in elementary school, sat stone-faced and silent in his usual seat. I took note of Phil's reaction but chalked it up to his customary stoicism and his well-known poker face.

---

6   It's worth noting that these outrageous statements were met with approving silence from Republicans like John Boehner and Paul Ryan. If you could footnote a footnote, I would point out that they are cowards.

7   I viewed it more as a rebuke of being president and doing tough stuff to fix a shitty economy.

We hustled to announce the dinner invite as soon as possible. The morning of the announcement, Phil's staff went to call the staffs of the congressional leadership. The Democrats immediately accepted the invite. The Republicans, on the other hand, were unenthusiastic and noncommittal. We gave them a proposed date when Obama was free and Congress was in town. They said they would get back to us.

They didn't.

Turning down an invitation for dinner at the White House is just not done. I have seen people fly in from as far away as Singapore at the drop of a hat for a White House dinner. People skip family obligations and change plans because they know that dinner at the White House is a once-in-a-lifetime opportunity. Every day in our morning meeting, someone would ask Phil if Boehner, McConnell, and their deputies had gotten back to us. Every day, Phil would tersely say, "Not yet."

After a few days, I started to get annoyed. I had bumped heads with the legislative staff during the previous year because of the natural tension that comes between the people trying to pass bills through an unpopular Congress and the people trying to keep the president popular.

Every time Obama engaged with the very unpopular Congress, he got a little more of their shit on him, which was not great for his public image.[8]

Because this idea came from the communications wing of the White House staff, not the legislative staff, I thought they were slow-walking our idea.

I fired off an e-mail that was a touch too hot to a group that was a touch too large, demanding to know when we would get an answer on the dinner invite we'd announced with much fanfare. Phil had spent years working on some of the most important

---

8   It's a conundrum: you need high approval ratings to pass your agenda, but doing the things it takes to pass your agenda hurts your approval ratings.

congressional investigations, and based on that experience, he was very careful on e-mail. Phil knew better than most that an out-of-context e-mail can lead to a congressional subpoena.[9] If you got a response from Phil, which was pretty rare, it was almost always one line: "Please call me."

Upon receiving that e-mail, I didn't call; I stormed upstairs to try to get an answer. Phil was seated behind his desk scribbling on one of the legal pads he carried everywhere. He explained that this dinner was not going to happen. The Republicans did not want to be seen breaking bread with Obama because it would upset their voters. They were petrified of being tossed out in a primary challenge if they were photographed treating Barack Obama like a human being.

There you have it, the simplest explanation for why Republicans couldn't and wouldn't work with Obama.

Their voters hated Obama so much that it paralyzed the Republican Party. Now these Republicans should have had the courage to stand up to the rabid fringe of their party that believed Obama was a secret Muslim Manchurian candidate.

That failure is how we ended up with Trump. Before the Republican establishment knew it, the far-right fringe they tried to placate started calling the shots and mainstream Republicans like John Boehner served at the pleasure of the Breitbart birthers.

THE FEVER THAT WOULDN'T BREAK

During the 2012 election campaign, Barack Obama mused at one point that he hoped his reelection would "break the fever" of rabid opposition to him that came from Republican politicians and their voters. There was some logic in this hope. Mitch McConnell had declared that defeating Obama was his top priority. Not helping his constituents, saving the economy, or defeating Al-Qaeda, but

---

9   The DNC should have been more like Phil.

ensuring that Obama didn't win reelection. This was some of the most cynical hackery that can be found in politics, but we were burdened by governing with cynical hacks.

During heated budget negotiations in 2011 when Obama and Boehner were on the cusp of a historic deal, Paul Ryan, who was then chair of the Budget Committee, scuttled the deal because it would guarantee Obama's reelection—even though the deal would have been good for the country and accomplish some of Ryan's long-held policy goals.

In the Republican mind-set, beating Obama in 2012 wasn't just the primary political goal of the Republican Party; it was their only goal. It was their entire reason for being.

The idea of the "fever breaking" was ridiculed by cynical political pundits. Obama was always more hopeful and optimistic about the sincerity and integrity of some of his Republican colleagues than I was. But at first it seemed that Obama might have been right.

Right after the election, House Speaker John Boehner declared that Obamacare was now the law of the land and it was time for the Republicans to move on. Leading Republicans in the House and Senate and, more important, their overlords on Fox News began shifting their long-held positions against immigration reform and urged the party to take action.

In the ecstatic days after Obama's reelection, the possibility of putting the worst of the partisan wars of the previous four years behind us really did seem plausible and maybe even probable.

The first test of the new world order was fast upon us. Absent congressional action, taxes were going to go up on nearly all Americans at midnight on December 31, 2012. The media called this situation the "fiscal cliff," which was a terrible way of saying that Congress and the president had been kicking the can down the road and we were about to run out of road.

For much of 2012, the "fiscal cliff" was the least of my concerns. Sure, I went to numerous meetings about it where we gamed out strategies and potential compromise proposals to solve the problem, but I couldn't have cared less. Dealing with challenges that would come after the election seemed like a high-class problem to me—we had to win the election first. At least once a day for the previous two years, I had thought with dread about the possibility of losing the reelection, nullifying our work, and sending Obama to the consignment bin of history with the rest of the one-term presidents.

Reelections are unique experiences. The upcoming election hangs over the head of everyone who works in the White House and much of the government like the sword of Damocles. If the president loses, they are all out of a job within three months and the entire trajectories of their lives change. And while the campaign is happening and the president is absent much of the time stumping across the country, the same daily crises, policy problems, and management challenges that make the presidency such a hard job still happen.

Obama and Jack Lew, the former director of management and budget and seasoned government executive who became chief of staff in 2012, were very cognizant of the need to be able to walk and chew gum at the same time. The campaign staff, based once again in Chicago, had to focus on the election and the White House staff had to run the government, because one misstep within the government could negate all the work of the campaign team. To maximize success and ensure that we adhered to the law, only a small number of White House staffers were intimately involved in the strategy and decisions of the campaign—attending meetings, getting in on daily calls, and receiving daily updates on polling and other metrics. The group of designated White House staff were veterans from the 2008 campaign—David Plouffe, who was now senior advisor and coordinating strategy with the campaign; Alyssa Mastromonaco, who was leading the strategy on where Obama went and what he did there; Jon Favreau, who was traveling with the president and writing and refining the core message; and me serving as the connective tissue between the campaign and the White House on communications matters and helping coordinate on press strategy.

With this as the backdrop, most of the White House had been thinking and planning for the fiscal cliff for months. My view, which was admittedly irresponsible, was to win reelection and then figure it out.

Election night 2012 was a late night, with some of the OG 2008 gang emptying our mini bars and celebrating in Axelrod's hotel room till the sun came up. The next morning, I was woken up by a phone call from my assistant at 8:30 a.m.[10]

I answered the phone in an alcohol- and exhaustion-induced haze.

"Jack Lew has organized an eleven-thirty meeting to talk fiscal cliff strategy and he wants you to call in."

I said, "OK, I'll be on the call," but I thought, "Can't we have twenty-four hours to bask in our victory before getting back into the shit? Is that too much to ask for?"

After a perfunctory pat on the back for the election victory, it was right down to business. I noticed two things on the call. One, the economic and legislative teams had been chomping at the bit to lay out their strategy and thoughts about how to solve this problem. They had been at this for months without getting the attention of the political team, whose input they needed. Two, Plouffe had refused to get on the call, which was the first piece of evidence that he intended to live up to his long-held promise to exit the White House after the election.

Adding to my hangover, a lot of what I heard on the call was alarming me politically. Most of our economic team were veterans of the Clinton White House, and their political experience was in an era with a different, more moderate Republican Party. A time when the party had a coherent policy vision and compromise wasn't considered surrender. The potential deals they were talking about

---

10   Telling the bartender at our hotel that we were friends with Chicago mayor Rahm Emanuel and that he would want us to have another drink or six was entirely unpersuasive.

were great policy. These deals would help the economy and provide logical, rational solutions to a vexing policy problem at a time of divided government.

But we did not live in rational or logical times. This was not a logical and rational Republican Party. The president had tried to come to a grand bargain with Boehner and the Republicans back in 2011, and it had been a political and substantive disaster. Boehner was well intentioned, but his caucus led him as opposed to his leading them.[11] He simply wasn't strong enough to deliver on anything resembling a fair deal, and his caucus was out for blood, not bargains. Boehner was going to be much weaker now than he was then because even though the Republicans had held on to the House, they had lost seats and Boehner's narrow margin for error had gotten much narrower.

My second concern was that the deals being floated internally by our team were Solomonic proposals. I believed that after winning 332 electoral votes, Obama deserved more than half the baby and I knew that's what our base believed as well.

A deal that was viewed as weak would potentially cripple Obama heading into his second term, and a failure to get a deal would mean a massive tax increase that would potentially send the economy back into recession. Threading the needle was going to be incredibly challenging and would test the idea that the fever had broken.

This was also a critical time for me personally. Out of paranoid superstition, I hadn't allowed myself to think about anything that would happen after Election Day. I lived in fear of Obama losing the election. I had obsessed about it every day since 2010.

It was exhausting.

But now that the election was behind me, I needed to make some life decisions. I had been in the White House for four years plus two

---

11 Boehner was a better speaker than Paul Ryan, but a surgical sponge would be a better speaker than Ryan.

years on the campaign. In that period, I had been through a lot professionally and personally.

The end of the first term was potentially an ideal time for me to go out on a high note. I could get some sleep and get my life out of the state of suspended animation it had been in since I'd unexpectedly accepted that job offer to work for Barack Obama.

As appealing as an easier, fuller life seemed, I was also scared to leave. The adrenaline of the White House is like a drug. Plus, after six years together, my Obama colleagues were my family, and leaving them would be really hard. I legitimately didn't know what I would do every day if I wasn't waking up and going to the White House.

As I was beginning to wrestle with this decision, Plouffe asked me to come to lunch with him in the White House mess. This seemed consequential because in our years of being friends and colleagues, this was the first time just the two of us had ever shared a meal. This was going to be my best and perhaps only chance to pick Plouffe's brain on the question of whether to stay or go.

On the day of the lunch, I was not my best self. One of the consequences of internalizing six years of stress was that my digestive system was a disaster. My stomach hurt every day. Some days were worse than others, but this day was the worst. I could barely get up from my desk to go to the fateful lunch. It hurt so badly that I Googled symptoms of appendicitis (I didn't have it).

Desperate for some relief, I walked down the hall to Alyssa's office to ask for some medicine. Her purse was a virtual pharmacy, but she was not in her office, and even though she was one of my closest friends, I didn't feel like I could root through her purse for medicine in her absence.

At lunch, I nibbled on bread and sipped water while trying to suppress the look of distress on my face. Plouffe laid it out: He was going to leave right after the inauguration and asked me if I would be willing to stay and take over his job as senior advisor. He nicely said that my taking over for him would give him some comfort that there was someone who would help President Obama stay true to the ideals of the 2008 campaign.

This chance to take a new, more senior role and expand beyond communications was a very appealing reason to stay. I was flattered that Plouffe thought I could do the job. But at the end of the day, it wasn't Plouffe's job to offer. His endorsement would carry a lot of weight, but it was ultimately up to the president.

The battle over the fiscal cliff would be my audition.

Before the 2012 election, we were preparing the president for an event where he would take questions from the press. One of the questions would inevitably be about the fiscal cliff and the president's answer would set the stage for the upcoming negotiations. I pitched Obama on an answer that I had been thinking about for a few days.

Why not say something to the effect of, "Since we all agree on immediately extending the tax cuts for the middle class, there's no reason to wait. Let's do that now and worry about the rest later," I suggested, somewhat to the annoyance of some on the team who preferred a less aggressive position in order to preserve negotiating space for a bipartisan deal later.

Obama was taken with the simplicity of this message and the deviousness of the idea. This message put the Republicans in a terrible position. They would have to oppose this commonsense idea because they knew that the only way to pass tax cuts for the wealthy was to attach them to more popular tax cuts for the middle class. Obama would be able to (accurately) accuse them of holding the middle class hostage to protect tax cuts for millionaires and billionaires. This argument became a staple on the campaign trail.

With the cliff looming in the days after the election, Obama began to push the same argument more and more aggressively. We had momentum and Obama sought to press that advantage. But this was a risky endeavor—the president had pledged that he would not under any circumstances continue the tax cuts for the wealthy. If Obama backed off from that pledge, in search of a bipartisan deal or because he sincerely wanted to prevent a tax increase on all Americans, it would be a crushing blow to his second term before it even began.

I believed our best strategy was to take a maximalist position and call their bluff by forcing the House to try to pass a bill that the Senate had previously passed to extend the tax cuts for the middle class. Strength is the most important attribute in presidential politics. You have to look strong to get a deal. Obama's natural state of being is reasonableness—it's why he was a very good president and an even better person—but in certain heated political situations, there is a very fine line between reasonableness and looking weak.

For this strategy to work, we had to convince the Republicans of two things: Obama was willing to let taxes go up on everyone to prevent the wealthy from getting a tax cut, *and* he would be able to convince the public that it was their fault. We had to make them surrender.

After a few weeks of being hammered by Obama, Boehner called to offer a potential deal. Having heard that Obama was on the phone with Boehner, a bunch of us gathered outside the Oval Office, nervously waiting to hear the details. Obama opened the door to ask his assistant a question and saw a half dozen of us gathered awkwardly and anxiously outside his door. He chuckled and said in mock annoyance, "You all might as well come in."

Obama laid out the details of Boehner's proposal as we stood arrayed around his desk. Boehner said Republicans would agree to tax increases on incomes of a million dollars and above—something that had been verboten since the days of Reagan—in exchange for some entitlement cuts.

It made sense that Boehner would want to return to the table, because he had genuinely wanted this deal back in 2011 and might have been able to deliver it if he hadn't been stabbed in the back by Paul Ryan and Eric Cantor, his overly and obviously ambitious deputy.

Obama was excited, if skeptical, at this development. Most of the rest of the gathered senior aides were already thinking through counteroffers and policy implementation. I, on the other hand, did not share their enthusiasm and did not do a good job of hiding it. The president saw the look on my face and called me on it.

"Pfeiffer, what are your thoughts?"

"Maybe it's my PTSD from the failed grand bargain negotiations, but I am very afraid we are going to get burned again. Anything that smells like caving on the tax cuts for the wealthy will get us killed."

Our staff went back and forth with the Speaker for a few days before the negotiations blew up. They didn't blow up because the parties were at loggerheads or because there was a policy issue. They never got that far. The mere fact that Boehner was considering working with Obama was enough to cause his party to revolt.

Most of Boehner's members were not humbled by their electoral loss; they were angry. Many were still in a state of shock mainly because they got all their news from Fox, which had painted a very misleading picture of Romney's chances by claiming that the polls that showed Obama winning were skewed as part of a liberal media conspiracy.[12] The fate of the economy and even their own short-term political interests could not trump their hatred of the president.

We were about a week and a half away from the New Year's Eve deadline and back at square one.

Plouffe, who had been my partner in pushing for a strong deal, was heading off on a family vacation, where he intended to be unavailable. His original plan had been to leave the White House right after the election, but Obama had implored him to stay until the inauguration. Plouffe agreed, on the condition that he could go on the long-planned vacation.

As he headed out the door, Plouffe warned me against letting people, including some on the Hill, push Obama into a bad deal. "Try to land the plane while I'm gone," he said with a bit of a sympathetic smirk as he walked out the door.

Although he didn't say it explicitly, Plouffe's absence at this criti-

---

12   I no longer make fun of anyone who misreads the polls and gets an election prediction wrong. Out of the prediction game, as we say.

cal moment was also part of his plan to give me a shot to try out for his job in front of the president and, if I succeeded, make it easier for him to walk out the door in a few months.

The next ten days were a blur. I went home to Delaware to see my parents on the afternoon of Christmas Eve, spent much of Christmas on the phone and on the computer, including a call with the president at 10:00 p.m., and was back in the White House by 10:00 a.m. on the twenty-sixth.

The president continued to press his case to the public, expressing his willingness to go over the cliff and positioning the Republicans as the ones willing to raise taxes on the middle class to protect tax breaks for the wealthy. As we got closer to the deadline, I was in and out of the Oval Office multiple times a day, playing Plouffe's role as Obama's sounding board on the politics of the moment. I was on the high wire with no safety net, with the economy—not to mention my own job—on the line.

On New Year's Eve, there was finally a breakthrough. Mitch McConnell and the Senate Republicans had blinked. McConnell reached out to Vice President Biden with a potential solution. A bipartisan deal that was not perfect but much more palatable than what Boehner had offered and more palatable than raising taxes on the entire country.

We gathered in the vice president's office late in the night to hear the details of the deal. Biden was seated behind his desk, drinking a Gatorade. Obama was on speakerphone because he had retreated to the residence earlier in the evening. Biden laid out the details of the deal for the president. After he was done, the president put me on the spot:

"Is Pfeiffer in the room?"

Gulp.

While I appreciated the idea that the president wanted to hear my opinion, this was not how I wanted to share it with him.

I made my way to the vice president's desk so that I could speak into the phone.

"Yes, sir."

"What do you think of this deal? How will this sell?" Obama asked.

This was not what I wanted to happen. I had some serious concerns that a couple of elements of the deal would be seen unfairly as too favorable to the Republicans and the president would be criticized for being a bad negotiator. I also knew that I was in a distinct minority in the room, which included the chief of staff, the director of the office of management and budget, the Treasury secretary, and a gaggle of top White House aides—almost none of whom agreed with what I was about to say.

I was pretty sure I was about to get torn limb from limb by a group of very impressive people older and more experienced than me.

This was the moment of truth. I could either give my real opinion or go with the path of least resistance.

"Fuck it," I thought to myself and let it rip.

I laid out my concerns with a couple of the provisions. If we were going to give X, we needed to get more Y. The vice president vehemently disagreed with my view. I was standing about six inches from him and could feel him getting annoyed as I spoke into the phone. Who could blame him?

The vice president of the United States had been cutting deals in the Senate since long before I was born. As a kid from Delaware, I'd always looked up to Joe Biden. He was the first politician I'd ever met, had been either my senator or Obama's vice president my entire life, and was one of my political idols. I had been an intern in his Senate office while I was in college. The millisecond that I stopped speaking, the room erupted with disagreement from all corners.

Several members of the economic team were attacking my argument.

After a few minutes, Obama spoke and cut everyone off.

"Look, I think Dan is right about some of this. Joe, can you call Mitch back and see what else you can get?"

Obama didn't agree with everything I said, but in this showdown, he had taken my side. And I lived to fight another day.

McConnell accepted most of Biden's proposed changes and we had a deal. The House Republicans were furious but they were forced to swallow the deal. Most of them voted against it, but it passed with mostly Democratic votes.

While this could have been a sign the fever had finally broken, it turned out that this showdown only deepened their opposition. Their hatred for Obama consumed them and the politics of their party.

LESSONS FROM THE OBAMA WARS

The Republicans repeatedly declared war on Obama, but Obama usually came out on top. He was more popular than his Republican opponents, who had the approval ratings of pond scum. His agenda was in line with the majority of the American people. And he was smarter and better than the Republicans. If Obama played chess, Boehner, McConnell, and Ryan played tiddlywinks with mittens on.

It wasn't a fair fight.

But every Obama win came at a long-term cost. The Republican base got angrier and more radicalized. Not just at Obama, but at their own leaders. Faced with this revolt, Republicans like Ryan and McConnell decided to accommodate the crazy instead of confront it.

There are lessons from those victories—even the Pyrrhic ones—for the coming battles against Trumpism. Defeating the hateful, nihilist philosophy that led to Trump is much more important than beating the man.

Can't join 'em, beat 'em. By the end of 2013, it was clear that the fever would not break. We made attempt after attempt to secure bipartisan legislative successes, but each time we got tantalizingly close to progress on broadly popular issues like background checks for gun purchases and immigration reform, the right wing of the Republican Party would revolt.

When the president took off for his annual holiday trip to Hawaii, his frustration with the state of affairs was palpable and understandable. And it was shared by all of us. I felt like I had failed in my new job and not found a better, more successful path for the president.

Searching for answers over the holiday break, I read two books about presidents in their second terms to look for some historical guidance: *The Survivor* by Politico editor John Harris about the Clinton presidency, and *Days of Fire* by *New York Times* correspondent Peter Baker about the second Bush presidency. The books were a revelation to me. A common thread was that at some point in every second term, a president and his team must learn to make an impact without Congress.

Inspired, I sat down and pounded out a memo with my assessment of what went wrong in 2013 and charting a path forward for 2014.

The memo argued that it was time to give up on the Republicans in Congress and chart our own course through executive action. Politics is about understanding the incentives of the various actors, and Republicans had no incentive to ever work with Obama. Their political peril lay in challenges from the rabid anti-Obama base of the party.

Compromise was dead and we pursued it at our own peril. This memo made the rounds of the White House and became the foundation for our "Pen and Phone" strategy of going around Congress. We knew it worked because it made Republicans insane with anger.

The fact of the matter is that this Republican Party is incapable of working with Democrats. Their rabid base will not allow it. This is not what the framers intended, but until the defeat of the cancer at the heart of the Republican Party, confrontation is the only option. Bipartisanship is dead. The

Republicans killed it. If we want to make progress, we've got to beat Republicans at the ballot box, elect more Democrats, and move this country forward without their help.

Go high. At the 2016 Democratic Convention, Michelle Obama described the Democrats' response to Trump's infantile antics and vulgar insults as "when they go low, we go high." In the end, the side that went "low" won the election and a debate ensued in the Democratic Party about whether going "high" was the right response to Trump.

Democrats cannot and should not try to be a paler shade of Trump (i.e., slightly less orange). I can see some of the temptation of this approach. Doing the right thing is hard and can be painful. People like Al Franken resign from Congress for allegations of misconduct, while Donald Trump gets to stay in power. Trump and the Republicans violate norm after norm and lie in ways never seen before in American politics, seemingly without consequence. It's tempting to try their approach after ours failed in 2016, but we cannot give in to that temptation.

First and foremost, it's the wrong thing to do, and call me naïve but I believe—as Barack Obama does—that in the long run, doing the right thing is the best politics. Hopefully, sooner rather than later, Republicans will pay a steep price for embracing Trumpism and cultivating the worst instincts of Americans for short-term political power.

Second, this strategy won't work for Democrats. It's a simple question of math. Democrats do better when more people turn out to vote—there are more Democratic-leaning voters out there. Republicans, on the other hand, have fewer voters, but their voters are more reliable and turn out more often. Therefore, the parties have different strategies.

Democrats need to inspire people to turn out to vote. Republicans want to foster cynicism about politics and government and convince periodic voters that all politicians are terrible and their vote doesn't matter.

Going "low" wouldn't work in the short term and it would do tremendous damage to the long-term health of the party as tens of millions of millennials are making a decision about whether to get involved in politics. Millennials will decide the future of the country. If and only if they vote. They may never vote for the racism, misogyny, and retrograde thinking that dominates Trump's Republican Party, but they won't vote for a Democratic Party that doesn't aspire to a higher purpose either.

Don't cede the argument. The Republican Party is a contradiction. They control every lever of power, yet are on the verge of collapsing from within. There is huge tension at the heart of the party—the base is populist, but the agenda is corporatist. Donald Trump squared this circle by appealing to nativist sentiments and bashing elite institutions like the media and academia. But in the long run, this tension is unsustainable. It's easy to look at the polls that show unwavering support for Trump among his base in the face of incompetence, corruption, and absurdity and give up on those voters. It's true that we may never get them to vote for a Democrat, but we can raise real doubts about their affinity to the Republican Party.

The Message

A core part of the Democratic message needs to be showing that we are the party of the working class—of all races; that we will stand up to special interests and we will fight corruption in Washington and on Wall Street. If this message sounds familiar, it's because it's pretty damn close to Obama's from 2008 and 2012.

In 2016, Democrats up and down the ballot failed to make the argument persuasively enough to convince voters to trust us to fight for them. We can't afford to do that anymore. We don't need to convince all of the voters—80,000 voters in the Rust Belt states of Michigan, Wisconsin, and Pennsylvania decided the election. Winning enough voters to tip those states back into our column seems like a very solvable problem.

The Republican Party is now the Party of Trump. This may be a painful fact for the Republican lobbyists in expensive suits on K Street who believe in supply-side economics and worship at the altar of Ayn Rand. But it's fact. The party of Reagan, Romney, and both Bushes is dead.

All that's left are Donald Trump, Breitbart, and a bunch of mini-Trumps. Even the Republican politicians who argued against Trump's racism, mysogny, and indecency have fallen in line and become avatars of Trumpism (I'm talking to you, Paul Ryan). It's a party based on the idea of white victimization and trolling for the sake of trolling. And the Republican establishment let it happen. They actually encouraged this transformation during the Obama era because they wanted to harness the newly found energy of the Tea Party and to placate those in their base who believed the worst lies they peddled about Obama.

Trump is a symptom of the plague that has infected the Grand Old Party, but he is not the disease itself. Trump didn't take over the party; he is the end result of a party that weaponized racial anxiety to motivate their base during the Obama era. The good news is that this is not a sustainable strategy in a country that is getting more diverse by the minute. Obama's America is the future. Trump's America is the last throes of a bygone era. But we have to survive it.

And I don't just mean that in the sense that we need to prevent the world from blowing up out of pique or incompetence or both. We need our governing institutions and societal norms to survive the Trump era without so much damage that the new normal isn't illegal, unethical behavior and shameless lying.

And while we might be able to survive four years of Trump, I'm not sure we can survive eight years. This means Democrats have no choice but to confront the Republican Party for who they have become and win the next election. A normal win is not enough; it needs to be by a big enough margin to knock the GOP upside the head and convince them that they have to abandon not just Trump but Trumpism.

CHAPTER 8

TWEETING WHILE ROME BURNS

"DELETE YOUR LAST TWEET ASAP," screamed the e-mail from a White House reporter that I saw on my BlackBerry right before I fell into the deep sleep of anesthesia.

I had just committed the greatest Twitter faux pas in recent political history.[1] How it happened and how I ended up in that hospital bed tweeting moments before going under the knife is a great lesson on the dangerous addiction that American politics has to Twitter.

On a mild September night in the swamp of Washington, DC, I was the guest of honor at a dinner organized by a group of White House reporters to grill government officials over copious amounts of wine and overpriced faux French entrées.

The topic this evening was the crisis in Syria and President Obama's response to the reports that Syrian President Bashar al-Assad had used chemical weapons on his own people. To be clear, we were not discussing military strategy, the appropriate global response to the humanitarian crisis spreading like a cancer across the region, or the potential ripple effects of a US missile strike against the Assad government.

---

1   Donald Trump repeatedly retweeting anti-Semitic memes trumps my historic typo.

The topic of debate this evening was one of those weighty subjects that occupy Washington during times of national crisis.

Will the president address the nation seated or standing?

If you think this debate seems trivial, congratulations, you have not yet become a denizen of the swamp of stupidity.

By the fifth year of his presidency, Obama had delivered nearly a dozen televised addresses to the nation from the grounds of the White House. He had announced the death of Bin Laden, celebrated the passage of the Affordable Care Act, and heralded the end of combat operations in Iraq. But he had delivered only two of those speeches from behind his desk in the Oval Office.

The reporters at this dinner—and in Washington more generally—believed that the Oval Office addresses were somehow more presidential than the ones delivered standing in the other rooms of the White House.

"This is a debate from the eighties. I promise you no real people care where the president delivers the speech. They care about what he says and how he says it," I argued with visible exasperation. I had been having this debate for five years, and it was just as dumb on this evening as it had been five years earlier.

What I didn't say was the truth. The two speeches Obama had delivered from his posterior had not gone great. He looked a little awkward, and his delivery was not as crisp or forceful as usual.

In mid-argument, I started to feel weird. The entire right side of my body felt tingly. Sort of like my leg was asleep, but worse. The weirdest part was that my face was tingling.

This had never happened before. I thought I might be having an allergic reaction. I had this vision of my face swelling up. I excused myself to go to the bathroom.

It was surprisingly hard to walk because the muscles in my right leg weren't moving when my brain told them to. I didn't want to let the reporters see me limping, so I did the best I could to avoid it.

Once in the bathroom, I checked myself out in the mirror with dread:

"Thank God," I thought to myself. Staring back at me was not some swollen balloon of a face. Instead, I looked totally normal—or at least like my pale, haggard self with the dark circles under my eyes from a presidential campaign and six years in the White House.

I returned to the table with some relief and reengaged in the debate, which got more heated and less coherent as the wine continued to flow. At one point, I looked down and saw that my loafer had fallen off my right foot, and unbeknownst to me, I had been sitting with my sock touching the concrete patio.

I couldn't move my leg with enough control to put my shoe back on.

Now I was scared. I had a choice: tell these reporters that I might need medical attention and risk reading about that fact in the newspaper, or leave and fend for myself.[2]

"Umm. I hate to do this, but I have to get on a conference call. Thanks so much for dinner," I said suddenly, catching people off guard since we weren't yet through the entrée.

One of the advantages of working in the White House is that no one ever doubts that you have a conference call even at 9:30 at night.[3]

My big fear was that I wouldn't be able to get out of the restaurant on my own power. I gingerly stood up and carefully made my way to the exit. Halfway there, I almost collapsed but caught myself on an unoccupied table. I glanced behind me to see if any of the assembled reporters had noticed, but luckily they had turned their attention and inquiries to Katie Beirne Fallon, another White House aide also attending the dinner.

Once outside, I was nearing a state of panic. I vaguely remembered some long-ago acquired piece of knowledge about tingling

---

2   In hindsight, this was a dumb fear. These were all good people, who would have helped me without using it as fodder for future clicks.

3   I learned later that one attendee thought I was leaving to do my Fantasy Football draft.

limbs meaning the onset of something terrible. I just couldn't remember exactly what the terrible thing was.

Not sure what else to do, I e-mailed Alyssa Mastromonaco and asked her to call me. Alyssa is exactly the right kind of person for a situation like this. She is calm in a crisis and always knows what to do. She has also been my closest friend since the early days of the 2008 campaign. And as the deputy chief of staff of operations, she oversaw the White House doctors who took care of the first family and the White House staff.

In typical Alyssa fashion, she called me in less than a minute.

"Hey, buddy, is everything OK?" Alyssa asked before I could even say hello.[4]

"I need some help. I think I am fine but something weird is happening. Half my body feels like it's asleep and I can't really move my arms and legs."

"OK," she said calmly. "I'm sure this is no big deal, but I'm going to call the Medical Unit and run this by them just to be sure."

Thirty minutes later, I was lying on a gurney at George Washington University Hospital as an army of deadly serious doctors frantically checked my vitals and shouted questions at me. My blood pressure was at a level so high that the nurse audibly gasped when she saw it. Alyssa, who had met me at the hospital, was quickly ushered out of the exam room.

The whole thing was an out-of-body experience. Like watching myself in an episode of *ER*.

I was rushed from the emergency room into an MRI to see if my "stroke-like" symptoms were an actual stroke. The MRI was clear and eventually my blood pressure dropped to normal levels.

I was discharged at 3:00 a.m. with a diagnosis that was essentially the shrug emoji and told to get some sleep and take some time off.

I didn't.

---

4   Alyssa knew that after years of endless conference calls at all hours of the day, I hated talking on the phone more than anything.

There was a meeting in the chief of staff's office that morning to debate if, when, and how the president would address the nation about his decision on Syria. Essentially a repeat of the conversation that had gone so well for me the night before. I wasn't going to miss it even if it meant disobeying doctors' orders.

I was admittedly a bit of a masochistic workaholic. In fact, I had not missed a day of work or school[5] due to illness since my freshman year in high school when a nasty stomach flu caused me to miss one day of school and a basketball game. My team lost, which still bothers me, and I never took another day off.[6]

I took pride in this monomaniacal streak and didn't want it to end. Word of my medical "incident" had already spread across the White House. The president, who was traveling abroad at the time, had called to check on me. I wanted to show people that I was still alive. Proof-of-life attendance, if you will.

After the meeting, I followed Alyssa into her office to vent. As I paced around her spacious office[7] ranting about the dumb debates, political optics, and the Republicans, Alyssa nicely humored me while she caught up on her e-mail with her back to me. This had been a core part of our friendship over the previous eight years, listening to each other complain about things big and small. It was a release valve in the pressure cooker of the White House.

Then mid-rant, I abruptly stopped ranting. Alyssa turned around, took one look at me, and said, "Are you OK?"

"Can you please call Dr. Jones. It's happening again," I muttered. Moments later several members of the White House Medical Unit came sprinting into her office, alarming everyone in their path. A quick diagnosis suggested that I needed to be back in the hospital.

---

5 Apologies to the hundreds of coworkers I infected over the years.
6 It's also safe to say that my presence would not have changed the outcome of that game anyway, but a boy can dream.
7 This would become my office when Alyssa left, and it was some of the best real estate in the West Wing. Spacious with a coveted window and closest to the Oval Office. The last part didn't really mean anything, but people who didn't know any better thought that was important.

I had three thoughts as I was being practically carried by the medical staff down the colonnade next to the Rose Garden with Alyssa in tow.

First, they had to take me out the back and not use the sirens because I didn't want the press who gathered on the North Lawn in front of the White House to hear the noise. Every time there was any sort of incident at the White House, the press went into full freak-out mode for fear that something had happened to the president. I definitely didn't want my mother to learn about her son having a near-death experience from Wolf Blitzer.[8]

Second, I needed Alyssa to tell my new girlfriend what was happening, since I had been hustled by the doctors right past her desk in the West Wing. Howli Ledbetter and I had just started dating a few weeks before this, and after a few playing-it-cool texts from me in the hospital the night before (Nothing to see here just a quick trip to the ER, dinner this weekend?), Alyssa had been keeping her in the loop with actual updates from the doctors so her role as my best friend and medical intermediary was already established.[9] Alyssa put me in the makeshift ambulance and went right back to Howli's desk to talk to her.

"Holy shit, this could be it," I thought with some sense of sad irony that a debate about political optics was going to kill me.[10] Well, that would be a demise fitting of the politics of the time.

I spent the next three days in the Stroke Unit at George Washington University Hospital hooked up to more tubes than I'd imagined was physically possible. The eventual diagnosis was that I had a blood vessel in my brain that would spasm when my blood pressure reached a certain level, shutting down one half of my body. I

---

8   "HAPPENING NOW: TOP OBAMA AIDE RUSHED TO THE HOSPITAL," seemed like a bit much.

9   I had two goals that night: (1) don't die, and (2) don't eff up my chances with Howli. Two for two isn't bad.

10 Part of my medical regimen is fewer salty foods, no diet soda, and no getting worked up over optics debates. I am better at adhering to the first two.

was prescribed a cocktail of blood pressure medicines, a better diet, more sleep, and less stress.

When I returned to work, things had only gotten crazier for Obama. The Republicans had shut down the government in an ill-fated and inept attempt to repeal Obamacare. We were in the middle of a political and PR battle about who got blamed for the shutdown. If we lost, it would have been crippling to the president and millions of Americans would lose their health care. Needless to say, this environment was not consistent with the doctor's prescription of more sleep and less stress.

Before too long, the symptoms returned—although more minor than before. At first, I hesitated to tell the doctor because this was a make-or-break moment for Obama's second term and I didn't want to be taken off the field. I had pushed really hard—against the advice of some—for Obama to adopt a maximalist position in the shutdown negotiations. Obama had spent the last three years in a never-ending series of budget battles with Republicans, and this was going to be the war to end all wars. If Obama forced the Republicans to concede, it would establish a level of governing normalcy for the rest of his term, but if he failed, the presidency effectively would be over. I felt like it was pretty shitty to push for this high-risk strategy and then go check myself into a hospital.

The symptoms, while still not as bad as before, were getting less minor and more frequent. Finally, during a strategic debate in the chief of staff's office, I was in the middle of making what I'm sure was a very important point when I started to lose feeling in my face. Straining to keep my train of thought, I mumbled through the end of my argument and then got up and walked right to the White House Medical Unit to see the doctor. Within the hour, I was checking into the hospital for three days of tests.

Only seven people in the White House knew where I was— Alyssa, Denis McDonough, the chief of staff, Jennifer Palmieri, who replaced me as communications director, Barack Obama, Clay Dumas, who worked for me, and Howli.

My previous hospital visit had generated some unwelcome media coverage—so much so that CNN did a story off a tweet that said I was back to playing pickup basketball.

I hadn't even told my mom.[11] I was going back into the hospital and I really didn't want her to find out from the press. Since I wasn't going to be in meetings, quickly responding to e-mails, or talking to reporters, I was concerned my absence would be noted. I developed a proof-of-life strategy.

Tweeting.

This was not a doctor-approved strategy since high blood pressure was undoubtedly somehow related to my mysterious condition. Twitter is many things, but relaxing is not one of them. Regardless, I hatched a plan to send a few tweets a day so that it seemed like I was still in the game.

The primary purpose of the hospital stay was to conduct every test under the sun to figure out why I was having these mini-strokes and so we could develop a course of treatment. On my second day in the hospital, I was getting my liver biopsied, which is a minor surgery that requires anesthesia. Because there was a decent wait for the doctors to arrive, I brought my BlackBerry with me to catch up on e-mails and perhaps even send some tweets. To give you a full visual, not only was I cloaked in a hospital gown, but I also had my head wrapped in a turban that was covered in electrodes and connected to a beeping machine to see if I had epilepsy (which was a leading theory of some of my doctors).

After being given the anesthesia, I saw a tweet from *New York Times* reporter Jonathan Martin:

Glad @NBCFirstRead acknowledged a major factor in polarization: How Americans get information, rise of the Internet—@JMartNYT

I responded:

@JMartNYT It's a very smart point and a massive factor in political polarization—@Pfeiffer44

---

11   Mom, if you are reading this, I should have told you.

Mission accomplished—tweet sent. Maybe it was the anesthesia talking, but I couldn't leave well enough alone. The idea that political polarization is equally the fault of Democrats and Republicans drives me insane, and that notion was implicit in the original tweet.

My intention was to tweet Also a bigger factor on the right. I hit Send and put my BlackBerry down next to me in the hospital gurney and waited to fall into a deep, chemically induced sleep.

For once in my life, my obsessive-compulsive phone addiction worked to my advantage: As my eyes were rolling back into my head, I took one last look at my phone. That's when I saw the e-mail: DELETE YOUR LAST TWEET ASAP.

My stomach sank. It was the worst mistake I could have made. See, the B key and the N key are right next to each other, and I have fat thumbs even when not under the influence of heavy medication.

My tweet read: @JMartNYT also a n%@@#r factor on the right.

In that moment, it was a battle between my abject panic over a possibly career-ending and deeply offensive mistake and the very strong drugs flowing through my system. Luckily, I managed to hit Delete and send an apology tweet just as I went under.

I woke up sometime later with a hole in my side and a deep sense of anxiety from what I thought was a dream about the Twitter typo to end all typos. When I picked up my phone and saw multiple missed calls and dozens of e-mails from reporters and colleagues, I knew it wasn't a dream.

For a few days, I became a well-deserved object of ridicule. Most of the reporters and even some of my Republican counterparts were generous in their interpretation. The conservative propaganda machine and the Republican Twitter trolls who were three years from putting #MAGA in their bios less so. There was a parade of soon-to-be Trump supporters who would tweet that my typo meant that I was a secret racist. Working to elect our first black president was a strange life choice for a closet racist, but whatever.

I never told anyone the circumstances of the typo to end all typos. I didn't think anyone would believe that I was dumb enough to tweet under anesthesia, but if they did, that probably wasn't a good thing either.

When I returned to the White House a day or so later, I was very anxious about my first encounter with Obama. I was called down to the Oval Office early that first day back. I walked in with trepidation. The whole thing was so mortifying, and rehashing how I'd tweeted the N-word with the first African American president seemed like an unbearable experience.

Obama didn't bring up my typo in that meeting or in any meeting in the years since—not even as a joke. Just one of the many signs of the core decency of the man. Presidents have much bigger problems than the stupidity of their aides, so in fairness, it may never have crossed his mind again. But I like to believe that he knew it was a mistake, that I had learned my lesson, and there was no need to make me feel worse about it. And for that, I am eternally grateful.

The fact that I couldn't put Twitter down long enough to get my own liver biopsied is a sign of the times. American politics is addicted to Twitter. It is the primary forum for politicians to communicate, reporters to pontificate, and partisans to mobilize. That addiction has only gotten deeper and more dangerous in the years since my tweet.

PUTTING POLITICS ON STEROIDS

Twitter is a performance-enhancing drug for politics. It has made all the good parts of politics a little better and all the bad parts much, much worse.

The good parts of Twitter may seem hard to fathom in the Trump era, when America and the world wake up every day and grab their phone or tablet, open the app, and look with dread to see what insane thing the president has tweeted. It's not absurd to think that the next world war will start with an intemperate tweet. WWIII aside, Twitter is an important tool in democratizing information. Anyone, anywhere with a phone can break news or share photos or videos of what is happening in the world. Much of what we know about what is happening in far-flung parts of the world or war zones like Syria or in totalitarian countries like those in the Middle East comes bubbling up from the Twitter ecosystem. An army of citizen journalists who document the stories and the places previously ignored by the mainstream media is a positive development.

Twitter also removes a layer between politicians and the public—creating a closer relationship that is not filtered through the mainstream media and potentially offering an opportunity for conversation or engagement that is normally reserved for elites and the lucky few who find themselves in a town hall. These are all positive advances for politics and journalism.

On the other hand, Twitter makes politics louder, meaner, and faster. It distorts reality, hypes the trivial, and obscures the important. Thanks to Twitter, we've become a nation of pundits. And I say this as a card-carrying but self-hating member of the pundit class—that is a very bad thing.

Presuming we don't all die because an errant tweet starts a nuclear war between a nation run by an irrational authoritarian despot and North Korea, understanding how and why politics became addicted to Twitter is key to understanding politics today.[12]

TWITTER TAKES HOLD

I've never done meth,[13] but I imagine the experience is much like using Twitter.

You start it casually because you heard good things; next thing you know, you have been up for ninety-six hours, have lost all your teeth, and are living in a shopping cart outside the local supermarket.

---

12 Before the faux outrage machine flares up, this is a joke. I am not comparing Trump to Kim Jong Un, the murderous North Korean dictator. I am comparing him to a generic irrational authoritarian despot.
13 I make no promises if Trump is reelected in 2020.

The irony of Twitter's importance in the Obama era of politics and its utter dominance in the Trump era is that in the 2008 campaign I never tweeted, I never looked at Twitter, and I am pretty sure I didn't know it existed. After Twitter had blown up and I had dedicated an unhealthy portion of my life to consuming and thinking about Twitter, I would often tell people that the 2008 Obama campaign had not sent a single tweet. After telling this story in about three dozen interviews and panel discussions, Teddy Goff, who was one of the campaign's digital gurus, e-mailed me to very nicely tell me that I had no idea what I was talking about.

The campaign had tweeted and had a Twitter strategy; I just hadn't been paying attention. But no one else had either. Twitter wasn't just an afterthought. It wasn't even a thought.

That changed pretty quickly once we were in the White House.

Some of the more tech-savvy White House reporters started live-tweeting the White House briefing in early 2009.

At the time, I found this incredibly annoying. Robert Gibbs and his team spent hours prepping for every possible question under the sun. They took the briefing incredibly seriously and here these reporters were tweeting witty asides instead of listening to what Gibbs had to say.[14] The reporters would tweet back and forth to one another, as opposed to the public, because frankly there hadn't been sufficient adoption for Twitter to be a means to communicate news to the masses. Instead, it was brand building.

At first, we didn't even know the reporters were tweeting about us because Twitter, along with Facebook and Gmail, was blocked on all White House computers. The IT folks believed them to be vulnerable to hacking from foreign powers like Russia—just to pick one random example from around the globe.

Eventually, we had to make a special appeal to allow our research staff to get access so that they could send tweets of interest around to the rest of us. Even as Twitter was picking up steam in the brief-

---

14   Get off my lawn.

ing room, I continued to think Twitter was pretty dumb. It felt like a bunch of media and tech types talking to one another in a conversation that could not be more removed from how the American public was consuming and interpreting news.

But as time went on, more and more reporters started using it, so there was really no choice—the White House had to get in the game. The media was our constituency, and we thought of ourselves as cool early adopter types. Gibbs led the way by being the first senior White House staffer to get an account—@PressSec.

This turned out to be a very big deal. It was rightly viewed as a major innovation in how White Houses communicate with the public. On the night of the announcement, I watched the followers pour into Gibbs's account, and before long, he had well over 100,000.

Pretty soon Gibbs was communicating directly with an audience nearly as large as some cable news shows. He didn't need the press to decide what people heard or saw.

Twitter was the first real opportunity to cut out the middleman and go straight to the American people with a few keystrokes. The public was the one to decide if the information was interesting, valuable, and relevant to their lives. This was a critical development because the media's bias is toward conflict, politics, and what's new to them. The public, which doesn't consume every utterance of the president or the minute-by-minute ups and downs of legislation, often wants different information than what the media provides them.

After pulling some strings, I "persuaded" the IT overlords to get me a Twitter account—@Pfeiffer44—the "44" because Obama was the forty-fourth president.

I didn't start tweeting right away. I just used my account to monitor what was happening on Twitter. I would see a White House reporter tweeting something snarky or factually incorrect and I would run down to the lower press office, where the assistant press secretaries sat, and bark at them:

"Chuck Todd just tweeted something wrong about our housing policy. We gotta fix it."

"Jake Tapper is complaining that we didn't do a press conference with the leader of Poland because we didn't want to take health care questions. Can someone call him and explain it's because POTUS had to go to Walter Reed?"

"Everyone is whining because Obama's event is an hour late."

However, this was not a sustainable approach. Mainly because I was so annoying that the staff, which included *Pod Save America*'s Tommy Vietor, were soon going to bludgeon me to death with my own BlackBerry.

As a matter of self-preservation, we got all the press staff Twitter accounts. But they weren't allowed to tweet. Other than the press secretary's, the only public Twitter account was the official White House account—@WhiteHouse—which tweeted only basic announcements.

The President will begin speaking in the Rose Garden at 12:10 EST—@WhiteHouse

Read more about President Obama's plan to help American homeowners here—@WhiteHouse

The challenge with Twitter was that it had great potential as a communications tool, but to use it most effectively, you had to take more risks than most politicians and political operatives were comfortable with. High risk, high reward.

My initial approach was low risk, no reward.

Since no one else wanted the job, I designated myself the person who signed off on who in the White House could have a Twitter account, and I was being a real dick about who could get access.

The White House chief technology officer (CTO) came to my office on multiple occasions to plead for his own account so that he could tweet out news about all the work his team was doing to bring the federal government into the age of the Internet. His argument was incredibly reasonable—Twitter was how the tech community communicated, and it undermined his case that the White House was innovating when the person doing the innovating wasn't allowed on Twitter.

He wasn't wrong, but I continued to deny him out of a strong sense of risk aversion for the White House. Every person who works at the White House, from the press secretary to the person who organizes tours for school groups, represents the president. Whether they are speaking to a reporter, tweeting, or talking too loud at a restaurant, they are White House spokespeople. Everything they say can be construed as official White House policy.

One wrong word or misfired tweet could take the president off message for days and potentially permanently damage an individual's career.[15] Being a public face of the White House was a high-wire act, especially with the Republicans and their patrons at Fox News chomping at the bit to find any cudgel with which to beat Obama over the head. It was unduly risky and put an unfair burden on people who were not spokespeople by trade. This was a lesson I learned the hard way a couple of times.

In 2011, I decided to come out of the shadows and start tweeting. The political conversation had fully moved on to Twitter at that point, and it made sense for me to use my position as communications director to shape that conversation by trying to pull the curtain back on White House strategy. Reporters spend a ton of time and energy trying to intuit the reasons behind why politicians do certain things, and most of the time they are wrong. So why not just tell them by tweeting out some strategic thoughts? The idea would be to tweet things that seemed more authentic and showed more personality than what people had seen to date from the official spokespeople accounts. After a couple of years of mainlining Twitter, I thought I knew what the people wanted.

I kicked off my tweeting by doing an official Twitter Q&A about the State of the Union speech. Most of the questions were strictly policy related, and since I got to pick the ones that I answered, it was pretty hard to screw up. One of the first questions

---

15   This notion seems quaint now that Donald Trump got elected president because of and not in spite of his long history of embarrassing tweets.

submitted was from my buddy Chris, who played on my rec league basketball team and with whom I shared my Georgetown basketball season tickets. Chris was just messing around, and he asked me,

@pfeiffer44 Georgetown laying 8.5 to St. John's. Who do you like?

I started to type an answer and then realized, as a White House official, I probably shouldn't condone illegal gambling. This is exactly why a trained professional like myself should have a Twitter account and amateurs like the CTO should be protected from themselves.

The following Saturday I was sitting in my apartment, doing a little work after a very late night in the White House, when Chris tweeted at me again, asking about the Georgetown basketball game against Villanova University scheduled to start a few hours later:

@pfeiffer44 gtown-nova. What's your confidence level?

Without thinking too much, I responded:

Tough game on the road, but Nova is very beatable if the guards shoot well—@pfeiffer44

This tweet did not go over well.[16]

The Middle East was in even more turmoil than usual this Saturday morning. Pro-democracy protesters were being brutalized in Egypt. Twitter was one of the only ways the protesters could tell the world about what has happening. The Obama White House hadn't made an official statement, and here was the top communications official tweeting about a meaningless regular season Big East basketball game.

People were pissed at the White House for not doing or saying more about what was happening in the Middle East, and I had tweeted myself into being the target of that anger. The Twitter hordes turned on me quickly, and then some of the reporters on Twitter started tweeting about the reaction to my tweet. Chagrined

---

16   And not just because my basketball analysis was rudimentary at best.

and worried I was going to be in trouble at work, I apologized. Luckily the anger faded before too long and before too much damage had been done.

The next week when the CTO stopped me in the hallway to make another appeal, it was a short conversation and he returned to his office in the EEOB without a Twitter account.

Despite my errors, I ultimately let loose of the reins, and in the months that followed I gave a Twitter account to almost anyone who wanted one, with the freedom to tweet.

My fears about White House aides making errors that would throw the White House off message were totally unfounded. By 2013, the entire political conversation had moved on to Twitter. Every reporter, politician, and observer was sharing their views and having their views shaped by what was said on Twitter. To participate in that conversation and perhaps bend it in a more favorable direction, we needed to flood the zone with more people out there tweeting, retweeting, and sharing what the Obama White House was thinking and doing.

TWITTER AS THE FUN HOUSE MIRROR OF POLITICS

In those first few years, Twitter seemed like a great net positive for our political discourse. It made politics more approachable and democratic (small D). Some of the conversations between reporters and their sources were happening out in public for all to see, instead of in smoke-filled DC bars.

But it wasn't till the night of the first debate between Barack Obama and Mitt Romney in 2012 that I realized that Twitter had also fundamentally changed politics in ways that were disturbing and predictive of what was to come in 2016.

On that evening, I was in the temporary debate "war room" in the Obama campaign headquarters in Chicago. Most of the campaign senior staff were in Denver with Obama and preparing to rush into the spin room after the debate to offer their take on why Obama had won in a high-speed, anachronistic effort to shape coverage. I had been dispatched to Chicago to help with the rapid-response effort since I wasn't needed in Denver. I wasn't really needed in Chicago either—the campaign rapid-response team had their shit more than together and did not need a White House babysitter. But the idea of sitting on my couch like some civilian on the most important night of the campaign was more than my ego or blood pressure could possibly take, so I happily accepted my assignment in Chicago.

A subset of the research and communications team gathered in the conference room, which had been outfitted with TVs and Ethernet cords, just in case the Wi-Fi went out and crippled our operation. Even before the debate began, the room smelled pretty rank—a combination of too many bodies and not enough ventilation.

Heading into the debate, I was bouncing off the walls with nervous energy. Historically, incumbent presidents lose the first debate. It's hard to prep appropriately with the overflowing inbox of the leader of the free world. Plus, there's something about standing onstage next to a president that elevates the challenger.

Romney had also been getting the shit kicked out of him for months. The press was saying that if Obama won the debate, the race would be over. The combination of raised expectations for Obama, lowered expectations for Romney, and my Spidey sense telling me that there was no way the media was going to let the campaign be over with a month to go added to my nerves. I knew they would never leave all those clicks on the proverbial table.

As I walked out of the pre-meeting, the dinner spread was being set up.

"What the fuck is this?" I said to the nearest staffer. Before me was a massive buffet from Chipotle.

My state of near panic was totally unrelated to any possibility of a life-threatening E. coli infection.[17]

It was due to the long-running tradition in Obama World that on big nights—election nights, State of the Unions, and debates—we ate chicken tenders for good luck. This started in 2008, because the chain restaurant Houlihan's, which makes phenomenal Buffalo chicken tenders, was in our building. If Michelin knew anything, Houlihan's would have a star for these tenders. We ate the tenders for lunch on the day of Obama's shocking landslide victory in the South Carolina primary and never looked back. When we got to the White House, we substituted Houlihan's with the chicken tenders from the White House mess for special occasions. Superstition abounds in politics, perhaps because so often your fate is decided by things well beyond your control. I took this superstition so seriously that I would walk around the White House communications offices on the night of big speeches to make sure everyone had tenders on their desk. My wife even sent me chicken tenders on our wedding day to make sure we got our marriage off to the right start.

Given all that, you can imagine my horror at arriving to find Chipotle on the menu for dinner.

The debate started slow. Obama seemed tight and he had the tired look that any of his close aides know well. Playing off his campaign pledge, we used to joke that Obama was the "most transparent" president in history, because if he was tired, he couldn't hide it. Romney, on the other hand, was on his game. After months of being a punching bag, he showed up ready to punch back. Romney was a man debating like he had nothing to lose; Obama was playing not to lose, which is a strategy in the history of sports, wars, and political campaigns that never works.

I was focused on the combination of what was happening on TV;

---

17   I don't care what burrito snobs in my adopted home of California say, Chipotle is delicious.

in my e-mail in-box, where there was a steady stream of fact-checks and press responses being circulated for approval; the chat room where we were debating possible responses; and the open conference call line with the staff onsite at the debate. Due to this sensory overload, I was not as focused on the actual debate as I should have been.

But my sense was that Obama had started slow and was not delivering Romney the ass-kicking that I'd hoped for. It was a B performance for Obama once he hit his stride after the first ten minutes or so. Romney was certainly aggressive, but he was a little like an overeager Chihuahua with great hair. He was also lying left and right about Obama's record and his own policies—surely that would hurt him with the figure-skating judges/reporters who score debates.

I was concerned, but not panicked.

Then I checked Twitter. Things were not going well there.

It was a massacre.

The onetime conservative columnist turned ardent Obama supporter Andrew Sullivan was melting down.

How is Obama's closing so fucking sad, confused, lame? He choked. He lost. He may even have lost election tonight.—Andrew Sullivan (@sullydish)

Sullivan was not alone in his assessment, but his reaction was influencing the tone and tenor of the Twitter hot takes. The idea of one of Obama's strongest and smartest supporters panicking shifted the narrative from a middling performance to a disastrous one. Forty minutes into the ninety-minute debate, Ben Smith, the editor in chief of BuzzFeed News, a media company that didn't exist when Obama started running for president, tweeted a story declaring Romney as the winner of the debate.

Political pundits and reporters were savaging Obama's performance, and Obama supporters were in full panic mode because of the savaging, and then reporters would get more savage because of the panic from Obama supporters. Both sides kept egging each other on until the conventional wisdom was that Obama had delivered the worst debate performance since Adam Sandler in *Billy Madison*.[18]

After the debate, the campaign staffers and surrogates were rushed into the spin room to talk to the assembled media and appear on cable news, but it was too late. The judgment had been rendered and it had happened on Twitter.

Additionally, what happened on Twitter didn't stay on Twitter. When the debate ended, Chris Matthews—clearly influenced by the hot takes on Twitter—went on MSNBC and completely melted down. The disappointment and panic were oozing from his pores as he declared, "I don't know what he was doing out there. I know he likes to say he doesn't watch cable television, but maybe he should start. Maybe he should start. I don't know how he let Romney get away with the crap he threw at him tonight about Social Security."

This was a stark change to how politics and political coverage happened in the four years since Obama was last on a debate stage. Previously, the media would watch the debate in isolation in a large adjacent room at the debate site. And while they would be inundated by press releases from the campaigns via e-mail or runners, they made their judgment in isolation and they had no way of knowing what their colleagues, political experts, or the voters thought about what was happening until hours or even days later.

Twitter created a feeding frenzy that changed how the reporters viewed and covered the debate, which in turn affected how voters watched and judged the debate. Perception became reality and it all happened in thirty minutes. Obama went from cruising to reelection to being in danger of losing, and Twitter was a major contributor to that fact.

---

18 Look it up, millennials.

@POTUS

By 2015, most of the White House press and political and policy staffers had Twitter accounts with thousands and in some cases tens of thousands of followers. The heads and deputies of the Domestic Policy Councils had Twitter accounts, the president's photographer had a Twitter account, and the CTO (finally) had a Twitter account.

But there was still one notable person who didn't: Barack Obama.

There was @BarackObama, which was the Twitter handle that had been around from the very beginning in 2008 and at the time had the third-largest Twitter following in the world, right behind Katy Perry and Justin Bieber.[19] But that handle was owned by the campaign, and due to a very strict and cautious reading of laws written long before Twitter was invented, our lawyers wouldn't let Obama tweet from that account in his role as president.[20]

Therefore, the president of the United States, who could order an armada to sail across the world with one phone call, was not allowed to tweet. Periodically, the White House would send tweets from the official @WhiteHouse account and sign them "BO," which indicated that those particular Tweets were in his voice. It was just weird.

First, "BO" is the name of his dog, so it could be very confusing as to why one of the two Obama dogs had so much to say about health care and tax policy.

Second, that's not how Twitter works. You either have your own account or you don't. Guest appearances are not a thing.

---

19   Taylor Swift and Lady Gaga were numbers 4 and 5. I'm not sure what this says about Twitter or the musical tastes of the online global population.

20   I would note that Trump tweets from his @RealDonaldTrump account all the time, and if he is in jail by the time of the publishing of this book, it will not be because of which account he tweeted from, but that's neither here nor there.

Right after the 2012 election, the digital strategies staff, which I was technically responsible for,[21] came to see me with this problem.

Twitter was critical to getting our message out, and our biggest weapon was on the sidelines. Since it is never a good idea to come to a meeting with a problem and not a solution, they proposed the creation of an @POTUS account that Obama would tweet from periodically. This account would belong to the Office of the President, not Barack Obama personally, so that the next president would take the account and all the accrued followers once Obama left office.

This was really a good idea in theory, but it had some complications in execution.

Would it cause confusion for the 50 million or so people who already thought they were following Barack Obama on Twitter?

How often would Obama be expected to tweet?

Were we going to put Twitter on his BlackBerry?

Would the Secret Service even allow it?

We were in the middle of preparing for the second inaugural, trying to prevent a massive tax increase, and attempting to pass legislation to mandate background checks for gun purchases. The presidential Twitter account was a nice to-do, but not a must-have.

Every few months the digital team would bring it up with me, and every time I would demur. Most of my reticence came from prioritization. It was going to be a real pain in the ass to get this done, and I didn't have the energy to push this through the system. The second term was not off to an awesome start—our legislative agenda was stalled, the president's poll numbers were nearing the toilet, a couple of yahoos in a far-flung IRS office were accused of targeting conservatives, and Edward Snowden had walked out of the NSA with a thumb drive of all the nation's secrets.

Getting three dozen people to sign off on getting the Twitter app

---

21   They reported to me in the organizational structure but were more than a communications function and serviced the whole White House and most of the government.

installed on the presidential BlackBerry seemed like more than the system could bear at that moment.

I also wasn't sure this was a good idea.

Obama would need to tweet in a way that was authentic or at least authentic enough that it felt stylistically different from a typical presidential statement. Jumping into Twitter and failing at it would be embarrassing.

Obama was Internet savvy, as far as presidents go. He was the first president to spend most of his adult life using the Internet like a normal human as opposed to being an overly staffed politician who had interns and aides to read and write their e-mails and do research tasks that most Americans turn to Google for. When I went to work for Senator Evan Bayh in 2005, he had sent one e-mail from his phone in his life. It was to his chief of staff and it said, "I don't think this is safe."[22]

This is why Obama fought hard to keep his BlackBerry and have the ability to e-mail a subset of his aides as well as family and friends. But he was also the social media equivalent of the *Saturday Night Live* character Unfrozen Caveman Lawyer. He became president before people of his generation started really using Facebook, Twitter, and Instagram so he never spent any real time on those platforms to understand their language and culture.

Other than a couple of Twitter town halls, where he answered questions on the White House or campaign Twitter accounts,[23] Obama had never spent any time reading Twitter, but everything he had heard made him think it was some sort of dystopian hellhole. To make a point about how the media environment had changed for the worse, Obama would often gesture toward me and say with palpable pity, "My communications guy has to spend all day on Twitter."

---

22   He had a good point.

23   Ever competitive, Obama was very proud of his ability to get a twoosh, which is a tweet that is exactly 140 characters on the first try. This was a little too Rain Man–esque for my tastes, but he loved it.

I also didn't want Obama to start regularly reading Twitter for the same reason I appreciated the fact that he didn't regularly watch cable news. It could be a major distraction from the tasks at hand. I could just imagine Obama sending me tweets from White House reporters that annoyed him and I would spend the rest of my days playing a game of Internet whack-a-mole.

I kept thinking this was one of those ideas that looked great on Day 1, when everyone got excited about a presidential Twitter account. But by Day 2, it would be a hassle.

For months I continued to avoid the decision, generally getting more annoyed each time the digital strategies team did their job and brought it up with me.

Finally, in 2015, right before I left the White House, I pushed aside my indolence and reticence and started the process for launching the @POTUS handle. To be perfectly honest, I was motivated a little by senioritis. It if turned out to be a disaster or Obama became obsessed with his mentions, it wouldn't be my problem to deal with. I planned to be sitting on a beach in Thailand or Vietnam by the time his Twitter account went live.

The launch and everything that happened afterward proved without question once and for all that it was the right thing to do. @POTUS was huge news and changed how presidents would communicate with the public going forward.

Little did we know that we were handing matches to a subsequent presidential baby to burn down the body politic and possibly the world.

TWITTER IN THE AGE OF TRUMP

A few months after Trump took office, I was at one of those gatherings of Silicon Valley types and politicos where we were supposed to be planning the "resistance," but we were really just having yet another endless conversation about how we got into this mess.

In this meeting, someone brought up the idea of starting a movement to push Twitter to ban Trump from their platform. The initial argument was that Trump had violated Twitter's policies against hate speech and bullying. This led to a heated debate about free speech and the dangers of Silicon Valley making Trump a Twitter martyr. The underlying assumption of the whole discussion was that without Twitter, Trump would not have won.

I believe this. Without Twitter, there is no President Trump. He managed to use the platform to dominate the political conversation to the point where his Republican primary opponents could never get enough oxygen to mount a real challenge and Hillary Clinton was forced to respond to him so often that her own positive narrative fell by the wayside. But it's more than that. Twitter facilitated a coarser, less substantive political culture that significantly benefited Trump, who is at his very core a Twitter troll.

Hillary was a serious policy wonk who didn't love to put her guard down. She was a politician from a time before Twitter—and frankly before the Internet. Throughout the 2016 campaign, Twitter never felt like a natural fit for her. She had never participated in and consumed Facebook, Twitter, or Instagram like a civilian.

This put her at a disadvantage against Trump, who is legitimately good at Twitter, because for good or for ill, he is his authentic self on Twitter. And that is what the platform calls for.

Authenticity is the coin of the Twitter realm.

The second argument for taking Twitter away from President Trump is that denying him access to it would somehow make America safer. After Trump got into Twitter fights with Ted Cruz's wife, Megyn Kelly, and the Pope, the Democrats argued that Trump could stumble into a war through some ill-advised tweets.

But to borrow a flawed and morally bankrupt argument: Twitter doesn't start wars; unstable presidents with Twitter start wars. Kicking Trump off Twitter, which Twitter would never do, wouldn't

solve the problem. Trump says dumb, dangerous things, and sometimes he says them on Twitter. If there were no Twitter, Trump
would still act like a maniac with verbal diarrhea at press conferences or during his frequent appearances on the state-sponsored
television network also known as Fox News.

Twitter doesn't make Trump act like a fool; he is a fool who has
Twitter on his phone.

Despite Twitter's paltry returns on Wall Street, it is here to stay,
and it will only be more important in politics going forward.

This means that Democrats, the media, and Twitter need to adjust
their approach to reflect a new and dangerous era in politics and try to
prevent authoritarian despots like Trump from gaming the new system.

If progressives have any hope of taking back this country, we all
have to get better at Twitter. As gross as this feels, we can and should
learn some (but not all) lessons from Trump's Twitter strategy. And admit it, there is a certain appeal to beating him at his own game.

Tweet yo self. Jon Favreau always urges politicians to "talk like a
human." Favreau's point is that too many politicians talk like they
think politicians should sound—poll-tested mush with slogans and
phrases that pollsters said people would like—and deliver speeches
written by speechwriters with visions of Kennedy ghosts in their
heads.[24] In the end, they sound more like Mayor Quimby from *The
Simpsons* than JFK.

Obama, who certainly had the ability to hit high rhetorical
flourishes, avoided sound bites and clichés like the plague. This
Favreau Maxim extends to Twitter, too: Tweet like a human. Be
normal, be funny, be a little snarky, use a meme, be like everyone
else on Twitter. Most politicians have their tweets written by their
staff and approved by a committee of people including a lawyer
and a pollster. This fact is obvious to the voting public, which has

---

24 I guess I think it is cool that bad Democratic speechwriters will try and
    fail to bite Obama's style in the coming years. Better to be imitated than
    forgotten.

a great bullshit detector. Trump, on the other hand, wakes up and tweets his feelings. He howls at the TV via Twitter like any political junkie or sports fan. One of the lessons of 2016 is you can't fake Twitter. People have no interest in following or engaging with content that doesn't feel authentic. The best political follows on Twitter are those who clearly write their own tweets.

Some of the politicians with natural Twitter talent include established stars like @BernieSanders, @MaxineWaters, and @SenWarren; rising stars like @JasonKander, @brianschatz, and @ChrisMurphyCT; and nonagenarian @JohnDingell. The next president not named Trump will be good at Twitter.

Break news. In the Obama White House, we loved to use our Twitter accounts to break news. By going around the media, we could give the public the feeling that they had as much right to the information as the professional reporters who covered the White House. Twitter democratized the distribution of information. We never fully committed to this strategy because we tried to find a balance between using this new tool and managing our relationship with the White House Press Corps, who did not appreciate losing their role as the middleman. Trump took this to the next level in both the campaign and the White House. If you want to know what Trump is doing or saying, all you have to do is follow his Twitter account. Even though it's a little—OK, a lot—like a car crash, America can't turn away from Trump's Twitter.

Caution to the wind. Pre-Twitter politics rewarded risk aversion; Twitter rewards risk taking because it rewards authenticity and interestingness. There is an inherent risk in being yourself in politics, which is why so many politicians speak in platitudes and avoid taking positions for fear of pissing off the wrong people. I'm not sure that was ever a good political strategy, but it certainly isn't a good strategy on Twitter, which can have a vicious, mob mentality reaction to inauthenticity. Putting down one's guard—particularly in a hypercritical place like Twitter—can be profoundly uncomfortable for a politician. But there is no option—Twitter is the medium and language of politics. Important note: You don't have to be an asshole, but you do have to be interesting. Too often people on Twitter (including you know who) confuse the two.

Twitter has also changed political journalism in ways that enable Trump and his ilk to game the system, and the media needs to adopt new rules to protect their important role in the process:

Report first, analyze later. Back in the old days of newspapers, there were three types of people who wrote about politics:

- Reporters, who told the story of what happened. This is classic objective, "Just the facts, ma'am," Joe Friday–style reporting.
- Columnists, who offered up clearly demarcated opinions. Think George Will, Maureen Dowd, and Charles Blow. The newspapers thought it was so important that these pieces not be confused with the reporting function of the paper that they put these columns on an entirely separate page.
- Analysts, the most senior reporters with the most experience, who were periodically given the opportunity to write a piece analyzing why something happened or was likely to happen. This privilege was earned from decades of experience and granted to the smartest reporters, and this work was clearly labeled "Analysis" because it fell somewhere between objective reporting and subjective columns.

Twitter changed all that because it was for a long time a failed state, ungoverned by the normal rules of journalism and ignored by the powers that be at the papers. Reporters opined and even the most junior reporter was free to offer their political analysis of the most complex situations. Sometimes this analysis crossed the line into opining. The downside of this approach is that it erodes the authority of fact-based reporting and makes journalists no different from the talking heads that populate cable TV networks. When the lines between facts and opinions blur, it provides an opening for those who view facts as obstacles and not pillars to an argument.

Just in case I was too subtle: yes, I am talking about Donald J. Trump and his MAGA minions.

Don't fuck up. In 2013, I was slated to do all five Sunday shows to respond to allegations about political interference at the IRS. This was my first grilling on the Sunday shows, and it was going to be a high-wire act. I e-mailed David Plouffe to get some advice on how to handle this challenge. His response:

"Don't Fuck Up."

I would offer this same helpful advice to the media. Twitter makes it easier to get information to the public. This faster, easier process also means more mistakes—bad reporting, misunderstood information, and less context. Errors are not new in journalism. There is the famous case of *60 Minutes* using forged documents about George W. Bush's military service. There is the *New York Times'* scrutiny-free regurgitation of cherry-picked intelligence about WMD in Iraq. And there are garden-variety mistakes that come from the fact that journalism is a human enterprise. But Twitter has removed the checks and balances of the editorial process. All a reporter has to do is type out 280 characters of info and hit Tweet. Less oversight means more mistakes, and the media has been slow to recognize that a mistake on Twitter ends up being much more consequential than one made in the paper or on the air. The Twitter error circulates via retweets long after it is ever fixed. These errors provide a cudgel for the Right to discredit accurate reporting about the flaws in their policies and the foibles of their president.

Now everyone makes mistakes, but media outlets need to treat mistakes on their Twitter feed the way they would treat those errors if they appeared in the paper or were broadcast on the air. Fix them fast and be transparent about how they happened.

Twitter the platform also has a lot of work to do to protect itself and the public from the worst elements of our society.

Stop the bullying and ban the trolls. Twitter the company has utterly failed to police their own platform. Scroll through the mentions of a woman or a person of color on Twitter and you are bound to be horrified by what you read. There is racism, misogyny, and threats of violence and sexual assault. This problem existed long before Trump, but his rise enabled and empowered far-right hate accounts to be more public. Twitter has even verified some of these hate mongers, giving them the vaunted "blue checkmark."

Twitter has been impossibly slow to act in part because kicking a bunch of people off the platform would exacerbate the problem of anemic user growth. But this is a solvable problem:

- Enforce their policies against hate speech and bullying with a consistent zero tolerance policy.
- End the anonymity granted to users. There is no valid reason to let people spew hate anonymously. Much of the hate, abuse, and trolling would immediately disappear if people had to do it for the world to see using their real names.
- Ban hate groups identified by the Southern Poverty Law Center. I am sympathetic to Twitter's views about the First Amendment, but the Constitution doesn't grant people the right to use Twitter for their speech.
- Stop the bots: With the help of Russia, thousands of automated accounts shifted the conversation on Twitter in ways favorable to Trump. This is probably the easiest problem to solve. Twitter just has to want to do it.

OK, so Twitter seems terrible. It reminds us of everything we have come to hate about politics in the Trump era. I never feel better after I open the app. I also can't stop myself from opening it. Twitter may have gotten us into this mess, but it may also be the way out of it.

On the first weekend Trump was president, Americans swarmed airports across the country to protest the patently racist Muslim travel ban that Trump had announced late the night before. Howli and I went out to the San Francisco Airport. Like so many others, we were offended and alarmed by Trump's action. It was the exact opposite of the ideals we had worked so hard for in the previous administration. But we also wanted to be with people who shared our outrage and fear about the direction the country was rapidly headed. Sitting on the couch and scrolling through Twitter in anger felt like a mistake.[25]

I expected that there would be a handful of people—maybe a hundred, which would be impressive for a protest on a Saturday against a not yet implemented executive order.

When our Lyft arrived to pick us up, the driver saw that we were headed to the airport with no bags.

"Are you guys going to the protest? I'm going to head there later this afternoon," he said.

"What are the odds of that?" I thought to myself.

When we pulled up to the airport, we could hear the chanting.

Inside were well over a thousand people from all walks of life. Older, former hippies who'd probably come out to San Francisco during the summer of love and never left; tattooed hipsters; tech types in their hoodies and branded T-shirts; and millennials, alternately protesting and documenting the proceedings on their phones.

The whole scene was incredibly emotional. Like the Women's March of the week before, this was not a protest of anger. There was no cursing, vandalism, or threats. Just pure civil disobedience. People were happy to be a part of something bigger than themselves.

I was struck by how this many people could end up here so quickly. How did they know about the Muslim ban? It was a Saturday during the NFL play-offs, not exactly a time when people are glued to cable TV. It was also clear that there was no group organizing the protest, which is frankly how most protests happen these days. Yet somehow all these people from all these different walks

---

25   Often my natural state.

of life had gathered together at a moment's notice. A flash mob for equality and decency.

I heard a group of people standing near Howli and me talking to one another.

"How did you hear about all this?"

"I saw it on Twitter and it felt like somewhere I should be, so I came."

Twitter. It's not all bad.

CHAPTER 9

FROM 1600 PENN TO
KEEPIN' IT 1600

Not long after I returned from my hospital stay, the president called me down to the Oval Office. The ostensible purpose of the visit was for the president to check in with me on the news of the day and get a sense of how the government shutdown was playing out in the press.

Or so I thought.

"How are you feeling?" Obama asked me.

"Not bad. The press seems to be in a good place. They get who's at fault here and think the Republicans have completely fumbled the ball."

"No. How are *you* doing? What are the doctors saying?" Obama pushed.

Caught off guard, I stammered, "I feel better. I'm tired, but what else is new? The doctors don't have a great answer, but they believe I have a blood vessel in my brain that spasms when my blood pressure gets too high."

As I said these words out loud, I realized how scary this sounded and that I might have been so focused on returning to work that I hadn't thought through just how dire my situation was.

"Blood vessel in the brain sounds kinda serious," Obama said with some understatement.

"I mean, yeah, but I am now on medication which will deal with the blood pressure issue. It will be fine," I protested a little too much.

"You have been with me for a long time, from the very beginning of this journey. You have given as much to this endeavor as anyone. If you need to leave to get your health in order, I want you to do that. My first choice, of course, is for you to stay, but I want you to put your health first."

"I hear you. Dr. Jackson says with medication changes and some lifestyle adjustments, there is no reason I can't do my job," I responded, referring to the president's personal physician, who had been monitoring my treatment.

"Look, I'm not old enough to be your father, but I could be your older brother." This was how Obama started all of his very valuable life advice to me, just to make it clear that he was only fourteen years older than me.

"This is important work, probably the most important work we will ever do, but it's not everything. You have to think about the rest of your life, too."

I didn't decide to leave the White House right there in the Oval Office, but it was where the seed was planted. It was the first time I thought about how much life there was outside the eighteen acres of the White House and how little of it I was experiencing. I wasn't ready to leave yet, but for the first time I let the thought enter my mind.

A lot of my White House colleagues used to joke that I was going to be the one to turn out the lights at the White House. I always responded that I would leave the White House like Matt Damon at the end of *Good Will Hunting*. One day, everyone would show up to the morning senior staff meeting in the chief of staff's office and I just wouldn't be there. But I knew deep down that my colleagues were probably right.[1]

I loved my job. I loved walking into that building every day.

---

1 I did "go see about a girl," in a way.

Every time I boarded *Air Force One* or landed on the South Lawn late at night on *Marine One* was the thrill of a lifetime. It never got old. But the White House was my entire life. I had put everything else on hold for nearly a decade now. Barack Obama came first, second, and third. I had missed countless family trips, weddings, reunions, and just being there when my friends and family needed me.

Senior White House aides work in two-year increments. Come, stay till the next election, and if you stay after that, you are signing up to stay until the next election. In my mind, I circled the 2014 midterm elections on the calendar. This was the last exit on the highway. I either left around then or agreed to stay till the end.

Obama had always talked about the presidency as a relay race. There comes a time to pass the baton to the next person. As the calendar counted down to decision time, it was becoming increasingly clear to me what the right decision was.

After six years in the White House and two on the campaign, I was physically and emotionally exhausted. The normal wear and tear was worsened by the emotional stress of my health issues. I couldn't sleep for months afterward, in large part because when you check out of the Stroke Unit of a hospital, they tell you that if you feel the symptoms, come to the hospital immediately because there is a lifesaving treatment that they can give you if it is within a few hours of the onset of the stroke. But—and this is a big but—they say that if the stroke happens while you are sleeping, there is no way to know when it started, so no medication for you.

How could anyone sleep well after that? I woke up dozens of times a night for months, afraid I was having a stroke. Yet, ironically, one of the things that can prevent strokes—is getting sleep.

I was burning out quickly. The extraordinary was starting to feel a little more ordinary. The abnormal of the Republican reaction to Obama was starting to feel a little too normal for comfort.

The other argument for leaving was Howli.[2] A lot of relationships blossomed among White House staffers because only another White House staffer understood the pressures and commitments of the job. Howli understood when I had to mysteriously and suddenly cancel a beach weekend with no explanation given (I was going with Obama on a secret trip to Afghanistan). When my life blew up because of some work thing, she understood because it usually meant that her life was blowing up, too.

Our relationship was new, but it was a long time in the making. And it changed everything. When President Obama learned that we were dating, he told me that she had a great spirit, which is a perfect way of describing her infectious energy, kindness, and humor. She is the brightest light in every room she enters.

We started working in the same office in late 2011; before that she was on the first lady's staff. On Howli's first day working in the West Wing, Obama stormed into the office suite where we all sat together and called for Jay Carney and me to come out of our offices. We were in the middle of a big fight with the Republicans over the extension of a tax cut. Even though Republicans had never met a tax cut they didn't like, they were opposing this one because it (1) had Obama's name on it, and (2) seemed to be helping the economy in the run-up to his reelection campaign.

The president stood directly in front of Howli's desk and began a twenty-minute, not entirely family-friendly rant about the opposition party. The only thing dividing Howli from the president of the United States was her computer monitor. I was standing on the other side of Howli's desk from Obama. As I engaged in the discussion with Obama, I could see Howli out of the corner of my eye. She seemed totally unfazed by the president. She was sitting with perfect posture and continuing to type away on her keyboard, not

---

2   When editing this book, Howli commented "great point" about this
    sentence.

allowing Obama to distract her from the work at hand or look to be eavesdropping on the very lively conversation taking place inches from her.

Who was this perfectly poised woman who had joined our team?

Then I looked at her computer screen.

Gjsokposkpgojgonofjzososjfhohfo

She was just typing gibberish over and over again.

I didn't know it at the time, but I had just fallen in love.

We became colleagues and then friends bonding over our shared love of hip-hop and television shows such as *Sons of Anarchy* and *The Wire*. Before too long, it was clear that we were both interested in more than just a friendship.

About eighteen months after the typing incident, we went on our first date—in New York City. We were both going to be visiting friends there at the same time. DC is a small town and the White House is even smaller. We had no idea if our chemistry worked outside of the office and we wanted to find out without everyone in the White House knowing.

It was a long weekend and Obama was on vacation. We coincidentally ended up on the same train to New York, so we had a drink when we got to the city—sort of a pre-date if you will. We had dinner on Saturday night, and after dinner we walked all over the city with Howli showing me her favorite haunts from when she'd lived there after college. The next day, she took me to her favorite pizza place before I was supposed to go meet some friends, so she came with me. Then I went to meet her friends. We had another date Sunday night and then the same thing on Monday. We returned to DC on Tuesday and decided to order Thai food and watch a movie.

Needless to say, we still had the chemistry.

A few weeks after we'd started dating, I planned our first weekend away together. I invited Howli to come to my family's home on the Outer Banks of North Carolina for Labor Day Weekend. This was my favorite place on the planet. It was where I escaped whenever we got a break at the White House, and I wanted to share it with her. We were both pretty excited about the upcoming trip, but like so much in the White House, events intervened. A few days before we were supposed to leave, Syrian president Bashar al-Assad used chemical weapons on his citizens, precipitating a potential military conflict with the United States.

Vacation canceled. I was going to have to spend the weekend waiting around the White House working on the announcement of a potential strike against the Syrian regime. Deputy National Security Advisor Ben Rhodes and his team on the National Security Council were taking the lead, but I certainly couldn't be lounging on a beach with my new girlfriend when it happened. If it happened.

Howli—who can find fun in any activity and is always (I mean always) planning something[3]—proposed a staycation at my apartment (in between trips to the White House for meetings). We (mostly Howli) planned every minute of the weekend—the food we were going to eat, the cocktails we were going to make, and the movies we were going to watch. The plan was that Howli and I were going to meet at my apartment on Friday after work and get takeout from somewhere nicer than the usual rotation of Chinese and Thai places. Around 7 pm on Friday, Howli texted me to say she was walking out the door.

Leaving in 10. Meet you at my apartment in 30, I responded.

I shut down my computer, packed my bag, and bade farewell to Clay Dumas, my special assistant, who sat outside my office. I was halfway down the hall when Clay called for me:

"POTUS wants to see you. He's in the Oval."

I put my bag and phone on Clay's desk and walked to the hall for what I assumed would be a brief meeting. Obama was rarely still in the office this late, because he was religious about getting home for dinner with the family before working late into the night in his

---

3 Howli planned a July 4, 2017, trip to Montreal with our friends in February—of 2016.

study. But as his daughters had gotten older, they were often doing things in the evening, especially on Fridays, and Obama lingered longer before heading to the residence.

When I walked into the Oval Office, Obama was standing at his desk.

"Hey, sorry to blow up your Friday night, but I was just taking a walk with Denis and I had an idea. I asked the rest of the team to come down so I could run it by you guys."

What ensued was a nearly two-hour meeting about seeking congressional approval for a missile strike against Syria. Because no phones are allowed in the Oval Office and this wasn't the sort of meeting you walked out of to text your date, I was stuck sitting there with no way to tell Howli what had happened. With every passing minute, I got more anxious that I was about to blow it with this woman.

The second the meeting ended, I hustled to my desk, grabbed my phone, and sent an apologetic text. I couldn't explain the gravity of the subject matter because it was classified. But it didn't matter. Howli hadn't doubted me or assumed I was blowing her off.

She took matters into her own hands, picked a restaurant, ordered food, and was on the way to my apartment. I picked her up mid-walk and we ate a very late, very cold dinner on the roof deck of my apartment. We talked about everything—except work, which was so great.[4]

The abbreviated staycation weekend was when it became clear that Howli and I were on a path to start a life together. I wanted us to go to the movies without having to leave in the middle to get on a conference call, to go on uninterrupted dinner dates and not have to cancel vacations because of world events. I wanted a life that resembled normalcy and I wanted it with her.

During the holidays in 2014, Howli and I had taken a few days

---

4   This was a hallmark of our early relationship. We left work at the gates of the White House.

and headed to her native Bay Area. Miraculously, it was a quiet week in White House–adjusted terms. We wandered the streets of San Francisco, we saw friends, we went wine tasting. We lived life in a way that just wasn't possible in our current jobs. This was a joint decision: we were going to leave the White House together and start the next chapter of our lives.

I knew this was the right decision, but I was still nervous about it. I had seen friends leave the White House and go into a deep depression as they detoxed from the narcotic adrenaline of working in the most important building in the world. But I was willing to take that risk for a life with Howli. I was ready to pass the baton to the next person.

All that was left was to tell the president.

I kept making excuses not to tell him and Howli started to worry that I was going to change my mind. On the day after the State of the Union, I was traveling with Obama on *Air Force One* when I went into his cabin to break the news. He was seated at the desk and I plopped down on the couch. The president knew why I was there; the rumor mill had been churning about my departure for a few weeks.

He looked up from the briefing book he was reading and muted the TV, which was showing ESPN.

"Do you have some news for me?" he said knowingly.

"Yes, sir, I do. Working for you has been the greatest privilege of my life, but the time has come."

Obama pointed out that other than him, I was the only one left who had started on the first day of the campaign and served in the White House for the whole six years. He was more than kind about my decision.

"Look, I owe you a lot. I wouldn't be here without you," Obama graciously told me. Even though I knew this wasn't completely true, it meant the world to hear him say it.

Right when I was about to get emotional, we both started laughing and reminiscing about the past eight years—the good times, the bad times, but mostly the funny times. Right before we landed, Obama asked me what I was going to do next.

"Honestly, I have no idea," I replied on my way out of his cabin.

DETOX

Howli and I came up with a pretty ingenious plan to detox from the White House.

Leave the country and don't look back.[5]

Within days of turning in our BlackBerrys and White House badges, we were on a plane for a six-week journey of eating, drinking, and relaxing across Southeast Asia.

We ate Michelin-starred dim sum in a mall food court in Hong Kong.

We rode elephants in the jungles of northern Thailand.

We went to Muay Thai boxing matches with the locals.

We cruised down the Mekong in Laos drinking homemade whiskey fermenting with snakes and scorpions.[6]

We toured the ruins of Angkor Wat in Cambodia.[7]

We lounged on the beach, reading books and sipping cocktails on an island off the coast of Vietnam.

We ate pho and drank homemade beer in the old town of Hanoi.

It was amazing. I never missed or even really thought about what was happening in the White House. We didn't get international cell phone plans (the president had told Howli we should never take our phones out of the hotel safe), so our only access to the Internet was in the morning and evening at the hotel.

When hotel staff or airline attendants would offer us English lan-

---

5   If I don't pick up a meth habit, this is also our Trump Gets Reelected Plan.
6   We snuck some of the scorpion whiskey back into America as a "gift" for some friends who were still in the White House.
7   Obama never forgave us for not putting a stop at Angkor Wat on the itinerary for his 2012 trip to Cambodia.

guage newspapers, we would reject them the way Trump would reject a salad not served in a taco bowl.

Ignorance—for once—was bliss.

When we returned to the United States, I started to do some paid speeches and was serving as a fellow at the Institute of Politics that David Axelrod started at his alma mater in Chicago. I was writing some freelance pieces for *Grantland*, the now defunct ESPN-owned sports and pop culture website started by Bill Simmons. And of course, I was active on Twitter with my new civilian account.[8]

I was adjusting much better to life on the outside than I had imagined. Whenever I thought about leaving the White House, I remembered a *Washington Post* story from 2008 about a trio of Bush aides who had recently left government service. One of those aides was Dan Bartlett, Bush's longtime communications advisor. Bartlett shared an anecdote about going golfing on a weekday. After several hours, he realized that he hadn't received a single e-mail. Assuming his phone wasn't working, he called his wife and asked her to send him a test e-mail. It arrived right away. This anecdote always stuck with me about the challenges of going from being in demand 24/7 to being a normal human.

Much to my surprise, I loved not being in demand. I loved being able to go to a restaurant without spending half the meal outside on my phone. And I loved sleeping so much. After five or so hours of sleep a night for eight years, every time I woke up after the sun came up felt like an amazing luxury.

Another thing I noticed with my speaking and tweeting was how much I loved speaking for myself—saying what was on my mind and not trying to channel what was on Obama's. It felt so liberating. Barack Obama never asked me to say anything I didn't believe—far from it. I wouldn't have been there if I didn't believe

---

8   The very cautious White House lawyers made me give up my @pfeiffer44 Twitter account with its 70,000 followers when I left. I am reminded of this injustice every time Trump tweets government business from his personal Twitter account from an unsecure personal cell phone.

in him and his agenda. But there was a freedom in speaking for myself and not for a president, absent the scrutiny that comes with being an official spokesperson for the entire United States government.

With this in mind, I accepted an offer from CNN to be a political commentator for the network. I did this with some trepidation, mainly because I was scarred from the pressure that comes with being trotted out on TV as the tip of the White House's spear.

I'd appeared on the Sunday shows a handful of times during my tenure as senior advisor. I prepped for these appearances as if they were the bar exam.

I would take home a thirty-page briefing document and read it all Friday night before returning to the office on Saturday for another several hours before going home to study all night. On the morning of the interview, there would be a conference call with the communications staff and the National Security Council to prepare answers for anything that happened overnight. Needless to say, Clay, my hero of an assistant, and the press staff didn't love when I signed up to do the shows.

In March 2014, I was on *Meet the Press* right after Vladimir Putin and Russia had invaded Crimea, which heretofore had been part of the independent state of Ukraine. I was given a set of very pugnacious talking points by Ben Rhodes, which I appreciated because a lot of the approved talking points for delicate national security situations sounded exactly like what they were—verbal applesauce designed to say nothing and offend no one.

A few days later, the Russian government announced that they had sanctioned a number of US government officials, banning them from traveling to Russia. On the list were several US lawmakers including Democratic and Republican congressional leadership; the White House official responsible for coordinating and implementing US sanctions on Russia; Ben Rhodes; and me.

The role of White House senior advisor comes with many duties, but US-Russia policy is not one of them, so I was more than a little surprised to be included on the list. I had never been to Russia and had no plans to travel there, but it was a weird feeling to know I was personally banned from visiting another country.

"How the hell did I end up on this list?" I asked the national security aide traveling with us on *Air Force One* when the list came out.

"You talked shit about Putin on *Meet the Press*."

I have no idea if that is true, but it made me choose my words on television even more carefully going forward.

A few days into my new role as a paid pundit, I was on my way to the CNN studios when I got a news alert on my phone saying that Donald Trump was going to run for president. I knew from Trump's ill-fated birther crusade from a few years earlier that everything else in politics was about to be put on pause. It was going to be all Trump, all the time, for what I assumed would be a brief foray into politics as part of a PR stunt.

Like everyone else in Democratic political circles, I saw Trump's entry in the race as a great political gift. A reality TV star running on a racist platform, espousing conspiracy theories that spoke to a large part of the GOP base, would pull the entire field to the right, making the eventual nominee (who, of course, wouldn't be Trump) entirely unelectable.

KEEPIN' IT 1600

In early 2016, I got a particularly interesting e-mail from Jon Favreau. It was a forward of an e-mail exchange he was having with Bill Simmons, who had just started a new media company, asking if Jon had any interest in doing a political podcast with me as part of Simmons's new podcast network.

I was a huge fan of Simmons, who'd pioneered a new style of Internet-friendly writing that mixed sports and pop culture. I would read his columns and mail bag articles when I ate lunch at my desk in the White House. I consumed his 700-page book on basketball in a weekend.

Simmons was also very prescient about how the Internet was changing the kind of information people wanted and how they wanted to consume it. Back in 2008, he was one of the first people to experiment with a new format called podcasting.

Simmons had pitched us on getting Obama on his podcast in 2008 and we were all set to do it before management at ESPN, which hosted the podcast, nixed the event because they didn't want to get involved in politics.[9]

In 2012, Jon and I made another run at getting Obama to appear on Simmons's podcast to talk sports, pop culture, and politics. Because the campaign was not yet in full swing and Obama was president, not just a candidate, ESPN agreed.

The Obama appearance was a huge hit and served as a fairly explicit contrast to Mitt Romney, who was too stiff to engage in such a conversation and used the term "sport" instead of "sports," like everyone else. Romney sounded like he was talking about croquet and dressage instead of basketball and baseball.[10]

As a test, Simmons invited Jon and me onto his incredibly popular podcast. Through the years, I had been on *Meet the Press*, the *Nightly News*, and most every major news program, but being on Simmons's podcast beat them all. I heard from more friends and family about that appearance than any other media I had done in my career—if you don't count the time Jon Stewart ridiculed me for two minutes on *The Daily Show* because of a less than stellar appearance on the Sunday shows.

The response was good, so Simmons asked us to tape a test

---

9   This may be where the saying "Stick to Sports" was born.
10 The Romneys actually owned a horse named Rafalca that competed in the 2012 Olympics in dressage, which is the equine equivalent of synchronized swimming. For fun, I made my computer password some version of Rafalca for over a year.

podcast of the two of us just talking about politics. Jon and I were initially confused about how to do this. We didn't know how to podcast, so we just talked about the news like we normally would.

When we'd finished, I felt pretty good about it. It had been fun, and thanks to Trump, there had been no shortage of things to talk about. I was glad it was a dry run, because I was sure we had a lot of kinks to work out.

Except it wasn't.

Simmons's staff posted it on the Internet, and a few hours later, *Keepin' It 1600* was born. Well, actually, it started untitled. Our first choice for a title was *Politics as Usual*, naming it after the Jay-Z song, but that was taken. Then we named it *Playing Politics*, which was an ironic homage to an Obama-ism that politics isn't a game. After we announced that as a title, we discovered that the Minneapolis *Star Tribune* editorial board had a podcast by the same name, which made it impossible for listeners to search for it on iTunes. Out of desperation we asked people on Twitter for suggestions and one very talented user suggested *Keepin' It 1600*. It made absolutely no sense to anyone, but that's why it was funny.

The podcast was essentially the conversation about politics that Jon and I had been having for years in person or over text, but now for all the world to hear.

We were shocked, to say the least, that people actually listened to it. Our immediate family and former Obama administration colleagues, sure, but people we didn't know? That seemed impossible. Yet for some reason they did.

After a few months, we added a second weekly episode and brought on Jon Lovett, a former Obama speechwriter who'd been the chief architect of all of Obama's White House Correspondents' Dinner speeches, and Tommy Vietor, who'd started out as a junior press aide on Obama's 2004 Senate race and risen all the way up to being the spokesperson for the National Security Council before leaving the White House to start a consulting firm with Favreau.

They added new perspectives, Tommy's deep knowledge of foreign policy, and Lovett's sense of humor and unconventional takes.

In this hour a week of unfiltered, uncensored discussion with an engaged and enthusiastic audience, I had found the perfect place to observe and analyze the 2016 election. The early days of the podcast were more than a little ragtag. I conducted our first interview with then Labor Secretary and current DNC Chair Tom Perez on my cell phone from the supply closet of the tech company I worked for at the time. We had to stop the interview whenever someone came in to get a pen or a mouse pad. I had to explain to one potential guest what a "podcast" was—it's like radio, but on demand. Eventually, people became familiar with what we were doing. I had even gotten an actual microphone, but we didn't get too fancy. I continued to record at my kitchen table (and still do).

It was fun as hell, though.

Podcasting would, of course, just be a temporary gig until Hillary Clinton's inevitable win in November, and then I would retire from podcasting and politics.

Oops.

INTERLUDE 3

ADVICE YOU CAN BELIEVE IN

Barack Obama has many opportunities in the postpresidency phase of his life. He will be an author, a speaker, and the leader of a foundation. Maybe he will get to fulfill his dream and own an NBA team, but if none of those things work out for him, I have a suggestion:

Advice columnist.

My last day at the White House happened to fall on a day when the president was traveling to South Carolina. I decided to go along for one last flight on *Air Force One*, and being out of the office seemed likely to reduce the number of awkward good-byes that I wanted to avoid at all costs.

There was some symmetry to this visit—it was Obama's first visit to the state since his shockingly large victory in the South Carolina primary propelled him toward the Democratic nomination. The staff had also arranged a surprise meeting for Obama with Edith Childs, the South Carolina city councilwoman whom we called the "Fired Up and Ready to Go" lady. Ms. Childs was the star of the story about how one voice could change the world, and it ended almost every speech Obama gave on the trail in '08. By the end of the campaign, the entire staff—and press corps—could recite every word of the story from memory.

All in all, it seemed like a fitting last day at the White House.

After the last event in South Carolina, I rode in the presidential limo with Obama to the airport for the flight back to DC. I was telling him about my post–White House trip to Asia and that Howli and I were debating where to move when we got back.

"What's on the list?" Obama asked.

"New York and San Francisco," I replied.

"Can't go wrong there. Two great but very different cities. New York is a lot, so it's less relaxing. I love San Francisco, but the time change is a real thing."

I dismissed the time change argument out of hand, but I would learn years later that Obama was right when I would wake up at the crack of dawn in fear of what war or national embarrassment Trump had caused from his Twitter account while I was sleeping.

"So are you guys moving together? This is the one, huh?" Obama was always very proud of the hundreds of relationships that had sprung from his campaigns and his administration. As one example in 2016, I went to four different weddings of people who met working for Barack Obama. One of those was mine.[1]

He continued, "Here's the advice I give everyone about marriage—is she someone you find interesting?"

I was initially confused by the question, but I figured he must have a point.

"You will spend more time with this person than anyone else for the rest of your life, and there is nothing more important than always wanting to hear what she has to say about things," Obama continued.

"Does she make you laugh? And I don't know if you want kids, but if you do, do you think she will be a good mom? Life is long. These are the things that really matter over the long term."

We had just pulled up to the plane, and the world was waiting for us to get out.

---

1   She's the one.

"Howli is incredibly interesting, funnier than I am, and will be a phenomenal mom," I told the president.

"Sounds like she's the one. Lucky you," Obama told me as he exited the limo and headed up the stairs to get on *Air Force One*.

A year later Howli and I were engaged. And this is the advice I now give everyone about relationships. I credit Obama (most of the time).

CHAPTER 10

THE 2016 CAMPAIGN CLUSTERFUCK

On Election Day, I was woken up by my alarm in an old, but not charming, DC hotel. I had been in town for nearly a week making multiple appearances on CNN to explain with great confidence why Hillary Clinton was undoubtedly going to be the next president of the United States.

Sleeping soundly the night before an election was incredibly disorienting. For the first time in my professional life, I wasn't about to head to a campaign headquarters to monitor returns from key precincts or hit the road with a candidate stumping for last-minute votes. Other than appearing on CNN to fill dead airtime until the results started coming in, I was going to experience this election just like everyone else.

It was game day and I was on the sidelines. It made me personally uneasy, but I had zero doubt about the results. To be honest, I had never been more confident of anything in my political career.

I had spent the last many months assuring everyone that Hillary was going to win and win easily. It was the hallmark of our podcast. Every week, we were the antidote for the "bed wetters" who were panicking about the latest news or the slightest movement in the polls. *Keepin' It 1600* became Xanax for nervous Democrats.

That afternoon, I texted with a senior Clinton campaign aide who had also been involved with Obama 2012 to ask how the campaign was feeling.

"Let me put it this way: I am more confident than we were on Election Day 2012," the aide responded.

That was exactly what I wanted to hear. On Election Day 2012, we were almost certain about Obama's victory based on our sophisticated data modeling.

No reason to worry.

Later that evening, I went to Cody Keenan's apartment to watch the results come in with Ben Rhodes and Anita Breckenridge. This seemed fitting: Anita, Ben, and Cody, who had replaced Favreau as Obama's speechwriter, had been huge parts of my Obama experience going all the way back to 2007. We had been together through good times and bad. Traveled hundreds of thousands of miles together, seeing the sights and shutting down bars in far-flung corners of the world.

The fact that we were watching on the couch and eating pizza also symbolized how much we thought the whole election was a done deal. I have been to more elaborate *Game of Thrones* watch parties.

The early results were not great, to say the least. I e-mailed David Plouffe—the person whose political judgment I trust most. Plouffe was the ultimate anti–bed wetter. When people were really starting to get nervous during the campaign, we would invite Plouffe onto the podcast to soothe the anxious souls of our listeners. We did this as much for the listeners as for ourselves.

"You still feeling OK?" I wrote to Plouffe.

"Yes, but this could be under 300," he responded almost immediately, referring to the number of electoral votes.

That level of optimism was short-lived.

The biggest warning sign that we were fucked was that Plouffe had stopped responding to my e-mails.[1] Unfortunately for me, I was scheduled to do a very late-night CNN hit. I e-mailed some friends on the Clinton campaign to say I was going on TV in a few so if they had some optimistic spin, I would love to have it.

The answer I received was that Wisconsin was probably gone, but Michigan was still in play. I didn't want to be the one to tell them that without Wisconsin they weren't getting to 270.

I was texting with Howli about what I could possibly say on TV about this disaster. She was imploring me to come up with something, but I had nothing. One of the skills you develop in a career in politics is being able to divine some decent message out of any situation no matter how dire, but I was coming up blank.

No words described what was happening.

Right before I was ushered onto the set, a CNN exec stuck her head in to tersely tell me that my services would no longer be needed for the night. They were going to stick with the panel that had been on since 8:00 p.m. Many people would be annoyed about trekking across town after midnight, putting on gobs of TV makeup, and then sitting in a room with nothing more than tiny bottles of water for over an hour for no reason. Not me. Not on this night. It was a last-minute stay of execution.

Not long after, my phone blew up with push notifications informing me of the outcome I'd never imagined possible. An outcome I'd persuaded everyone would not happen—could not happen—had happened.

Donald Trump was the president-elect of the United States.

Fuck.

How did this happen?

---

1   Rereading my e-mails from election night as part of my research for this book was a truly terrible experience. With each e-mail, you can see the hopes of all the participants getting progressively more crushed. I would reprint them here, but you all deserve better.

EXPLAINING THE UNEXPLAINABLE

I could not have been more wrong about the 2016 election. Fortunately, I was not alone in being incorrect. It's not just about getting a prediction wrong—that's pretty irrelevant in the grand scheme of things[2]—it's about figuring out what has changed in politics that led to Democrats losing the most winnable race in history so that we can figure out how to make sure Trump is a one-term president. A couple of important caveats:

First, Hillary would have been a great president. As Barack Obama would often say, she was more qualified than any other person to ever run for the office. Even more importantly, she had the empathy, humility, and intellectual curiosity necessary to do the job well.[3] I supported her, donated to her, and knocked on doors for her. I wish she had won.

Second, if the Russians had not intervened and FBI Director Jim Comey had not decided to violate Department of Justice procedure to announce a short-lived and irrelevant reopening of the e-mail investigation, she would have won the White House and perhaps by a sizable margin.

Finally, there has been a lot of dancing on the graves of the Clinton campaign by people who opposed her in the primary; that is not my intention. I have nothing but respect for the Clinton staff in Brooklyn and across the country, who fought so hard to protect us from Trump.

If Democrats are going to win future elections and the larger battle against Trumpism, we need to understand how the political firmament shifted and why we missed the shift.

With that in mind, here are five things I missed and why I think I missed them:

---

2 I'm out of the prediction business anyway.
3 Notably, Trump has none of these things.

1. Underestimating Obama's Appeal and Hillary's (Unfair) Baggage

"Hillary the bad candidate" has become shorthand to explain the loss. It's worth unpacking this narrative, because it's more complicated than that.

Yes, Clinton made mistakes. She was overly cautious and played not to lose. She didn't have a clear message or rationale for her candidacy other than that she would be a good president who would do good things. This is as rational a rationale as you can get, but it is far from electrifying. Her decision to give speeches to Wall Street banks like Goldman Sachs in exchange for large sums of money was out of touch. And finally, her decision in 2009 to use a private e-mail server was catastrophic because it meant she spent most of the 2016 election under some form of FBI investigation, which was less than ideal to say the least.

But she also had numerous strengths, and I gave these more weight. Yeah, there were going to be challenges, but she was a skilled politician who was willing to put in the work. In the end, I assumed the balance would fall in her favor.

In 2008 and 2016, despite narratives to the contrary, there were millions and millions of voters who were passionately excited about her candidacy, and in 2016, she excelled in the most important moments of the campaign—the three nationally televised debates.

It's also impossible to talk about assessments of Hillary Clinton's abilities as a candidate without mentioning the insidious effect of sexism in the media and the voting public. Behavior, body language, and tone that were applauded in male candidates were derided in Clinton. At every turn, she was held to a different and unfair standard. She carried the baggage and scars of decades of partisan attacks on her and her husband. Clinton had been portrayed entirely as the Devil incarnate—a combination of Lady Macbeth, Claire Underwood, and Cruella de Vil. We can't forget that right-wing radio spent years convincing people that Hillary Clinton murdered former White House aide Vince Foster (she didn't), and then right-wing Twitter and Fox News spent four years convincing people that she was responsible for and glibly insensitive to the deaths of Americans in Benghazi (she wasn't).

The e-mail server and the paid speeches to Wall Street banks powerfully reinforced the preexisting negative perceptions of her.

But despite all this baggage, I thought Clinton had found an ideal opponent in Donald Trump. If voters didn't trust Clinton, they trusted Trump less. If some voters weren't excited to vote for Clinton, they were more excited to vote against Trump. On top of all this, Obama was very popular and the economy was doing well— both of which historically meant that the incumbent party would retain power. While the Clinton coalition might look a little different from the Obama coalition, it seemed certain there would be enough overlap to get her well north of 270.

Inside Obama World and the chattering class more generally, it was an article of faith that Obama represented the nadir of Democrats' performance with white voters and particularly with older white voters who lived in rural areas. As a young, hip African American with an unusual name and even more unusual background pushing a very progressive agenda, Obama was a poor fit for the more conservative white voters who tend to bounce back and forth between parties. Only 39 percent of whites voted for Obama in 2012, which was the worst performance for a Democrat in history. It had to get better, right?

Nope.

Shockingly, Obama got a higher percentage of the white vote and did significantly better in the rural areas that seemed most likely to improve for Hillary Clinton. According to postelection studies, only about three quarters of the white Obama voters with a high school diploma voted for Clinton. Her support among these voters was even lower in the Rust Belt battleground states.

I have been accused many times—always fairly—of being an unrepentant Obama Kool-Aid drinker, but even I underestimated Barack Obama's appeal to independents and conservative Democrats. Instead of causing older, more conservative white voters to flee the Democratic Party, Obama was holding on to these voters, who might otherwise have left years ago. There was something unique about him that transcended race and ideology. It was this allure that fueled his insurgent 2008 campaign. It was why I went to work for him in 2008, and by 2016, politics had become so partisan that I took for granted his unique appeal. Winning back these voters won't be easy and won't be enough to win, but has to happen if we want to succeed.

2. The Death of Electability

The traditional definition of electability is dead.

We think about political campaigns through the prism of electability—what specific traits or positions do voters consider preferable and what things are deal breakers? But like most political analysis, on questions of electability we tend to look backward as opposed to projecting forward.

For a long time, this made sense. Or at least we thought it did.

The first forty-three presidents were all very similar. They all had similar backgrounds—senators, vice presidents, or governors. Many had served in the military. They were all white male politicians who looked not that different from all the people who grace our money.

After John Kerry lost the 2004 election, the conventional wisdom among Democrats was that the only way for Democrats to return to the White House in 2008 was to nominate someone from a red state with experience winning over independents and Republicans.

Three years later, Barack Hussein Obama, from the South Side of Chicago via Hawaii and Indonesia, won the White House.

Eight years after that, Donald J. Trump, a dotty old racist[4] reality TV star, won the White House.

A man who had never served in public office, never served in the military, never served his country or his community in any way big or small. A man famous for being famous.

Although as a white male, Trump looked like all the guys on our money, nothing else about him fit the definition of electable. And it was that fact that polluted all the coverage of him.

Because I (and almost everyone else) thought Trump was too loud, too crass, too inexperienced, and ultimately too ridiculous to be elected, I discounted his strengths as a candidate and the power of the political forces that propelled his candidacy. In some ways, Trump is an accidental president, winning on a technicality with help from the Russian judge. But he did beat the best and brightest the Republican Party had to offer in 2016,[5] and, in doing so, re-shaped one of our two major political parties.

Until recently, electability was a bit of a self-fulfilling process. Campaigns are fueled by money and media attention, and the only candidates who had access to either were the ones donors and members of the media determined were electable. This thinking ultimately affected voter preference—voters in primaries are the most engaged of all voters and they pick only candidates they think can win.

As it has done to so much else in politics, the Internet also has upended who can be elected president.

Candidates now have the ability to bypass the political tastemakers and go directly to the voters to make their case. Candidates can bypass the big political check writers and raise money on the Internet from

---

4   H/t Jon Lovett.
5   I wouldn't be me if I didn't point out that this is a little like being the tallest of the Seven Dwarves.

grassroots donors. If the media won't take their candidacy seriously enough, candidates can communicate directly with the public through Twitter and Facebook.

Applying an outdated filter of electability was a fundamental error and a particularly foolish one for someone who'd had a front-row seat to Barack Obama's rise. Using that same filter in 2008, I wouldn't have bothered moving to Chicago.

In the future, when some pundit (or podcaster) tells you not to bother supporting some candidate because they can't win or that the election is in the bag because the other party nominated some "unelectable" candidate, DO NOT LISTEN.

3. Best Messenger Wins

After the 2016 election, whenever I would appear on some post-election panel, I'd give the audience an exercise.

First, I would ask them, "What was Donald Trump's positive argument for himself?"

The audience would unanimously shout back, "Make America Great Again."

Then I would ask them if they knew what Trump's argument against Hillary was.

The audience would respond by saying, "Crooked Hillary" and "Lock Her Up."

Next, I would do the same exercise for Hillary.

"What was her argument against Trump?"

The audience would respond with a cacophony of responses: unfit, racist, sexist, liar, thief, bully, and on and on.

When I'd ask the audience about Hillary's argument for herself, it would be near silence. A few would murmur "experience" or "qualified," but without much conviction or enthusiasm.

For all of Trump's offensive statements and absurd tweets, he had a clear and consistent message that broke through. And the candidate with the more clear and consistent message always wins.

Most of Trump's positive message was without a doubt nonsensical bullshit, but it was memorable enough to be emblazoned on hats and abbreviated into a hashtag. Trump's argument against Hillary Clinton was also unfair and inaccurate, but he was swimming with the current. It fit with an existing narrative about her that was believable to a large portion of the populace. The most effective political attacks are ones that fit into what people are already willing to believe.

The 2016 political environment was unique—the incumbent Democratic president was historically popular and incredibly popular with the Democratic voters Clinton needed to turn out, but they were also hungry enough for change that they backed Vermont senator Bernie Sanders in large numbers in the Democratic primaries. Clinton struggled to find the right balance between appealing to the voters who loved Obama and showing the broader electorate how a Clinton presidency would be different and better than Obama's.

Trump certainly offered the Clinton campaign no shortage of opportunities to attack him. In fact, that may have been part of the problem.

Every campaign starts the day with a call, a meeting, an e-mail chain, or a Slack channel to discuss what the opponent did or said that they should go after that day. In most campaigns, you are lucky if you have one good "hit" a day and are often scraping the bottom of the barrel to find a negative message to drive that day. I always imagined the Clinton campaign just had a rolling twenty-four-hour meeting, because every three minutes Trump would say something outrageous or dishonest or a story would emerge about some past outrageous behavior that would have disqualified every other previous candidate from continuing their campaign.

The ethos of modern campaigns is never to let a pitch go by. Hit your opponent and hit them hard. Don't stop until the election is over. Trump's flaws, gaffes, and moral outrages were so numerous that the Clinton campaign found it almost impossible to drive a consistent narrative against Trump.

One day he was an intolerant, deplorable racist. The next day he was temperamentally unfit for office. The day after he was a misogynist who bragged about sexually assaulting women and a rapacious businessman who profited off the very same working-class voters he claimed to champion.

These critiques were true and some of them Clinton was morally obligated to make even if they weren't the "message of the day." It would be wrong not to call out bigotry and misogyny.

But in the end, these various arguments were never woven into a single coherent narrative about why Donald Trump shouldn't be president.

During the campaign, I supported and encouraged the Clinton campaign strategy, but in hindsight, I lost track of one of the core lessons of Obama's success—campaigns are about telling the American people a story—a story about where we are, where we are going, and why you are the right person, and your opponent is the wrong person, to take the country there. It's a story that needs to be compelling, but also easily understood, and then driven home by the candidate and the campaign with relentless discipline.

In 2008, Obama's message against Clinton and McCain was so simple: Change versus the Status Quo. Clinton represented the same old politics that had led to missed opportunities and lost elections, and McCain represented a continuation of George W. Bush's failed policies at home and abroad. In 2012, as the incumbent president, Obama could no longer run as the change agent against the status quo. Every time he stood behind a podium with the presidential seal or boarded *Air Force One*, it reminded the world that Obama was now the establishment, not the insurgent. That's why Obama needed to turn the 2012 election into a debate about competing economic theories and which candidate would fight for the middle and working class.

Democrats are rightly and reflexively repulsed by the idea of learning anything from Trump or drawing parallels between Trump and Obama.[6] Yet we cannot discount Trump's success at having a message that worked in 2016 or ignore the failure of the Democrats to turn their very worthwhile policy agenda and their even more legitimate arguments against Trump into a message that fit in a tweet or on an ugly red hat.

Simple is better, but simple doesn't mean simplistic.

4. Too Much Science, Not Enough Storytelling

Up until Election Day 2016, I had a real pet peeve about modern political journalism.

In the modern era, political campaigns are high-tech affairs that use highly sophisticated data analytics to understand the political environment and craft strategies and messages. Campaigns are now more science than art. Yet they are covered by English majors who treat campaigns like Shakespearean dramas with dramatic plot twists.[7]

The gap between the science of campaigns and the art of journalism was never clearer than in the final weeks of the 2012 campaign. The press believed that Romney was surging toward the finish line, citing anecdotal evidence such as rally crowd sizes, the frequency of yard signs, and the slightest movement in often flawed media polls. In phone calls, coffees, and late-night discussions in hotel bars on the campaign trail, we would try to convince the media that they were focusing on the noise, but we could see the signal. The data we saw was very clear that Obama was headed for a sizable electoral victory. The media presumed this was just spin.

They were wrong.[8]

The election perfectly mirrored what we told reporters was going to happen, down to a shocking level of specificity on things like the early voting margin in states such as Ohio, Florida, and Colorado.

---

6   Writing that sentence made me throw up a little in my mouth.
7   There are exceptions to this rule, most notably Nate Silver of FiveThirty-Eight, who pioneered the idea of data journalism.
8   We weren't above spinning; we just weren't doing it here.

This was the first time the media realized how far campaigns (or at least Obama's campaign) had advanced and how the amount of data at the campaign's fingertips so far outpaced anything the media could ever know. The media was covering the tip of the iceberg with no capacity to see what was happening below the surface.

Data became the new big thing in politics. Reporters wrote about it and campaigns became obsessed with it. Math majors had never been more in demand.

If the lesson of the Obama campaign was that data could be decisive, the lesson of the Clinton campaign was that it wasn't perfect.

In 2012, analytics was new enough that the Obama campaign still wanted a three-part system in place to constantly check on what the data was telling us. We were not yet ready to put all of our eggs into the data basket.

Part one was the data itself, which was refreshed nightly through tens of thousands of robo-calls asking voters who their preference was between Romney and Obama in every battleground state. Part two was the traditional polls that campaigns have used for nearly a century—live people asking approximately 1,000 people per state about the race. Part three was the massive army of volunteers and field organizers who were talking to voters on the phones and at the doors every night. If one of those three data points was out of line, it was cause for concern that something was afoot, and we would dig in deeper with additional research to see if it was an anomaly or a real problem.

As more of our lives move online, the ability of campaigns to predict who you will vote for and what issues you care about will only grow. One misfire isn't going to mean that campaigns will go back to using an abacus.[9] But there is a second lesson about the dangers of relying so heavily on data in campaigns.

---

9   The counterargument is that this misfire elected Trump and we may never have another election again because we will die in a nuclear attack or Trump will seize power in an authoritarian coup.

The vast amounts of available data and sophisticated models can divine with great precision which message voters most want to hear, and social media and other technologies give campaigns the ability to target individual voters with those individually designed messages.

Millennials in urban areas want a president who believes in climate change.

Female voters over the age of fifty but under the age of sixty-five who are unmarried, have a college degree, and live in rural areas care most about education.

White male NASCAR fans care about health care and are worried about terrorism.

These new tools provide campaigns with the dangerous temptation of telling each voter what they want to hear, instead of developing an overall message that is broadly appealing. Political campaigns are ultimately about inspiring people to get off their couch and go wait in line, often for hours, to cast their vote. This is a big ask. It's much different than selling soap or affordable razors. It can't be paint by numbers.

The folly of this strategy was perhaps best explained by Jason Kander, the former Missouri secretary of state who lost a tough race for Senate in 2016 but impressed everyone by outperforming Hillary Clinton by 16 points. On a postelection episode of the podcast, when Jon Favreau and I asked about what went wrong for Democrats in 2016, Kander described two different approaches.

Imagine, he said, a lawyer making a closing argument to the jury and that lawyer makes a different argument to each juror trying to individually convince them with slightly different rationales with the whole jury watching. Now, imagine an attorney who makes one argument that attempts to persuade the entire jury. Which do you think will work better?

Campaigns are run on science and tech. That's never going to change, nor should it, but no matter how precise the data or advanced the technology, campaigns will always be decided by who tells a more compelling story about America.

As Democrats, we may have lost sight of that important fact.

5. The Economy, Stupid

On the 1992 Clinton campaign, strategist James Carville hung a sign on the wall of the Little Rock, Arkansas, headquarters that outlined the three crucial messages for the campaign:

- Change vs. More of the Same
- The Economy, Stupid
- Don't Forget about Health Care

This strategy propelled Bill Clinton to a surprising win in 1992, and these principles became the bedrock of Democratic campaigns. Axelrod, who was Obama's Carville, didn't write those exact principles on the wall, but they were at the heart of the Obama 2008 strategy.

With the possible exception of the period right after 9/11, the economy has been the most important issue on the minds of voters. It's the prism through which voters judge candidates.

In 2012 against Romney, the overwhelming majority of ads the campaign ran, every speech Obama gave, and every tweet the campaign sent out was about the economy. Obama's plan versus Romney's plan. The core argument of the campaign was that Obama fought for people like you and Romney fought for people like him and the proof was in their very different economic policies. To Axelrod's great credit in the decade we worked together, he never went a day—or even an hour—without reminding us never to lose sight of the economic message.

There is an irony that Hillary Clinton's campaign might have been the first Democratic campaign to diverge from those principles.

Since Hillary Clinton had been on the national stage so long and was running to replace a popular two-term president, "Change vs. More of the Same" was a hard message for her campaign.

It would be literally impossible to forget about health care since the Affordable Health Care Act was passed in 2010. Opposing that law has been the animating principle of the Republican Party ever since, while protecting it has been a litmus test for the Democrats.

In hindsight, the Democrats lost sight of the most important part of the Carville doctrine: "The Economy, Stupid."

This is not to say that Hillary Clinton didn't have gobs of great economic policy positions. She did.

And this is not to say that she didn't talk about those positions on the stump as she campaigned across the country. She most certainly did.

But the economic message most certainly didn't break through. There is no doubt the media is partly to blame because they simply wouldn't cover her policy positions or her policy-based critiques of Trump. To get coverage, she had to make personality-based attacks:

Trump is a liar. That goes viral.

Trump is a racist. That leads the news.

Trump bragged about sexual assault. That gets 100,000 retweets.

Trump wants to give tax cuts to wealthy people like him and balloon the deficit. Crickets.

In the wake of Clinton's loss, the Democratic Party has engaged in a self-defeating debate about whether the party should embrace a strategy that targets the "Obama Coalition" of millennials, women, and people of color or a strategy that uses an economic populist message to court working-class voters.

This is a stupid debate because it is both a false choice and not a choice at all. It is simply not an option for Democrats to remain silent on issues of racism and misogyny, particularly when those repugnant views are emanating from the Oval Office. We have a moral and political obligation to be a bulwark against Trump's hateful rhetoric.

Democrats must also recognize that despite the low unemployment and high Dow Jones average at the end of the Obama years, the economy remains the single most important issue in American politics. It is the connective tissue between all parts of society. Economic anxiety is very real and for good reason. The gap between the rich and the poor is growing larger. Advances in technology are changing what a job means in this country. Automation and globalization are taking away the blue-collar manufacturing jobs that used to be the bedrock of middle-class life.

We need policies and a message that explain why Democrats are the right party—and Republicans are the wrong party—to shepherd the country through an uncertain economic future.

If we lose that battle, Democrats will not see the halls of power for a very long time.

ARE WE PERMANENTLY SCREWED?

Politics is a fickle beast.

In the summer of 2006, a book came out called *One Party Country*, about how George W. Bush and Karl Rove were on the cusp of building a permanent Republican majority that would rule politics till the end of time.

A few months later, the Democrats took back the House and the Senate in a landslide. Two years after that, Barack Obama won a huge electoral victory, capturing states that no Democrat had won in decades.

The country that I saw traveling with Barack Obama bears no resemblance to the one that Trump describes. The American people are good and decent and want the best for one another and the country.

Are there exceptions? Of course. President Trump is one of them.

The path back for Democrats is pretty clear and it doesn't mean becoming more like Trump. Hate worked for him; it won't work for us. We need to be audacious, authentic, and inspirational. It's not an entirely new playbook. It's an update of the one that Barack Obama wrote.

There are reasons to believe hope is right around the corner.

On Inauguration Day, I was holed up in a hotel hiding from the reality of the end of the Obama era and the dawn of the Trump years between CNN hits where I got to look at the well-deserved shit-eating grins of Trump apologists. When I wasn't on CNN, I was in my room watching the news out of a sense of masochism and hiding from the red-hatted MAGA mobs who were marching through the streets as the conquering army they were. My only contact with an actual human who didn't work for CNN or deliver room service that day was with the hotel employee who stopped by my room to deliver the Inauguration 2017 gift that the hotel was providing to guests in town for this historic occasion.

I had been in this hotel for several days, and once a day the same young Latino would knock on my door and try to give me the gift of the day—an engraved flask, a framed picture of Washington, DC, an official inaugural tie, and so on. Every time I would decline the gift, and every time he would nod to me with a professional but knowing look of appreciation. The overwhelming majority of people in this hotel had come to Washington to celebrate a man who called Mexicans rapists and ran on a platform that demonized anyone who looked like the guy forced to deliver gifts to these very celebrants.

After he left with my commemorative gift still in tow, I turned off the TV and went to YouTube for some inspiration. When I was working in the White House and the world felt dark and depressing, it never lasted because hope was just down the hall. Now that hope had gotten on *Marine One* and left the White House for the last time, I turned to YouTube and started watching some of Obama's greatest hits.

I stumbled on a speech I had forgotten about because it happened during one of the crazier times in the White House. Obama was asked to speak at the fiftieth anniversary of the March on Washington. Talk about a tough speech to give. Martin Luther King is a hard act to follow, and Obama would be speaking from the very spot where King had delivered his "I Have a Dream" speech, which is one of the greatest pieces of political oratory in history.

Seems easy. No expectations at all, right?

Working on the speech almost killed Obama and Cody Keenan, who had been the president's chief speechwriter for only a few months at the time. I don't think either slept for a week, but what came out was a masterpiece.

One specific passage really hit me:

"The March on Washington teaches us that we are not trapped by the mistakes of history, that we are masters of our fate," he said. "The arc of the universe may bend toward justice, but it doesn't bend on its own."

We are masters of our fate.

The next day, cabin fever finally got to me and I decided I needed to leave the hotel and brave the new world. When I walked out of the hotel doors, I saw exactly what Obama was talking about.

The streets were filled with people, but these people weren't wearing red hats. They were wearing pinks ones. These were not Trump supporters. They were in DC for the Women's March to send a message to Trump that the resistance was here and would not be going anywhere. I had read about the grassroots effort to start the march. It had been organized not by politicians or interest groups, but by citizens who wanted to be masters of their fate.

I was blown away by what I saw. I hadn't seen this many people in Washington since Obama's first inaugural.

I was stopped by a woman from Ohio who recognized me from CNN. She was there with her daughter and two granddaughters. They had traveled all night to be there. One of the granddaughters was more than a little under the weather, but nothing could keep them from joining the march. Like everyone else I met that day, they weren't angry or depressed or cynical. They were hopeful and full of joy. They found comfort and solace in being part of something much bigger than themselves. I was deeply moved by this family and got choked up when they talked about how much they were going to miss Obama.

I saw on Twitter that the same thing was happening in blue cities and red towns all across America. Millions were marching for a better future for their children and grandchildren.

As I wandered through the teeming masses of people, I thought to myself, "One day into the Trump era, and we are already bending the arc toward justice."

CHAPTER 11

THANKS, OBAMA (SERIOUSLY)

After the political carnage of 2016 and the political carnival of the early days of the Trump presidency, friends, family, coworkers, Friends of the Pod, and even the woman who owns my local coffee shop would ask me the same two questions:

What is Barack Obama really like, and how did Barack Obama do it?

The first question is so freighted with hope and anticipation, especially in the Trump era. When he was running and then as president, Obama represented hope for so many Americans. In the Trump era, this is even truer. Many people are clinging to the idea that someone good and decent like Barack Obama was once president as evidence that America has not crossed a point of no return. People want to believe so desperately that the good, decent smart man they saw on their TVs and social media feeds is the same person off camera as on camera.

The good news is I can tell you with every bit of conviction that there is really only one Barack Obama. The guy singing "Amazing Grace" to help heal a nation in crisis is the same guy I sat in tens of thousands of meetings with. The guy that appeared on *Pod Save America* the day before he left office is the same guy I traveled around the country with in 2007. Eight years later, the only real change is that his hair is a little grayer.[1]

As Obama said in almost every speech he gave in 2008, he is not a perfect man and he was never going to be a perfect president. But he is a better man than he was a president, and he was a pretty great president.

Historians, journalists, and Obama's friends, family, and staff have all offered their assessments of Barack Obama, but I have always thought that Chance the Rapper, the hip-hop artist who has known Obama for most of his life, put it best in a 2016 interview with GQ:

"He's a good man. Even if he wasn't president, if his ass worked at, like, Red Lobster, he'd be just a good man working at Red Lobster."

If the first question was about the past, the second question was all about the future of the Democratic Party and the country.

As an Obama loyalist through and through, I love that this question is asked. Most presidents, even some of the more consequential ones, slink out of office weighed down by scandal, dismal approval ratings, or the burden of being a lame duck. Obama had his ups and downs, he was written off for dead by the pundits more times than any of us can remember, but in the end he will go down as one of America's most consequential presidents. His success is even more notable because it came exactly at the time that politics seemed to be coming apart at the seams.

Inherent in this question is the anxiety that grips the Democratic Party after the devastating loss of the 2016 election. If we can't beat Trump, how can we ever win again? This is a totally fair question. It's the one that keeps me up at night, but every time I am gripped

---

1   I am also a little—OK, a lot grayer. A few months before I left the White House, I was riding on *Marine One* with Obama, when he looked up from his BlackBerry and said: "Hey, Pfeiffer, I noticed when we were in the Situation Room yesterday you have a lot of gray hair." I'm not saying this is why I left the White House, but I am not saying it's not why.

with panic or the urge to throw in the towel, I remember that Barack Obama navigated all these treacherous waters and kicked the asses of the Republicans and the blowhards on Fox News.

At least once a week in the post-Obama era, someone e-mails, calls, texts, or tweets me urging Obama to speak out about Trump's most recent verbal or policy atrocity. They want Obama to somehow save us from Trump. Many people in this country would feel better if we could hear from Obama more often, particularly after times of tragedy. His voice provides a sense of comfort and helps us believe that we can come out of the Trump era without too much lasting damage to the country.

But Obama is not the solution. He cannot save the Democrats or the country. That job falls to the next generation, but there are lessons to be learned from Obama's success.

There are three stories that to me show who Obama is, explain why he was so politically successful, and lay out the lessons for Democrats looking to chart a path forward.

DON'T BE AFRAID TO PLAY TO WIN

Back in March 2007, when Obama had been officially in the presidential race for less than a month, he conducted an interview with *New York Times* columnist Nick Kristof.

Kristof told us he wanted to write a counterintuitive piece that Obama's nontraditional background made him uniquely qualified to be president. Our campaign enthusiastically jumped at this opportunity because the "experience" issue was going to be the existential threat to the campaign of a man only a few years removed from the Illinois State Legislature. Kristof, who most certainly would be referred to as a globalist cuck by Steve Bannon, wanted to argue that Obama's time living in Indonesia as a child and traveling the world provided him with meaningful experience that would help him do the job of president.

Kristof wanted to interview Obama for the column, and we had the sense that the interview was table stakes to get the column written.

The lead of the column was everything we could have hoped for and more:

The conventional wisdom about Barack Obama is that he's smart and charismatic but so inexperienced that we should feel jittery about him in the Oval Office.

But that view is myopic. In some respects, Mr. Obama is far more experienced than other presidential candidates.

His experience as an antipoverty organizer in Chicago, for example, gives him a deep grasp of a crucial twenty-first-century challenge—poverty in America—that almost all politicians lack. He says that grass-roots experience helps explain why he favors not only government spending programs, like early childhood education, but also cultural initiatives, like efforts to promote responsible fatherhood.

In foreign policy as well, Mr. Obama would bring to the White House an important experience that most other candidates lack: he has actually lived abroad. He spent four years as a child in Indonesia and attended schools in the Indonesian language, which he still speaks.

This was the exact case we were trying to make, and there are few things better in a Democratic primary than having a *New York Times* columnist make that argument for you.[2]

On the daily 7:30 a.m. campaign strategy call, the Kristof column was a primary topic of discussion, but people weren't patting themselves on the back for this obviously great column. Instead, there was a decent amount of concern about a passage in the middle of the column:

---

2   I recognize this validates the Fox News caricature of Dems as latte-sipping elites.

Mr. Obama recalled the opening lines of the Arabic call to prayer, reciting them with a first-rate accent. In a remark that seemed delightfully uncalculated (it'll give Alabama voters heart attacks), Mr. Obama described the call to prayer as "one of the prettiest sounds on Earth at sunset."

The concern was that this anecdote could be used by malicious Republicans (and Democrats using their playbook) to portray Obama as soft on terror. This is an utterly absurd and repugnant notion, but for multiple election cycles, the Republicans had beaten Democrats by questioning their patriotism.

Every Democratic operative remembered the ad that compared Georgia senator Max Cleland, a Vietnam veteran who'd lost three limbs on the battlefield, to Osama bin Laden because of some obscure Senate votes. If they could do it to war heroes like Max Cleland and John Kerry, they could certainly do it to Barack Obama. As a party, we were scared of our own shadow.

On the call, everyone acknowledged the absurdity of having to worry about something like this, but agreed that we had to worry about it nonetheless. The horse was out of the barn; we couldn't go back in time and have Obama unsay it. The only course of action was to talk to him about the answer and suggest that maybe he not use it again.

"Pfeiffer, will you talk to Obama about this?" Plouffe suggested.

"Good idea, we should do this today," someone chimed in unhelpfully.

I responded, "Sure," but I thought, "Shit."

At this point in the campaign, I was still serving as the traveling press secretary, so I was doing the call from some hotel lobby waiting for the then-senator to emerge from a fund-raising breakfast. I had known Obama for only a couple of months and was still trying to build a relationship of trust with him.

Being on the traveling staff of a campaign has a lot of perks, including a lot of face time with the candidate, but one of the downsides is being the one who has to deliver bad news or criticism directly to the boss.

Because I wasn't yet confident in my relationship with Barack Obama, I was dreading this task. The last thing I needed was to piss him off. We were in the early stages of the Democratic primary, and this was unlikely to be an issue anytime soon.

But I am a loyal soldier, so once Obama exited the breakfast and we got in the car to the next event, I planned to relay the message.

This was before Donald Trump was birthering or the e-mail chains claiming Obama was a secret Manchurian candidate–style Islamist were circulating, but the Fox News smear about Obama being educated in a madrassa gave a clear view of what was coming if he was ever seen as a threat to win the White House.

Obama got in the car with me and Reggie Love. He was in a great mood and launched into a discussion of the HBO show *Rome*.

While Obama was pitching Reggie and me on watching *Rome* because it was in Obama's view a show about politics, I gamed out my approach.

In the interim, I had gotten an e-mail from Plouffe, asking, "What did BO say about Kristof?"

In what was not exactly a profile in courage, I decided on a classic staff trick for the aide assigned to deliver bad news.

Sort of throwing my colleagues under the bus, I said, "Hey, Plouffe and Axe asked me to talk to you about something." This was a way of separating myself from the specific complaint. In other words, don't shoot the messenger.

I explained the situation and the concern from the campaign team. As I was talking, Obama didn't look upset or annoyed. He had sort of a wry smile on his face.

Before I could finish, Obama interjected with a bit of sympathetic chuckle:

"Look, I know why you guys are concerned.[3] I said it because

---

3   Obama did not fall for my trick and lumped me in with the rest of the team.

it happened to be true. I'm not going to play the game where I edit what I say because I am afraid of Republican attacks. That's their game. If we play their game, we lose. We have to change the game."

IT'S ALL ABOUT TIMING: BEING FUNNY AND COOL

The Internet helped create the Obama presidency and then almost ended it. And then it saved it again.

In late 2013, we faced perhaps the biggest political crisis of the Obama years. The website that millions of people were supposed to use to sign up for Obamacare was broken. Not "too slow" broken or "a little buggy" broken, but straight up totally broken. People could not sign up for health care. This was incredibly embarrassing, because it was a problem entirely of our own making. The public was pissed, the Democrats were pissed, and the Republicans were overjoyed, which was the exact opposite of where we wanted to be.

Health care was Obama's biggest accomplishment. An accomplishment so tied to Obama's legacy that it is named after him.[4]

The problem was bigger than optics and politics.[5] If we didn't get enough people—and especially enough healthy young people—to sign up for health care during the six-month open enrollment period, the system would collapse. Under the best scenario, this was going to be a challenge. After losing the first couple of months due to a broken website, our backs were against the wall.

And who do you turn to in moments of crisis?

Zach Galifianakis, of course.

As part of our full-court press, Obama and all of his surrogates,

---

4   The Republicans named it Obamacare because they thought that would make it more unpopular. That worked for a while and then Obama became the most popular politician in America and made it more popular.

5   This statement is always true.

yours truly included, were blanketing the media to tell people about the upcoming deadline and encourage them to sign up. In what probably isn't a surprise, young women were signing up on schedule, but young men were lagging. We made an effort to do as many interviews on sports radio, ESPN, and other media outlets that the data told us were consumed by our target audience.

This was the whole ball game. If we got enough of the right people to sign up, Obamacare would succeed and our presidency would be saved.

One day, Bradley Cooper was in the White House for some meetings before attending a state dinner that evening. White House Senior Advisor Valerie Jarrett was meeting with him to talk about some of his pet issues and because he is Bradley Cooper.[6] During the meeting, Valerie presented our challenge of trying to reach young men ages twenty-six to thirty and asked Cooper if he had any ideas.

Cooper responded immediately that President Obama should appear on a web show hosted by Zach Galifianakis called *Between Two Ferns*. Cooper said this was the single best thing we could do to reach our target audience.

Right after Cooper left, Valerie stopped by my office and told me of his idea and that she planned to mention it to the president. This was the first that Valerie had heard of *Between Two Ferns*, but because I was familiar with the show, I was initially skeptical.

Then I thought, "Fuck it. Why not?"

Not long after, I ran into Valerie in the hall.

"Great news. He said he would do it," she said.

I sent Obama some of the previous interviews in the hopes he would watch them and wrap his head around what he'd agreed to do. He never watched them.

---

6   Cooper was a few years ahead of me at Georgetown and was known around campus as Fabio, because he had long blond hair and tended to wear flowy linen shirts unbuttoned to his navel. This is not superrelevant, but I had to tell someone.

The day before the interview, I walked into the Oval Office with a borrowed iPad intending to force him. Obama was seated in his chair in the seating area of the Oval. I was seated on the adjacent couch. I cued up the video, hit Play, and handed it to him.

And then nothing. Obama handed it back to me. I hit Play again and gave it back. Same result.

Before I could get it to work, the attendees for the next meeting arrived. I had missed my chance.

"Sorry about that. I will e-mail you the videos and you are getting a briefing in your book tonight. I really think it's worth reading."

On the day of the appearance, I walked over to the room where the interview was going to occur, primarily to look Galifianakis in the eye and get him to commit to sticking to the script. There had been a lot of back-and-forth about which jokes were appropriate and how and when Obama would get to make his pitch for people to sign up for health care. There were some really funny jokes that we rejected because they went too far. The good news was that the *Ferns* staff, Galifianakis included, were more nervous about this than I was. The bad news was that Galifianakis made a joke when I asked him about sticking to the script. I had no idea what was about to happen.

"This is going to be a disaster," I thought to myself.

Thankfully, I was wrong.

When I walked into the Oval with Cody, Obama had a huge smile on his face.

Prepping for *Ferns* episodes and press conferences was most certainly not Obama's favorite part of the job, but he looked genuinely enthused for this one. Before we could even sit down, Obama told us that he had read the script and watched the videos.

"This is some pretty funny stuff," Obama told us. "But do I have to stick to the script?"

"Umm, I mean, not technically, but...," I said.

"Good. I want to have some fun with this."

It was a home run. The interview went viral, and, most important, we saw a surge of traffic to Healthcare.gov directly from the link included in the video. We hit our number of sign-ups, and Obamacare lived to fight another day.

First, Obama is at heart a gambler, not a reckless one, but the smart, methodical kind you never want to sit across the table from.

Second, comedy is Obama's superpower. The world knows this from watching him kill at the White House Correspondents' Dinner every year.

Finally, Obama may have some Dad jokes and wear his Black-Berry on his belt, but he is our coolest president since John F. Kennedy. He gets the rhythms of pop culture—he watches *Game of Thrones* and *The Wire*, he can talk knowledgably about musicians like Kendrick Lamar, and he has seen every movie of consequence in the last ten years.[7] He can talk hoops with the best of them and can sing Marvin Gaye songs at a fund-raiser to rave reviews. Most politicians (see Mitt Romney) interact with pop culture like aliens visiting Earth for the first time; Obama was never more at home.

Of course, Obama was going to kill it on *Between Two Ferns*. It's just what he does. And it's exactly the sort of approach we need to beat Donald Trump.

OBAMA THE OPTIMIST

In the dark weeks after the 2016 election, Howli and I got invited to an Obama communications staff reunion at the White House. We debated whether we should make the trek from our new home in San Francisco and visit DC, which was about to become enemy territory. The idea of seeing a bunch of ecstatic Republicans in their

---

7   This is what happens when you can't leave your house on a Saturday without a thirty-car motorcade, a police escort, and a calvacade of armed personnel. And that house has a movie theater.

Brooks Brothers blazers and pleated khakis[8] seemed like more than we could possibly stand. But Howli wisely convinced me that this could be the last time we walked into that building while Obama was president—or maybe ever again.

We decided to turn it into a longer trip, because there was a separate event hosted by the first lady for all of her current and former staff and Howli had worked for the first lady before coming over to the West Wing. If we were going to be angry and depressed about the election, we might as well be angry and depressed with our Obama family. Frankly, it was good to get out of San Francisco. Everywhere we went, people who knew our background in politics wanted to talk about the election and what was to come. They wanted to hear something hopeful about the future, but I was pretty much out of hope for the first time since I had met Barack Obama.

DC was exactly as we'd feared. Dark and dreary. The depression and fear were palpable. The city of Washington, DC—as opposed to the town of politicians, reporters, and lobbyists—is one of the most Democratic and diverse in the country. The transition from Obama to Trump, who had run by stoking racial fear against the very residents of the city, had cast a pall over the place.

On our first day in DC, I went to the White House. This was my first visit back to the West Wing since moving to California in 2015. It was hard to avoid the elephant in the room. To get in the building, you had to walk past the construction site for the reviewing stand where Trump would watch the parade on Inauguration Day. This was a particular punch in the gut. They actually start the construction before Election Day, and my old office when I was communications director looked out onto the construction. In 2012, the idea of Mitt Romney sitting there while I packed up my office haunted my dreams. Now, a more perverted version of this nightmare had come true.

---

8   Almost no one in politics—the author included—dresses well, but Republican staffers are keeping the pleated pants industry afloat.

Once I was inside, the reality of Trump's electoral win and the dangerous future to come hit me again. I checked in with the ROTUS—the receptionist of the United States—as we referred to the staffer who sat in the West Wing lobby and greeted guests—and then sat down on the couch to wait for someone to come get me. A few moments later a familiar-looking man sat down on the couch next to me. I definitely knew this guy, but I just couldn't place him. At first I assumed that he was just another administration appointee or a denizen of DC that I knew around town.

Then it dawned on me. I know this guy.

It's Michael Fucking Flynn. The retired general and future felon whom Trump had just appointed as his national security advisor. The man who had famously led the Republican National Convention in a chant of "Lock her up," referring to Hillary Clinton.[9] He was here to meet with Susan Rice, Obama's national security advisor, as part of the transition process. This was real. It was happening, and it was happening fast.

The White House was lacking its normal addictive buzz. It was a quiet-ish time of the year, and normally at this point there would have been tons of transition work going on, but the Trump folks hadn't gotten their shit together yet, so most people were out having networking coffee to get advice and find jobs.

After having some meetings and seeing some friends and dispensing a decent amount of career advice, I popped my head in to see the president. He had just finished taping a podcast with my old friend David Axelrod, and the three of us joked in the outer oval that it felt like 2008 all over again.

Later, the president and I went into the Oval Office. He sat behind the desk, and I sat in the chair next to the desk that I had sat in so many times over the years.

I hadn't seen Obama since his birthday party in August and hadn't spoken to him since the election. He asked me about life as a newly-

---

9   Oh, the irony.

wed with Howli and our recent wedding and told me how he'd heard it had been a hell of a party from his staff that went. I told him I'd heard the same thing since it was all a bit of a blur to me.

We talked about the surprising success of the podcast. And while Obama didn't listen to podcasts, he said Pete Souza, his photographer and good friend, had told him that *Keepin' It 1600* was funny, if a little profane. I appreciated this because entertaining if a little profane was exactly what we were going for.

After a while, I could sense that our time was coming to an end, so I finally asked the question that I needed to know the answer to:

"Sir, how are you doing?"

The tone of my voice made it clear that my question was about something bigger than how his day was. I was trying to get at two things that had been on my mind since the election.

Basically, I was asking him, "How fucked are we?"

Obama knew what I was asking, and he sighed and shook his head and said, "Look, this isn't an ideal situation to say the least," and then we both laughed.

Understatement for the purposes of gallows humor is a tried-and-true Obama-ism.

Then he said, "Maybe I am just looking for a silver lining, but I am hopeful that this will be the clarifying event that will show the public the two different visions for the country."

And there it was: the eternal optimism and unending faith in the American people.

I am going to miss him.

We are going to miss him.

EPILOGUE

There was a point during election night 2018 when it felt eerily similar to election night 2016. I was at the Crooked Media headquarters with Jon, Jon, and Tommy to watch the results and do some periodic live streaming. The Crooked staff had invited their friends and family to watch the (hopefully) happy results over pizza and beer.

For a group of pretty-superstitious individuals, this was an audacious tempting of the fickle political Gods. My *Pod Save America* cohosts had (in)famously decided to participate in a live stream on election night in 2016. The entire nation was able to bear witness to them in real time as they experienced the wrenching, emotional trauma of Trump's victory. For some reason, we signed up to do it all over again.

Much like in 2016, this election started joyous. All the models and polls pointed to a victory. There were anecdotes of turnout in all the right places as far as the eye could see. The mood ebullient.

Then they started counting votes and that's when the PTSD[1] set in.

The race everyone was watching to read the tea leaves was the sixth district of Kentucky, where Amy McGrath, a fighter pilot and

---

1 Post-Trump Stress Disorder.

top Democratic recruit, was challenging a Republican incumbent. The polls close in Kentucky first in the country, and if McGrath was winning, it would be a very positive sign for what was to come.

She wasn't winning.

Florida was up next. Andrew Gillum, the mayor of Tallahassee, was running against Ron DeSantis, a Trumpkin known for spouting off racist comments. This was one that really mattered to us— politically and personally. Democrats hadn't held the governorship of Florida this century,[2] and winning would give Democrats a leg up in the 2020 election. But I was also so inspired by Gillum, along with Beto O'Rourke, who was running against human carbuncle Ted Cruz for senate in Texas, and Stacey Abrams, who was running for governor of Georgia, and thought they were the future leaders the Democratic Party needed. They were courageous, inspiring, and they were stars. O'Rourke and Abrams were longer shots, but Gillum had been leading in every poll for weeks. His victory seemed the most assured.[3]

This is when the 2016 déjà vu set in. Florida was where we realized that something was very wrong for Hillary. Trump was blowing the doors off in areas that performed well for Obama. The same thing was happening again. Maybe all the models, polls, and predictions were wrong and once again the Republicans would shock the political world.

It got dark very fast. So dark that at one point Jon Favreau's wife, Emily, had to come in and tell us to get our shit together.

"There are a lot of people out there looking to you guys for what is happening." She pointed to the area at Crooked HQ where everyone had gathered.

Emily was right.[4] But at the time I thought, "If this is all going to hell, why should we try to make them feel better. America is over."

---

2 Seriously. What the hell is wrong with us?
3 Plus his opponent had the political deftness of a manatee wearing mittens.
4 As she often is.

OK, that was a little dramatic. But I was legitimately fearful of what was to come if the Democrats didn't take control of the House of Representatives. Imagine what would happen if after all the controversy, corruption, and incompetence the voters rewarded the Republicans with more power. The last two years of Trump's first term would make the first two years seem like the good ole days. I was also concerned about the millions of Americans who had gotten involved in politics since 2016. The people who had marched for women and against guns, flocked to airports to protest, and knocked on doors and made phone calls. What impact would another loss have on them? Would they turn away from politics forever?

Unlike in 2016, this time things got better. Democrats started picking up seats all across the country. Before too long, the Associated Press made the call we had waited two years to hear: "Democrats will control the House of Representatives."

Nancy Pelosi would now have to sign off on every law that Donald Trump would want to pass. Checks and balances would be restored. The corruption and criminality would be investigated. Democracy would be saved.[5]

Most important, the victory in 2018 was proof that if enough people get involved and fight for their country—Yes, We (Still) Can.

So why did election night 2018 go so right, and what lessons can we learn to make sure that election night 2020 looks more like 2018 than 2016? Some thoughts:

RABBIT HOLES ARE FOR SUCKERS

In the waning days of the 2018 election, Trump threw a Hail Mary. He started tweeting and talking about a "caravan" of migrants from Central America headed to the southern U.S. border.

---

5 At least temporarily.

He claimed the caravan was filled with MS-13 gang members and terrorists. He called this caravan made up of mostly women and children an "invasion" and sent thousands of U.S. troops to the border to do . . . who the hell knows what.[6] This was an obvious exercise in cynical abuse of power. The goal was not subtle—scare the living shit out of white people (and excite the Trump base)[7] in the hopes of helping Republicans win an election.

In 2016 the Democrats chased Trump down every rabbit hole and responded to his every tweet, outrage, and scandal. But in the run-up to the 2018 election, Democrats across the country ran on a very specific and effective message: Republicans want to take away your health care and cut your Medicare to pay for a tax cut for corporations and billionaires.[8] This message put the Republicans on the defensive and opened up opportunities for congressional pickups all across the country. The Democrats refused to fall into Trump's trap. Instead of responding to his absurdities and changing the subject from health care (which excites our voters) to immigration (which excites his voters), more often than not Democrats stayed on message.

The lesson is clear. Trump's political superpower is turning the conversation to the topics that help Republicans and hurt Democrats. It helps Trump when all we talk about is Trump. In 2020 the Democratic nominee is going to need to tell a compelling and inspirational story about an America in which Trump is not the main star. The best candidates are disciplined. And that will never be more important than in 2020.

---

6 The military didn't know, either, and right after the election most of the troops went home.
7 Redundant.
8 Or "people of means" as person of means Howard Schultz calls them.

BEWARE OF FALSE CHOICES

The 2020 Democratic primary—like every one that has come before it—will be a minefield of hot pundit takes about Democrats divided over whether to be liberal or moderate. Whether to target base voters or swing voters. Whether to campaign in the Rust Belt or the Sun Belt, or to seek the votes of unregistered voters in urban areas or Obama-Trump voters in rural areas.

Let me spare you hours of scanning Twitter, reading tip sheets, and watching television pundits yell at each other—2018 gave us the answer to all of these questions.

Wait for it...

YES.

The answer to all of these questions is yes. Getting the requisite 270 Electoral College votes means doing all of the above.[9] It's how we won in 2018. We won blue, purple, and red congressional districts. We won in cities, suburbs, and exurbs. We won in the Midwest and the Southwest. We won by running candidates who could both inspire turnout from the base *and* persuade swing voters. The winners included liberal candidates who campaigned with Bernie Sanders and supported Medicare for All and moderate candidates who campaigned with Joe Biden and opposed Medicare for All. The point is that questions of ideology are much more relevant to pundits and podcasters than actual voters. It's not choosing between exciting the base and winning over swing voters. Get yourself a candidate who can do both.

IT'S UP TO YOU

Nancy Pelosi, Chuck Schumer, and Barack Obama aren't the reason we won in 2018. The Democratic National Committee

---

9   We should get rid of the Electoral College. It's anachronistic and antidemocratic. More on that later.

didn't single-handedly deliver victory. The pod didn't save America.[10]

Democrats were able to win up and down the ballot not because of some decision made in Washington, DC, but because of you. The most important lesson of 2018 is that activism works.

Democrats won because all across the country everyday Americans decided to do the hard work of citizenship. You believed America was better than Trump and decided to do something about it. You marched, you protested, you knocked on doors and made calls. And most important, you voted.

No matter who we nominate in 2020, no matter how much money the Koch brothers spend, no matter what the Russians do, no matter what Mueller does, you will decide whether Trump wins or loses. It's that simple. There are more of those who know Trump is a danger than those who think he is making America great again. All we have to do is put in the work.

Politics is ultimately a very simple enterprise. Showing up is the entire battle.

No pressure, but the fate of the entire planet is on your shoulders.

---

10   No matter what Jon Lovett says, the title is supposed to be ironic.

ACKNOWLEDGMENTS

This may be patently obvious to all of you who just finished reading, but I have never written a book before. I think the longest memo I wrote in the White House was five pages, and most of my written communications for the last few years have been around 140 characters. I never could have finished this book without the help of a lot of very patient and encouraging people. More important, I would never have been in a position to write this or any book were it not for so many people who gave me opportunity after opportunity. I have been so fortunate in my life and career because of the people I have met, worked with, and worked for.

There are too many people to thank individually, but here goes in no real order (if I've forgotten anyone, I will fix it in the paperback edition):

Sean Desmond, Rachel Kambury, and everyone at Twelve: Thank you for being so supportive of a first-time author who knew just enough to be dangerous and for talking me off the ledge multiple times. I couldn't have asked for a better (or nicer) editor.

David Larabell and CAA: Thank you for helping me take the vaguest notion of a book to an actual proposal to a new proposal after the election upended everything and, finally, to a book. You believed in this book even when I doubted it.

Howli: None this could have happened without your ideas, encouragement, patience, and top-notch editing. As with everything else in our life, you made this book better, brighter, and more fun. I love you and am so excited for what comes next (LD).

Gary and Lear Pfeiffer: Thank you for a) allowing me to believe that I could do anything, b) teaching me and Bob about our responsibility to something bigger than ourselves, and c) putting up with an outspoken, opinionated son who never knew what he didn't know (still may not), but letting him figure that out on his own.

Robert Pfeiffer: Thank for being the sort of writer and person I aspire to be.

Barbara and Howdy Ledbetter: Thank you for Howli and so much more.

Jon Favreau, Jon Lovett, Tommy Vietor, and Crooked Media: When I left the White House, the two things I thought I would miss most were working with my friends and talking politics with smart, funny people. Thank you for solving that problem and for having the courage and insight to start Crooked Media, which will eventually save America from a dystopian future where we are ruled by Sean Hannity's brain in a jar.

Alyssa Mastromonaco: It is hard to believe that we have already been friends for a decade and simultaneously hard to believe that we have only been friends for decade. No one could ask for a better, funnier, or more supportive friend. I would not have survived (figuratively and literally) without you. Thanks, buddy.

Pete Rouse: You supported me, mentored me, and hired me even after I helped cost you your job by losing Tom Daschle's race (worked out pretty well for us, though). Everyone should have a boss like you once in their lives. I was fortunate to work for you many times.

David Plouffe and David Axelrod: You guys wrote the book (literally) on how to win a campaign. Without your smarts and savvy, Obama doesn't become president, I don't get to work in the White House, and America is totally screwed (OK, that may have happened anyway).

Steve Hildebrand: The 2002 Johnson campaign taught me so much about politics and life and put me on the path to meet Barack Obama. I can't thank you enough for your friendship and support and for challenging me to do crazy things like eat Mexican food in South Dakota and get crazy words printed in the newspaper.

Anita Dunn: Thank you for hiring me repeatedly and for very generously helping me succeed you. You also saved me from law school after finding me a job at the darkest moment of my career.

Robert Gibbs: For teaching me that the best staff are the one's willing to have the hard conversations with the boss and for never peeing on my leg and telling me it's raining (my favorite Gibbs-ism).

Valerie Jarrett and Anita Breckenridge: Thank you for being great travel buddies and good friends and for always representing the original Obama crew.

Denis McDonough: Hats off. I should have known when you showed up in South Dakota in 2002 and promptly organized a massive GOTV operation before unpacking your car that you would eventually be running the world.

Cody Keenan and Ben Rhodes: Thank you for being great friends who always made me laugh even on the toughest days at the White House. No thank you for being such intimidatingly good writers.

Jennifer Palmieri and Jen Psaki: I couldn't have asked for smarter, nicer partners. Thank you for being great colleagues and always pushing me to look at things from a different perspective.

Clay Dumas, Lauren Thorbjornsen, and Dawn Selak: Thank you for putting up with a very particular often grumpy and demanding boss who never said thank you enough. You all deserve a medal.

Obama Communications Team: I am biased, but the communications team was always the best, smartest, funniest, and tightest-knit group in Obama-land. You fundamentally changed how communications was done and were a blast to work with every single day. You will rule the world one day (presuming there is still a world post 2020).

Chad Griffin: Thank you for showing me that a career in politics was possible, helping me get started, and being a great friend for a very long time.

Stephen Liset, Zach Korman, and Jim Steckart: For never letting me take myself too seriously, standing by me when I went missing for a few years, and always being down for a game of Buck Up.

Bill Simmons, Joe Fuentes, Tate Frazier, and everyone at the Ringer: Thank you for teaching us how to pod and taking a risk on *Keepin' it 1600* and for all the hours I will never get back from consuming all of your pods, mailbags, and other great content.

Vice President Biden: Thank for showing me you can be a great politician and a good person at the same time and for all the Delaware references in White House meetings.

President Obama: More than a decade ago, I packed up my life to move to Chicago on a whim after meeting with you for an hour. I put all of my faith and hope in you, and never once did I regret that decision. Thank you for the privilege and honor of a lifetime, for all the great advice, and for introducing me to my wife. Also, apologies for Georgetown repeatedly blowing up your bracket.

Friends of the Pod: The best part of the entire *Pod Save America* experience is all of the people we have met across the country who are engaging in politics at every level. You give me hope about the future of the country (especially when you are wearing merch).

Obama Family: A few weeks before the election in 2008, Dan Balz of the *Washington Post* told me that if Barack Obama won, I would forever be known as an "Obama person." At the time, I didn't appreciate the significance of that designation. I do now. I couldn't be prouder to be known as an "Obama person" and to be connected to so many smart, good people who did so much to make America a better place. Barack Obama may be out of the White House, but we will always be "Obama people" and you will always be my family. Two thousand eight was just the beginning.

In loving memory of Brandon Lepow and Alan Krueger.

ABOUT THE AUTHOR

Dan Pfeiffer is a cohost of *Pod Save America*. One of Barack Obama's longest-serving advisers, he was White House director of communications under President Obama (2009–2013) and senior adviser to the president (2013–2015). He currently lives in the Bay Area with his wife, Howli, and his daughter, Kyla.

TWELVE MISSION STATEMENT

Twelve strives to publish singular books by authors who have unique perspectives and compelling authority. Books that explain our culture; that illuminate, inspire, provoke, and entertain. Our mission is to provide a consummate publishing experience for our authors, one truly devoted to thoughtful partnership and cutting-edge promotional sophistication that reaches as many readers as possible. For readers, we aim to spark that rare reading experience—one that opens doors, transports, and possibly changes their outlook on our ever changing world.